La Merica

IMAGES OF ITALIAN GREENHORN
EXPERIENCE

La Merica

IMAGES OF ITALIAN GREENHORN EXPERIENCE

Michael La Sorte

TEMPLE UNIVERSITY PRESS

Philadelphia

Temple University Press, Philadelphia 19122
© 1985 by Temple University. All rights reserved
Published 1985
Printed in the United States of America

Library of Congress Cataloging in Publication Data

La Sorte, Michael.
   La merica.

   Bibliography: p.
   Includes index.
   1. Italian Americans—Biography.
2. Italian Americans—History.
3. United States—Emigration and immigration—Biography.
4. Autobiography.
I. Title.
E184.18L28   1985   305.8'51'073   84-16169
ISBN 0-87722-382-3

To Rosina, who created her own world in America, and to Cosmina, who went back to hers

CONTENTS

PREFACE

In this book I look at the phenomenon of the emigration of Italian men to the United States prior to the First World War from the perspective of the participants in the event, the migrants themselves. The focus is restricted to the greenhorn years—the initial encounter with the immigrant status. The first exposure to the host country was the most trying and turbulent period for the immigrant as he strove to make a functional adjustment to his new environment. What he experienced during the first months and years and the way he responded to those experiences served to shape his immigrant personality and to determine, to a large extent, his subsequent behavior and actions. I have sought in this book to engage the reader with the immigrants' world, to see their world as they saw it and to understand their behavior in terms of their own values and priorities.

Other books and articles have examined transatlantic Italian emigration from a number of points of view and have employed various data sources and methodologies. There have been numerous statistical analyses as well as historical surveys and monograph studies of Italian colonial life. And there is a substantial critical literature in Italian and in English. Taken together, these publications represent an invaluable contribution to our understanding of the entire process of migration. But a number of lacunae continue to exist. More attention should be directed to the individual. Much can be learned by turning the lens on the immigrant himself and allowing him to tell his own story without conceptual encumbrances.

Specialists in the field of immigration studies have often referred to the need for further documentation of the subjective impressions of the migrants. Richard N. Juliani has noted that studies of Italian migration have largely focused upon the larger institutional conditions without an adequate examination at the level of the individual.[1] Rudolph J. Vecoli speaks of the development of the history of the "inner life" of the immigrants,[2] and Rudolph M. Bell recognizes the value of the historical biography in any analysis of the dynamics of migratory movements.[3]

In recent years the use of the first-person account in Italian immigration studies has become increasingly more common. Virginia

Yans-McLaughlin[4] and Josef F. Barton[5] collected interview data as part
of their studies of Buffalo and Cleveland. Richard N. Juliani made extensive use of in-depth interviews in his investigation of the Philadelphia Italians.[6] Ann Cornelisen combined the techniques of observa-
tion and the unstructured interview for a successful study of the
adjustment patterns of Italo-Germans.[7] There have been several oral
history projects, including one by John Bodnar[8] of first- and second-
generation workers in Pennsylvania and a study by Nuto Revelli[9] of
270 Italian emigrants, born between 1880 and 1915, who returned to
their native northern province of Cuneo.

The literature produced by the Italian immigrants themselves is
not voluminous, but it does exist. There are autobiographies, diaries,
letters, interviews, and a large number of Italian colony newspapers
and pamphlets, as well as the published observations of Italian officials, journalists, and travelers to America, some of which are excellent in their depictions of everyday immigrant life. These materials
represent the primary data for this book, especially the autobiographi-
cal works by Italian immigrant men in which they describe their lives
in Italy prior to emigration and their first few years in the United
States. Most of these men were young and single; if they were married, they had left their families at home. They worked in the rural
labor camps, and they lived in the cities. They were sojourners who
returned to Italy after a few years, or immigrants looking for a new
life, or young men who had been lured across the Atlantic by what
America promised. Each one experienced his own America, and the
book focuses on those experiences.

Life histories as human documents have been called "the most
perfect type of sociological material."[10] The advantages of life histories are many: they serve to give substance and detail to the general
histories, and to give motive and purpose to impersonal documents
and aggregate statistics; actions and attitudes can be more fully understood and more deeply analyzed, since the life history presents the
development of a real person and reveals that which accounts for behavior. Yet every data source has drawbacks, and the life history—
whether it is offered by the immigrant or sought by the researcher—is
no exception. If the source is a diary, one must consider why it was so
assiduously kept. The memoir written in old age and the granted interview contain the potential problem of inaccurate recall. If a bias ex-

ists, its type and origin must be carefully evaluated. The value for research of the human document can be enhanced by corroborative
evidence, and by judicious and discriminating selection of the material.

Six autobiographies and a diary constitute one major set of sources
used in this book. These works were produced by men who came over
as ordinary immigrants and who have left behind fascinating and complex descriptions of their greenhorn years. Because their experiences
figure prominently throughout the book, a brief description of each
author is given here.

Pasquale D'Angelo was a youngster of 16 when he came to this
country in 1910 with his father and other sojourners. During the next
decade he worked as an itinerant laborer. Self-taught, he mastered the
English language, through diligent effort, quit unskilled work, and
moved to New York City to become a writer and a poet. He became
known as the "pick and shovel poet" after he won a prize for three of
his poems. D'Angelo's autobiography, *Son of Italy* (1924), details his
life in Italy and his initial years in America as a construction worker.
He died destitute in 1932 following a fatal appendectomy.

Constantine Maria Panunzio was born into a middle-class southern Italian family. His early desire to enter the priesthood was set aside
when he decided to go to sea as a *mozzo* (shipboy). At age 19, in 1902,
he left his ship in Boston and spent the next year traveling through
New England working at various immigrant jobs. Driven by a desire to
excel, Panunzio then entered school to learn English. In the years to
follow he became a preacher, a teacher, and eventually a professor of
sociology at the University of California. In his autobiography, *The
Soul of an Immigrant* (1921), Panunzio states that the book is an out-
growth of his interest in recounting the inner struggles of an average
Italian immigrant, who was neither too successful or too unsuccessful,
in his efforts to come to terms with his immigrant status. Such memoirs were very rare, and he hoped to help fill this deficiency. Panunzio's
depiction of his demeaning and harsh experience as a greenhorn is an
indictment of the indifference and hostility of American society to the
plight of the worker immigrant.

By contrast, the memoirs of Francesco Ventresca, *Personal Reminiscences of a Naturalized American* (1937), are instilled with high
hopes and a buoyant optimism. Ventresca always looked on the bright
side of every venture and saw life as a challenge, which he cheerfully

accepted. He did not consider oppressive the grinding manual labor that he performed in Italy and in America, but neither did he find it fulfilling. After a year of moving from one immigrant job to another, he decided that if he did not learn English, he would be doing the same repetitive work the remainder of his life. At age 20 Ventresca entered elementary school, and once he had perfected his English, he pursued his education to the university level. He became fluent in six languages and worked as a teacher and translator. Although the book was written some years after his greenhorn period, a number of the events narrated are based on a diary that Ventresca kept during the first years after his arrival in 1908.[11]

The book by Gabriel A. Iamurri, *The True Story of an Immigrant* (first published in 1945), documents his early life in the province of Campobasso and his eagerness to see the world, which finally won out over his thoughts of a career in the Church. Still in his teens when he landed in New York in 1895, Iamurri worked as a railroad hand for several years before deciding to enter school to learn English. Thereafter, his language skills enabled him to become a timekeeper and foreman on the railroad, a job that he fell back on often over the following years. He later entered college, studied briefly in a seminary, received a law degree but never practiced, and was trained as a detective. After service in the Canadian army during the First World War, Iamurri returned to the railroad for a few years before settling down with his wife in a candy store business. His memoirs are perceptive and critical, his descriptions of immigrant processing and his first few months in the United States very evocative.

Carmine Biagio Iannace emigrated to America in 1906 at the age of 16, returned to his village in 1907, and after a brief stay came back to this country to settle. With only a third-grade formal education, Iannace acquired during his immigrant years sufficient knowledge of written Italian to be able to produce an autobiography, *La scoperta dell'America* (1971). Professor M. Ricciardelli of the University of Buffalo, who contributes an introduction to the book, met Iannace two years before his death in 1968 and was instrumental in getting the manuscript published posthumously in Italy. Carmine Iannace was an unpretentious man who had spent a lifetime as an ordinary laborer and who had lived to see each of his American-born children enter the professions. At the age of 70, with free time on his hands, he suddenly

felt the strong urge to put down some of the events, which came flood-
ing back to his memory, of his first year in the United States and his
return to Italy. Halfway through his manuscript, his energy partially
spent, he had second thoughts about his skill in expressing those mental images in words. "Today is March 6, 1966. I have reread the pages
I have written and they have assaulted me with a sense of discomfort.
My words now seem inadequate to what I want to say. These anecdotes
of my youth have come back to me bit by bit until one day I got this
sudden need to express myself on paper. The thoughts came to me in a
rush—my life and the lives of others. I wanted to do so much more
with this, but my preparation is inadequate" (p. 124). Despite Iannace's doubts, the book succeeds admirably.

Antonio Margariti also decided to write his memoirs in his old
age. A farm laborer from Calabria with no formal education, Margariti left Italy in 1913 and, like millions of other immigrants, built a
life for himself and his family in America. He held a number of temporary immigrant jobs before settling after the First World War in Philadelphia, where he worked in an automobile plant until his retirement
in 1965. After the last member of his family died in 1978, Margariti
sat down and typed a 47-page autobiography, *America! America!*
(1979), in his own unschooled Italian. The sentences, and some of the
words, run together with no internal punctuation or terminal stops,
and there is no paragraphing. Margariti sent his typescript to an Italian
editor, who decided to publish together in a single volume Magariti's
original pages and the editor's version written in proper Italian. The
effect is dramatic, and both can be read easily and with profit.

In 1972 I acquired a set of diaries written in Italian that had been
kept by an immigrant known only as Totonno from 1906 until after the
Second World War. I have translated the 1906–19 diaries; the Totonno
excerpts in this book are from that translation (only the 1906–7 seg-
ment has been published; it appeared in *Attenzione* magazine, January
1981). Leaving his native village represented for this 19-year-old
butcher's son so decisive a moment in his life that on April 22, 1906, a
few days before his departure, he began a running record of his experiences. The diary opens with these words: "With my new life, going to
America, I want to write down for my old age, if nature permits me an
old age, my youthful adventures, so that one day I can read about the
life I have had." The diary is rich in detail. Totonno had an unerring

eye and a receptive ear, and could effectively capture a mood or a subject in a few well-chosen words. Although he was a man of many deep passions and fixed ideas, he was capable of lucid and impartial descriptions of people and occurrences.

Both Margariti and Totonno were lifelong socialists and idealists, not passive persons who took life as it came, and they were sensitive to the suffering of others. Both loved America and like many immigrants valued what America represented—freedom of thought and action. The two men differed radically, however, in their attachment to what they had left behind. Margariti never looked back, but Totonno remained emotionally tied to his village and to his Italianness. These diverse perspectives influenced the way in which the two men viewed their immigrant experience.

Throughout the research and writing phases of this project, I received assistance and encouragement from a number of individuals and institutions. Those who were most active in their participation, although a few may not be aware of my debt to them, are Gloria Condoluci, Franco Fido, Giuseppe Guarnieri, Egidio Lunardi, Jerry Mangione, Rudolph J. Vecoli, and the Campanella and Fumarola families. I am grateful to the National Endowment for the Humanities for summer fellowships in 1979 and 1983. These awards permitted me to study Italian dialects at Stanford University and to have access to the resources of the University of Minnesota Immigration History Research Center. I owe a special thanks to the staff members of the library at the State University of New York at Brockport, who labored tirelessly to track down my persistent requests for rare Italian titles. The translations from the Italian sources are my own.

La Merica

IMAGES OF ITALIAN GREENHORN
EXPERIENCE

ONE

Leaving Italy

> The land that does not have products to export, exports its own sons; the people who do not find in their own country their elevation will search for it across the ocean among other peoples.[1]
>
> Be good boys, young gentlemen:
> Discard your umbrellas
> and your gloves;
> you take our places in the fields,
> for we are going to America.[2]

The Decision to Emigrate

To understand why emigration from Italy commenced and grew steadily in volume, one must consider more than the broad societal forces that set the flow in motion. Time and again over the years, it was a combination of individual forces that triggered the decision to emigrate. Poverty, or relative deprivation, does not by itself create a sufficient or even necessary "push" to go elsewhere. However, if poverty is combined with personal goals and expectations that are perceived as not realizable at home, and if a place to relocate becomes available where such hopes appear to have a greater chance of realization, the desire to emigrate may become irresistible.

Rocco Boffilo, a Calabrian *contadino*, comparing what he had heard about America with the style of life in his district, found the former promising and the latter wanting: "Things go badly here. Many *contadini* here do not eat bread. They live on potatoes and beans. The salaries have increased, that is true, but one can only find work three or four months out of the year. Why do so many go to America? Because they are better off there. The work here, in comparison, is too much to bear. Up at sunrise, carrying your tools while walking several kilometers to the fields and then returning during the darkness in the evening, totally exhausted: that is the life we live here. And add to that a long, frigid winter season. When someone returns from America to tell us that the wages are superior and that there are fewer discomforts, many of the men cannot resist the temptation to go and find out for themselves."[3]

But even these remarks are too simplistic. Most emigrants did not set a straight-line path that led inexorably to the decision to leave home. Rather, history demonstrates that their lives—like ours—were at once more disorderly and varied and risky and interesting than fiction often dares to imagine.

If blatant economic deprivation had been the sole or dominant precipitating factor, workers of the lowest classes—both in the cities and around the countryside—would have departed to the last man, while those who were better off would have stayed home. This was far from the case; many stayed on even though their existence was marginal. Vincenzo Tucci was one of these; as a farm laborer, he had to support a wife and four children on the modest sum of one *lira* per day. The family, living together in one room, was at the edge of desperation much of the time. But when he was asked why he did not seek to improve his lot by going to America, as others were doing, he replied that what he had in Italy was more important to him than what he might hope to obtain in America.[4]

For every Tucci who remained, however, there was another Italian in much better circumstances who left, even though—in objective terms—remaining at home would probably have been the wiser choice. Unlike Tucci, such a man was likely to have skills that were more marketable in Italy than abroad. And certainly, staying put would have been less taxing on mind and body than gambling on success in immigrant America. So why did he go?

Some Italians felt that they could not live an honest life in their home country. The employment outlook was grim; the depressed wage system prevented many from fulfilling cherished goals, such as marrying when they wished to do so; for many, each day blended into all the others in one unending tedium. As one intending emigrant expressed the limiting features of his life to his priest, Father Giovanni Scalabrini, "I can be a thief or I can emigrate."[5] And he chose the latter alternative because it was less morally repugnant to him. Others wanted to improve their living standards, or were disturbed by the mediocrity of their society, or were embarrassed by the meaninglessness of their work. More than a few got swept up in the fever of emigration, fostered by the myths perpetuated by some returning emigrants who willingly presented themselves as solid proof that the streets of America were indeed inlaid with gold. Every remittance mailed home by an immigrant was a reminder of America's wealth and fired the zeal of at least one more person to want to follow after him.

By the decade of 1910 Italians in the United States were sending home large sums of money. One source estimated that over $85,000,000 a year went to Italy,[6] and for some families back home, this money represented a large portion of their total income. "Without America to send us money," a Calabrese *contadino* remarked, "we would now be eating one another."[7] Money became the prime topic of letters between the family members in America and those in Italy. It was believed that money was easy to come by in America; consequently, everyone at home had his hand out. Diego Delfino went to great lengths to satisfy his Uncle Cosimo's constant requests for small sums for this or that expense; when he discovered that the uncle had spent the money on pleasure, he sent him a very angry letter.[8]

On occasion the immigrants had to remind those in Italy of the sacrifices they had to make in order to keep the remittances coming. One son, in exasperation, wrote to his father that "it is not as you believe that here in America money is found on the ground." He was a dutiful son, he insisted; he labored "night and day" to earn money and had reduced his standard of living to an absolute minimum "in order to have a penny more" to send home. A complaining wife finally received this letter from her immigrant husband: "Dear Wife . . . I will not send you another penny for food. Because of this you take care, for I am one of those who means what I say when I have said something." When the remittances stopped because of unemployment, those in Italy would panic. A man named Domenico sought to reassure his wife that he had not forgotten her: "I want you to know," he wrote, "that during the month of January I did not make anything for food and for the house rent. The weather is bad and there is no work. Dear wife, as I make money I will send it to you."[9]

Fortune Gallo was typical of the impressionistic boys and young men who were quickly seduced into emigrating by the stories of the riches of America. Gallo was 17 years old in 1895 when a returnee to

Torre Maggiore, Puglia, visited his father. The man had accumulated a tidy fortune in the Buffalo, New York, produce business and was not modest about his accomplishments. Gallo listened avidly to every word, admiring the visitor's symbols of monetary success. "A big man, he dressed the part of the successful tycoon. His clothes were of the finest material and across his massive chest dangled a heavy gold chain. His hands sparkled with a glittering display of diamond rings. From his lips protruded a large, expensive cigar." Characteristically for his type, the man's boasting increased with each mouthful of wine until with a flourish he pulled out his bankbook to substantiate his remarks. "See," he fairly shouted, "here is evidence of what I say. Thirty thousand dollars!—the result of four years' work." The man urged young Gallo to leave Torre Maggiore and return with him to America, where his future would be limitless. The father was not impressed with the man's vulgar display of wealth, but he turned to his son and asked if he were interested. Young Gallo did not hesitate; the eagerness that had been gathering strength in his throat sprang out in an instant: "I told him yes so fast he seemed almost hurt." [10]

But not every Italian who eventually left went at the first opportunity. Some needed more sustained pressure than others; for them, the Italian proverb "*Chi esce riesce*" (He who leaves succeeds) had to be confirmed repeatedly. Before they took the first gingerly step, they let the pioneers go first to examine the "new ground" and to establish a colony of *paesani*. Any slight tremor, any setback or discouragement, might cause the timid ones to about-face and retrace their steps to the sanctuary of Italian village life.

Breaking Away

Their ship idled at anchor in the bay
towering above the chafing of the sea;
The lusty crew worked, frantic, in relay
loading the ship for the westward journey.
At last, the passengers moved from the shore.
A tense excitement stirred the milling throng,
as one heard high above the muffled roar
the tender strains of a romantic song. [11]

Acquiring a passport was one of the first steps in the preparation for departure (indeed, the intending emigrant had a greater need for a passport to leave Italy than to enter America). To get one, he first requested his birth certificate from the secretary of the municipality in which he had been born. The certificate was then forwarded by the subagent to the *questura*, the police headquarters, in the provincial capital, where the personal record of each man in the province was kept for purposes of military conscription and criminal vigilance. If a man's name was not on file, he did not officially exist and could not be issued a passport. Or if there was anything in the record to cause the *questor* to conclude that the man should be refused permission to depart, he was denied a passport.

Once their passports were in hand, the intending emigrants were the center of attention during the weeks before departure. New clothes were tailored for them (often never worn because they were dress clothes that proved to be out of fashion in America) and, unless they could take a firm stand, they were weighed down with various items that their relatives considered absolute necessities. Dinners would be held and special emigration masses celebrated at the churches before the men went to the railroad station or set off down the path that led to the railhead. Where railroads did not exist, the emigrants reached the ports on foot. Vito Ferrari and a companion packed everything in saddlebags on tiny donkeys and walked 200 miles over the mountain roads from Basilicata to Naples.[12]

Breaking away caused acute stress for both the emigrants and, especially, those who remained behind. At age 22, Enrico Fino left his small village near Foggia, Puglia, where his father was postmaster; he had become intrigued with America by handling the correspondence to and from the immigrants. His father refused to give him permission to leave: "It is not for you," the elder Fino insisted. "It is not as easy as it looks." Enrico went anyway.[13] And many decades later, Pietro Greco could still recall vividly the day of his departure. "My heart aches everytime I think about that afternoon when I left my parents and friends to go to the railroad station. My mother kissed me goodbye and then stood by the doorway as stiff as a statue sobbing as my father and I left the house. At the station even my father as hard as he tried could not keep the tears from filling his eyes."[14]

Carmine Iannace's father never accepted his decision. Iannace was born in 1890 in the region of Campania near the small village of Belvedere. His father was a typical *contadino* of the district who farmed and kept a few animals. Iannace left school after three years to work with his father, just when the rural proletariat of the province were catching the emigration fever. Hundreds were departing each month; many of his relatives and friends had gone, and each time Iannace watched another person leave, he felt a desire to go along. Caught up in romantic images gleaned from returning emigrants and transatlantic correspondence, the young boy ignored the admonitions of his older brother, who had already worked in America, and his father, who saw no reward in going to that "cold country." Each time Iannace broached the subject, his father cut him short. He was too young to engage in such a foolish venture, the boy was told; furthermore, he was needed in the fields.

But Iannace was not to be deterred. He was convinced that the advantages of emigration were there for all to see. Money was to be made in America. Over there one could earn $1.25 for ten hours of labor, the equivalent of six *lire* and 25 *centesimi*, whereas a day laborer in Belvedere could hope to earn only one *lira* for a full 12 hours. Iannace visualized himself returning home in grand style, as others had done, impressing his family with his worldly sophistication and resourcefulness.

Iannace wrote to his chum and relative, Cavuoto, in Pennsylvania in hopes that Cavuoto would lend support to his plan to join him. The reply was neutral—"If you decide to come, look me up"—but the 16-year-old boy chose to interpret the remark as encouragement and proceeded to make plans. At the village hall, however, he discovered that he needed his father's permission to apply for a passport. With the confidence of one who knows his mind, he set forth his argument: there need not be any worry about his youth, he concluded, because Cavuoto would take care of him. The father said nothing for a moment, and then with a sign of resignation told his son that he was needed for the grape harvest—at least he could do that much. Iannace was elated; his father had not said yes, but neither would he any longer block his son's path.

But as the day approached, the father suddenly became visibly upset: "I never saw my father so angry." When the morning of his departure arrived, Iannace picked up his heavy suitcases, which contained a large pecorino cheese and a sack of chickpeas (both thrust upon him by an aunt) as well as his few clothes, and began to walk with his father to Benevento, where he and other emigrants would catch the afternoon train for Naples. At the three-kilometer mark, however, without a word or gesture, his father abruptly turned around and started back to the village. Startled and not knowing how to interpret this action, Iannace yelled after him, but the man did not turn or respond. Iannace was in anguish; his father had "rejected" him. Seeing the young boy on the edge of tears, one of the men in the group tried to console him: "*Compare*, the best way to uproot a plant is to pull it out in one fast motion." Iannace did not understand the metaphor, so the man added, "You are now an emigrant. From today forward you are completely on your own. He [motioning to the father's receding figure] can no longer be of any help to you." [15]

Once in America, Iannace worked alongside men who were for the most part considerably older. The median age bracket in the Italian work gangs was 25 to 35. Many workers were single men who were planning to return to Italy to buy some land and select a bride as soon as they had earned enough money.

Matteo was one of these individuals. [16] Because his original plans to marry had not materialized, for personal and economic reasons, he decided at age 27 to go to the United States, where he worked for a number of years in order to earn enough money to return home and choose a wife on his terms.

Matteo was born in 1885 into a Sicilian farm family of six children in the village of Trappeto, province of Trapani, located on the Gulf of Castellammare. Because the plot owned by the family barely sufficed to meet its needs, especially during times of high costs and poor crops, the father frequently went out to sea with the local fishermen to supplement his income.

Matteo's father began to employ his son in a variety of capacities as soon as the boy could walk. At age five Matteo had the responsibility of collecting hay for the donkey and gathering manure. By age ten he was transporting grain to the mill to be ground into flour, and gathering firewood while in the fields with his father from five in the morning until evening. As a result, Matteo never attended school. Within a few years he had graduated to the status of full-time farm laborer.

At age 25, Matteo had no desire to leave home. He had become engaged and planned to spend the next few years saving his money in order to purchase a parcel of land on which he would build a house for his bride. The decision to emigrate was prompted by the father of his *fidanzata*, who one day called Matteo a cretin, an imbecile, and an ignoramus—a man incapable of carrying on a decent discourse. "Your brother is not a suitable prospect for my daughter," the father told Matteo's sister. "He cannot support my daughter." When Matteo heard this, he thought of the time wasted during the 18-month engagement, and of his awkward visits to the girl's house, when they would sit at opposite sides of the room avoiding each other's eyes and saying nothing. The insults stung him, and he refused to consider his family's suggestions of reconciliation. Over the strong protestations of his mother and sisters, Matteo decided then and there to leave on the first ship.

Unlike Matteo's firm decision, Totonno's was ambivalent; a combination of factors led him to emigrate, with the lure of America the least of them. For Totonno, America was primarily a place of refuge where he could take stock of himself, unfettered by the harsh opinions and prying eyes of the other members of his family. Totonno was the only member of his family to emigrate, and their opposition to his leaving was very strong. His parents and siblings had great pride in themselves and their heritage. In later years, when Totonno encouraged his siblings to join him in America, his arguments were met with dead silence. The immigrant in America was, to them, a slave who had given up his birthright in order to benefit from higher wages. Emigration indicated a flaw in one's character and an unwillingness to face squarely the challenges at home.

The sixth of 11 children, Totonno was born in 1886 in the Puglia village of Martina Franca, located a dozen kilometers inland from the ancient seaport of Taranto. For generations, Totonno's family had been in the meat business as vendors and butchers. Totonno's father had returned, in 1870, from eight years of service with the Italian *carabinieri* and had taken possession of the family's meat shop in partnership with an uncle. In 1887 the business failed, and the father spent the next six years trying unsuccessfully to start again in several cities in the region. In 1893 he accepted an offer to open a shop in the nearby village of Alberobello. The next year, at the age of eight, Totonno began to assist his father. At age 12 he left school to work full time, and by 16 he had become a skilled butcher who knew every aspect of the trade.

In 1904 his older brother was called to serve 18 months in the military, but after a year he wanted to get out and resume his education. The father decided to send Totonno as a substitute to serve the remaining six months. A very unhappy Totonno went to a military base in north Italy, near Udine, leaving behind the girl he loved. Thoughts of emigration began to form in his mind during that period. Once he had seen the big cities, his small village seemed insignificant by comparison. He returned to Alberobello to discover that his girlfriend did not want to continue their romance and that many of his peers were gone, having emigrated to Argentina and to the United States. (The outward flow had been steadily increasing since 1900; from 1900 to 1910 the population of Alberobello declined by 50 percent.) Friends sent Totonno photographs from New York depicting the good life there and urging him to join them. His best friend, who was living in the South Bronx, was particularly insistent.

Actually, Totonno had always expected to assume operation of the family shop. But the father, a stern and uncommunicative man, would not take his son seriously. He did not condone Totonno's rebellious behavior, his evening escapades, or his lack of discipline. What Totonno really wanted was his father's approval, for he did not look forward to a life of butchering animals; in fact, he had always had an aversion to the meat business. But what else was there in Alberobello for him? He did not want to study for a teacher's diploma, and he was too old to begin an apprenticeship in another trade. That left emigration, an excuse to leave home and an opportunity to show his father and the rest of his family that he could become a man worthy of respect.

His family chose to ignore his departure for Naples. Totonno arose early that morning and left the house quickly and quietly. Turning the corner, however, he encountered his older half-brother, who had been waiting to escort him to the station, and together they

> walked through the village to the railroad station. I had not made a point of my departure to anyone, so I was surprised to discover among the large crowd many of my friends. It was a beautiful day, and the parting was joyful and without strain. Our party of twelve emigrants arrived in Naples after dark.[17]

At 19, Totonno was the youngest of the 12 men, who ranged in age up to 42 years. Five of them were married, six were laborers, and eight could read and write. None had been in America before. Once in New York, each man would go in a different direction: the Bronx, Brooklyn, Utica, Scranton, Paterson, and a few small towns in upstate New York.

The drama of farewell was played out innumerable times at the provincial railroad stations throughout Italy. The platforms would be crowded with people—the emigrants, their relatives, and the curious, for the departures were significant events in the lives of the villagers. Bidding goodbye to a loved one who might never be seen again created unforgettable scenes at the stations. One observer described the atmosphere as "worse than a funeral." [18] Angelo Mosso was aboard a train that stopped at Castrofilippo, Sicily, in March 1905. His description contains all of the typical ingredients of the platform drama:

> The stationmaster told me that thirty emigrants were departing, including seven women. They had been waiting for two months for a ship, and last week they received word to go to Palermo for embarkation. When the train began to move, a piercing cry arose from the crowd along the platform. Each person had an arm upraised clutching a handkerchief. One woman broke away from the crowd and began to run alongside the train as it pulled out of the station, yelling out: "Say hello to him (meaning her husband); remind him that I am still waiting for him to send me the money for the steamship ticket. Tell him I am waiting, and tell him . . . tell him . . . that if I have to stay here any longer I will die." As the train chugged into the next station, Racalmuto, the anxious platform crowd broke out into a long, confused roar that sounded like a clap of thunder. Six or seven emigrants boarded, and the same tearful goodbyes were repeated. Several women ran alongside the train holding onto the emigrants who were themselves hanging out of the open windows. Only after the train had picked up speed did the women disengage. [19]

The drama did not end there. Up to the turn of the century, the port cities could not adequately provide for the ever increasing numbers of those leaving Italy. In the 1880s and 1890s the port of Genoa earned a notorious reputation: the dock area was woefully congested; the emigrants were treated like cattle; the sleeping and eating facilities did not provide for more than one-third of those awaiting transport. The situation changed little until the passage of new laws in 1901. The following description is from 1898:

Once the emigrants decide to leave home, they find themselves burdened with all sorts of unanticipated expenses, including the special trains that transport hundreds of them each day to Genoa, and the cost of food and lodging. The agents systematically fleece their charges. They are sent here a week before sailing and are directed to those merchants and innkeepers with whom the agents have arranged a sharing of the spoils. For twenty years now, this city has had to endure the spectacle of large groups of pathetic and famished emigrants, devoid of decent clothing and money, in the most immoral circumstances, stretched out wherever they can—on the floors of hotels, on the streets, in public places—and they are to be seen everywhere, day and night.[20]

By 1906, when Totonno and his *paesani* arrived in Naples, some of the major problems of emigrant processing at the ports had been alleviated by the construction of a number of communal facilities and the introduction of workable bureaucratic procedures. In 1907, Naples had 80 *locande* (third-class hostels) with 2,157 beds for emigrants, and 745 dormitory accommodations. Genoa had 31 *locande* that could sleep and feed 767 persons; Palermo, with 34 *locande*, had 1,121 beds and 334 dormitory posts; and Messina had two *locande* for 88 emigrants. But a number of problems remained. The hotels for the emigrants were rude, still overcrowded, and not always situated close to the port. Moreover, the hotel personnel often came from "suspect elements" who took the work for the opportunities it offered in fraud and theft. Even though the authorities were diligent in enforcing the regulations, the official statistics of violations were undoubtedly far fewer than the actual number. In 1906, the inspectors of emigration took 82 legal actions for irregularities against the hotels, calling for a suspension or revocation of the license to operate. During that same year there were over 400 declarations of fraud by emigrants against *locanda* proprietors and employees.[21]

Totonno and the others from Alberobello walked directly from the Naples station to a hotel managed by the ship company. After depositing their luggage, the men followed a crowd of people to the dining hall to eat the one meal a day that their steamship tickets entitled them to. Hundreds of emigrants were moving in and out of the hall, and Totonno waited for about half an hour before he could sit with the others around one of the large tables. Harassed, unkempt waiters brought plates of soup made with tomatoes and pasta. There was also a stew of goat meat and potatoes, and melons and sour wine. It was in Totonno's opinion a "tasteless and hurried supper." Back at the hotel, they slept ten to a room and two or more to a bed. The quality of the hotel can best be imagined from this notation in Totonno's diary: "The next morning I saw Rocco. An insect of some kind had bitten him on the right eyelid during the night. His eye was swollen closed."

Thieves and Rogues

Before boarding ship, the emigrants had to run the gauntlet of a small army of peddlers, thieves, and confidence men—the flotsam of Italian society—all of whom earned their daily bread by extracting every possible penny from their departing conationals.

Peddlers of all sorts offered—at inflated prices—food, hats, pillows, and numerous worthless objects and trinkets that they hoped would appeal to the innocent country bumpkins. The men who went about selling grass ropes did an especially brisk business. The suitcases that the emigrants had purchased at home, fabricated purposely for them, were of cheap construction and not meant to hold together for more than a few days. Made of cloth and paper pasted over frail wooden frames, a suitcase would be in two or more pieces by the time the emigrant reached the port of embarkation, and the grass rope was needed to tie it up.

The peddlers also profited by many emigrants' lack of precise information as to what should be carried on the voyage. Some knew what they would need on board ship and during their first weeks in America, but others were entirely ignorant of what was essential. Accordingly, there were those who arrived on the dock with little more than the clothes on their backs; at the same time there were families that brought everything—bags, trunks of food, clothes, mattresses, cooking utensils. All these possessions created insurmountable problems. The docks were choked with people and small mountains of luggage. It took hours for the emigrants to shift through the bags, boxes, and bundles to find their own and for the officials to check them through.

Frequently, baggage was lost or stolen, or never loaded on the ship. Pietro Moldotti, a Scalabrinian missionary, related one such incident. In the 1880s, arriving at the Genoa terminal, he came upon a mob scene—a jumble of emigrants, baggage, agents, officials, and dock people all competing for limited space.

> I could not comprehend anything that was happening before my eyes, but it was a spectacle interesting to watch. Suddenly, a young man from Cremona, with a yellow ticket in his cap, his arms outstretched, ran up to me asking for help. A sack of his had been taken, and his wife and children were missing. Without hesitation, I plunged with him into that Babylonian confusion of people, goods, and carts. The air was thick with yells, cries, and profanities from almost every dialect in Italy. After considerable searching and effort we succeeded, God only knows how, in locating his family and the delinquent, who was strolling about with the sack on his shoulder. A lively fistfight broke out during which I both received and delivered a number of well-placed blows. A gentleman came to our aid not a moment too soon, grabbed that rascal by the throat, and dragged him over to the police. Once it was over we began to shake and cry uncontrollably. They because of their desperate condition and I because of my rage.[22]

Thieves circulated freely among the emigrants, looking for any unattended item of value to snatch or a convenient pocket to pick or a poor soul to torment. Once one of these boys or men decided that a particular traveler was vulnerable, he would follow and pester his quarry until he received something for his labors. Even fairly sophisticated persons were often victims. Broughton Brandenburg, an American journalist who posed as an emigrant, was impressed by the expertise and persistence of the dock people in Messina and Naples. One young man pursued him relentlessly until in exasperation Brandenburg gave him a few coins. Predictably, in a few minutes the man was back for a second helping—which he received. Naples had long had a notorious reputation among tourists and other visitors. The emigrants called it the "City of Thieves," and the dock people worked hard to live up to that name. "Dishonesty is part of the air of Naples," Brandenburg noted, "just as is the smell that is famous."[23]

Totonno, the morning after his arrival, took a tour of the city and was impressed with the tempo of Neapolitan life and the large, ornate buildings. "The city is a delight," he wrote in his diary, "but the people are impossible." His language became stronger when, a few hours later, while standing in line during the final phases of processing, he passed his hand over the pocket where his billfold was supposed to be but wasn't. A pickpocket had taken every penny he had.

> I realized with a sinking feeling that my billfold, which contained fifty *lire* [$10], was gone forever. In vain, we looked everywhere. There are plenty of thieves in Naples who prey on people like us. I finally had to accept the fact that it must have been taken right out of my pocket. Now I will have to depend on my friends for money. I boarded ship in a state of despair. I could not even enjoy the cigarette I was smoking or admire the panorama as we sailed out into the Bay of Naples.

In addition to outright theft, hundreds of emigrants were subjected to fraud and deceit; large sums of money went directly into the pockets of unscrupulous men who took advantage of the emigrants' lack of knowledge of bureaucratic procedure, their timidity in the face of authority (or presumed authority), and their tendency to rely on hearsay and rumor. In the world they came from, persons of authority were corrupt or corruptible, and they were feared and distrusted because of the large amount of discretionary power they held, power that could be exercised arbitrarily on the basis of a pretext or a mere whim. The emigrants were sure that to insult an official or customs inspector, or to do the wrong thing, or to fail to do the right thing would result in their being summarily sent back home. This attitude made them susceptible to suggestion and therefore easily victimized by confidence men who, while posing as figures of authority in official-looking garb and insignia, worked on them a number of ingenious and time-honored scams.

Since labels were affixed to baggage by customs officials after it had been inspected, men posing as officials would go through the dock crowd casually slapping bogus labels on baggage, then asking for and usually receiving payment. The dupe did not realize that he had been deceived until he went through the legitimate customs procedure and had to face the anger and sometimes vindictiveness of the inspectors, who accused the emigrant of attempting to deceive them. The bogus labels would be ripped off and the luggage examined minutely, while its hapless owner sought in vain to convince the officials that he had not been party to any attempt to bypass the regulations but rather was an innocent and thoroughly confused victim.

The most lucrative of all the rackets, one engaged in by legitimate businessmen and even bankers, involved cheating the migrant when he exchanged his Italian *lire* for American dollars. In Naples, men presenting themselves as officials worked the crowds. If you hold on to those "old" *lire*, the emigrants were warned, you will lose money when you exchange them for dollars in America. To prevent that loss, you need only give me your *lire* and I will give you "new" drafts. That way your money is safe.

The drafts were indeed negotiable but their worth was reduced by the 10 to 20 percent profit that the sellers took as their commission. The peddlers on the docks and the businessmen in the surrounding area also gave change in American currency, with the commission built into the price of the article. For example, if an emigrant had 25 cents in change coming, the man would give him 16 cents, pocketing nine cents for himself. The seller thereby realized a double profit: one from the inflated retail price of the article, and another from the unnecessary money exchange.

The emigrant was not always merely an innocent victim; he was often looking for shortcuts through the bureaucratic maze of regulations. In some cases, out of superstition or misinformation or just plain stubbornness, he was not willing to comply with a regulation and would welcome, and pay for, advice to help him to beat the system. For example, a vaccination was required before one could board a ship leaving from an Italian port. The emigrants feared these vaccinations because, among other reasons, it meant a sore arm and a fever during the voyage, and they suspected that the ocean trip would be arduous enough without adding a high temperature to the discomforts of steerage and seasickness. So when young men walked up and down the vaccination line whispering, "For a *lira* I will tell you how to keep from getting a sore arm," a *lira* would indeed change hands. "When the doctor vaccinates you, rub your shirt sleeve down over the two scratched places quickly. Don't worry, he won't stop you." The advice was good. The vaccination was not likely to "take" if the person rubbed the serum off immediately. Those who waited a few minutes before doing so ended up suffering the soreness and the fever.

Brandenburg observed a man stopping emigrants on the Messina docks and asking if they had had their tickets stamped by the "American doctor." The emigrants knew that somewhere along the line a person would examine them and that he had the authority to turn them back. No, the confused emigrant would reply, in a voice rapidly approaching panic. Well, the man would continue, I can take care of it for you. For a small fee I will stamp your ticket, and the American doctor will take one look at the stamp and allow you to pass through without an examination. If the emigrant agreed, he would be taken to a small office where his ticket would be marked with a bogus stamp in a flourish of bureaucratic efficiency. The emigrant would go on his way with a somewhat lighter purse but breathing a sigh of relief for having found this out just in time. The procedure, of course, was a ruse. There was no American doctor.

Some emigrants were easily deceived by a confidence game because they were blinded by their own greed. Variations of the entrapment techniques were endless. Generally speaking, a man would strike up a casual conversation with an emigrant, using the "haven't we met someplace else" approach. By observing dialect, manner, and dress, the man would determine the emigrant's home province and shape his remarks accordingly. If the man could convince the emigrant that they had something in common, he could more easily set him up. They would talk; the man would do the emigrant a small favor, or buy him a glass of wine, or in some other way indicate a very friendly attitude. Once the friendship was established, an accomplice would appear and show a sum of money, saying that he had to deliver it to a certain address and needed directions. The first man would take the emigrant aside and suggest that they walk with the second man to a secluded spot and relieve him of the money. But the person who got beaten and robbed, of course, was the emigrant.[24]

On the Ocean

The great majority of Italians going to the Americas traveled in third-class steerage, rooms or large areas sometimes below the water line, where the air was foul and the accommodations meager and crowded. Few ordinary emigrants were found in cabin class unless they had previously made money in America and wanted to cross the Atlantic in comfort this time. When Totonno returned to Italy in 1910, he met only four other Italians in second class; the rest were huddled below. The total number of alien immigrants who came to the United States in cabin class was 82,055 in 1901 and 64,269 in 1902; of these no more than one-third were Italian.[25]

The conditions of travel differed, depending on the steamship company, the port of departure, the year, and the season. A number of Italians sailed from French and English ports, sometimes to shorten the sea voyage, but also to avoid Italian ships, which were thought to offer inferior services. In the early days of emigration, before the turn of the century and the construction of new fleets of carriers, ships that had transported cattle and horses in their holds were converted to carry passengers. Generally speaking, after 1890 the newer and larger ships made the Atlantic crossing more comfortable and less hazardous, even in steerage. The price of a third-class ticket rose during the peak months of transatlantic travel. Emigration to the northern hemisphere cost the most from February to June and the least in December and January; to the southern hemisphere it was highest from October to December and lowest in April, May, and June. About 50 percent of the Italians bound for the United States each year sailed in March, April, or May. In 1906, the third-class fare to New York during peak months was from 125 to 180 *lire* (the official exchange rate at the time was 5.44 *lire* to the U.S. dollar).[26]

What was life like on board the emigrant ships? Amy Bernardy, an Italian writer, who observed emigrant travel after the turn of the century, disagreed with those who argued that steerage was a wretched experience: "Seventy-five percent of the emigrants live better on board ship than they did at home," where they lived in humble huts and ate humble food. It is true, she continued, that one hears chronic complaints, but these complaints can be interpreted as mere vocalizations, the kind one would expect to hear from naive countryfolk who are bewildered by their new environment and anxious about what the future holds. She surmised that much of the griping was imitative behavior: one person would voice a complaint, and others would take up the chant and parrot his protestations.[27]

Other cabin passengers and crew members held the same opinion. Federico Garlanda, who crossed the Atlantic many times during the same period, went down to steerage to see with his own eyes "how these poor people are treated." Their circumstances "are fine," he concluded. "I feel perfectly safe in saying that these emigrants have much better conditions aboard than they ever had in their own houses." Their beds were comfortable, Garlanda observed; the food was abundant; and, above all, they were served meat twice a day—a diet they never enjoyed at home.[28]

Another cabin passenger offered a somewhat different perspective. Edmondo De Amicis was a celebrated Italian writer; his classic book, *Sull'oceano*, is a detailed account of his tedious 28-day voyage from Genoa to Argentina in the late 1880s (he found even his own first-class accommodations confining and uncomfortable). De Amicis wanted to document the psychological state of the departing Italians. Emigration, he argued, had been forced upon them by economic circumstances, and this radical uprooting from their villages and fields was taking a terrible toll. He climbed down the ladder to peer into the steerage compartments shortly after everyone had boarded.

> The emigrants were crowded together. Many were seasick, with sweating faces and ruffled hair, lying among piles of blankets and rags. Family members were bunched together in small, tight groups, looking lost and dismayed like those who suddenly find themselves without a roof over their heads. The husband is sleeping sitting up, his wife is beside him with her head on his shoulder, and the children are up on the sleeping planks, each with a head on the knees of another. They look more like deportees than emigrants. Here they are at the beginning of their voyage and they are already worn out, their energy spent in making the momentous decision to leave Italy, selling their possessions, arguing with the padroni and their priests, and still feeling the effects of the painful separation from their villages and relatives.[29]

Bernardy, Garlanda, and De Amicis were all affluent, educated Italians who were viewing the process of emigration as outsiders. To them, emigration was a fascinating object of study—to be poked and probed at their leisure but certainly not to be encountered directly.

There were some people of similar background, however, who actually traveled in steerage. In 1879, Adolfo Rossi and his friend Giuseppi, both from northern Italian burgher backgrounds, traveled across France to England, where they boarded an English ship. The two adventurers had wanted second-class berths, but because of insufficient funds they had to take third-class accommodations.

Along with a dozen German and Irish workers, the young men were installed below deck in a large room that was divided into several sleeping sections. The two Italians selected one and spread out the mattresses they had purchased the day before. Rossi tried to relax and adjust himself to his new surroundings but could not. He was not accustomed to the primitive sleeping arrangement. Nor could he stomach the odors emanating from the sweating Irish and German workers or the food that was served: salted meat, potatoes, fish, and an adulterated drink that "was supposed to be either tea or milk." Rossi and Giuseppi pooled their money and approached one of the ship's porters who agreed, for a handsome fee, to provide them with more suitable rations from the second-class kitchen. For the remainder of the voyage, the two men ate freshly baked bread and good cuts of meat and cheese, all washed down with the dozen bottles of a fine Bordeaux that Rossi had purchased at an English shop prior to boarding.[30]

Another man who endured the voyage in steerage, even though his emigration was motivated by a spirit of adventure rather than a background of poverty, was Francesco Ventresca. He was born in 1872 in the village of Introdacqua, Abruzzi. His father had served in the army for eight years; once released, he acquired a parcel of land, which gave him the prestige of a landowner and from which he derived a small but steady income as well as a minor position with the municipality. Although there were 11 children, the family did not want for basic necessities: "We had plenty to eat . . . but we had very little cash."[31] Each child received a basic education, and Francesco attended school to age 12.

The father had little to pass on to his sons, however, so as each boy came of age, he sought work wherever he could find it. At 17, Ventresca followed his older brothers to other provinces to labor on a variety of construction projects. His first job was digging drainage ditches on reclaimed marshland from dawn to dusk for 30 cents a day. The workers ate no breakfast; for lunch there was pizza, a cake made of cornmeal and rye baked in the coals of an open fire; and the evening meal consisted of polenta (cornmeal mush) with cheese, tomato sauce, and pork sausage. That winter Ventresca helped clear woodlands. Later the three brothers spent several months on a tunnel project near Naples.

Prior to 1890, those emigrating from Introdacqua went either to Brazil or to Argentina. New York first became an object of conversation when two men, who had left town hurriedly to escape arrest in 1880, reappeared after a ten-year absence to extol the virtues of the America of the North. Their tales of the sensual pleasures of New York City and the money to be made by immigrant workers caught the attention of many men of the village. To Ventresca and the others, $2.00 a day as compared to their 20 to 40 cents a day for the same kind of labor was the difference between the satisfaction of a large meal and the belt tightening to which they had become accustomed.

Ventresca's parents were against the idea of emigration. They did not believe that America was an enchanted land and argued with their son that he could establish himself in Italy much better than he could abroad. Nor would his American remittances be crucial to the survival of the family. A neighbor woman said much the same to him: "Francesco, why do you want to go to America and endanger your life? We cannot blame those who have very little at home and emigrate to look for something better; but you are so comfortable at home; why should you go?" [32]

It was true that Ventresca was not deeply discontented with his life in Italy; nevertheless, he found the concept of America fascinating. Even if he did the same work in America, there was something more appealing about doing it as an immigrant in a foreign land than in Italy. In addition, America could offer something new. Who could say what opportunities were awaiting, ready to be taken for the asking? The risk was worthwhile. Others were going, and he did not want to be left behind. In April 1891 Ventresca sailed from Naples on the French liner *La Champagne*, carrying a shoulder bag filled with salami and cheese.

Unlike Rossi, who was able to mitigate his situation through bribery, Ventresca experienced the full impact of steerage life:

> There were over a thousand of us on board. I recall only steerage. I did not venture to speculate on higher living. Most of us were

assigned to bunks—berths would be too refined a name for them. Some of the men were placed one story below deck and others two stories below. We managed to get a bit of light through the hatchway or through the portholes. No one could stay below for very long. We were all the time on deck, except at night and in stormy weather—and we had plenty of that.

We ate our three meals a day in groups of six. One man was given a big pan and he got the food while we looked for a good spot on deck. We just crouched or squatted like the Orientals. We could not very well say that we enjoyed the food, for only genuine hunger could have made it palatable, and in this case hunger was the best sauce.[33]

Brandenburg offered a fuller account of life aboard an emigrant ship. In 1902, having attached themselves to an emigrating Sicilian family, he and his wife experienced most, but not all, of the rigors of steerage life. Like Rossi, after a few days at sea they arranged with a steward to receive a more refined diet from the kitchen and, after a brief and uncomfortable acquaintance with steerage, bargained with the same fellow for better sleeping accommodations. Money bought them additional comforts and also served to smooth the way for better relationships with the crew. Less fortunate emigrants found most of the ship personnel uncooperative, impersonal, and rude. The sailors that Aldobrando Piacenza encountered, for example, were "very discourteous toward all of the Italians." The Italians retaliated, and a lively fistfight ensued after a series of "oppressive acts" by the sailors.[34]

The Brandenburgs were originally assigned to a steerage compartment that was ten feet in height, the size of six rooms—and occupied by over 200 persons. The beds were double-tiered in blocks of 10 to 20, constructed of iron framework with iron slats to support the mattresses which were burlap-covered bags of straw, grass, or waste. The cork life jackets served as pillows, and each passenger was issued a blanket made of jute, five and a half feet long and four and a half wide. There was no ventilation; the compartment was hot, and the air was heavy with the odor of oil and disinfectants. The engine noise was mixed with the crying of the babies, and the stink of vomit and rotting scraps of food, which the emigrants had dropped to the floor, were ever present.[35]

Meals were served on deck, the food ladled out of huge tanks by the steerage stewards. The *capo di rancio* (chief of rations), the man elected by the group of six to get the food, took the pan and bucket and passed along the food line. From the first tank the *capo* received Neapolitan macaroni; from the second, chunks of beef the size of one's fist; and from the third, red wine. Then came the bread baskets and finally the boiled potatoes. The *capo* would return to his group and distribute the food and drink to each tin plate and cup. Brandenburg felt that the quality of the rations was as good as the average Italian got at home.[36]

Iannace and Totonno would not have agreed. Both left Italy in the spring of 1906, Iannace on the liner *Europa* and Totonno on the S.S. *Bulgaria*. Iannace found the shipboard diet monotonous and tasteless. He had been reluctant to bring along his sack of peas and smelly cheese, which became riper each day, but now he was delighted that he could nibble on occasion from his food sack and find nourishment whenever his regular meal was spoiled by seawater splashing on that part of the deck where his group ate. The cheese also helped to mask the overpowering odor of the phenic acid used to disinfect the sleeping quarters.

The 2,500 passengers on Totonno's ship received two meals a day, one at eleven o'clock in the morning and the other at five in the afternoon. Most of the day was spent in eating or queuing up for the next meal. Dinners offered little variety—either pasta or rice in soup, or pasta with sauce. What meat there was Totonno found to be "putrid and inedible."

Breakfast, on ships that served it, was not much better. At eight o'clock the steerage cooks and stewards handed out biscuits and coffee. Brandenburg described the standard biscuit as a "disk of dough, three-quarters of an inch thick, and a hand's length broad. It was as hard as a landlord's heart, and as tasteless as a bit of rag carpet. Half the biscuits were moldy. About 3000 were served out, and for the next half hour disks went sailing high in the air over the sides and into the sea. We used a corkscrew to separate the biscuit into edible fragments."[37]

The aspect of the transatlantic voyage that the emigrants feared most was stormy weather. To ride out a storm in the crowded and oppressive atmosphere of steerage, with the hatches tightly secured, was an experience that few emigrants forgot. "The big event of our voyage across the turbulent Atlantic," Totonno noted in his diary, "was a terrifying night storm. The huge waves bounced our ship around like a cork in a vat of fermenting wine. We were knocked from pillar to post; persons were thrown from their bunks; the women were petrified, and cried, screamed, and prayed all at the same time." For Ventresca, what was to have been a 14-day voyage stretched out to 23 after a storm struck the ship in mid-Atlantic. For days everyone remained below as the ship rolled from side to side. The seasick emigrants spent much of their time in prayer, beseeching the Holy Mother, "*Madonna Santissima, aiutaci!*" (Most Holy Mother, help us).[38]

Seasickness was common; Brandenburg described the seasickness on his ship as "nothing short of frightful," and estimated that more than one-third of the steerage passengers were virtually incapacitated during some portion of the voyage. Totonno was ill most of the time; what little he ate he had to force down while holding his nose. "My luck took a decided turn for the worse as we passed through the Straits of Gibraltar into the much rougher waters of the Atlantic. The ship began to roll and pitch, and my stomach commenced the same rhythm. My routine has now changed completely. I arise in the morning and slowly make my way topside to find a quiet location where I can stretch out and breathe some fresh air. Then I crawl back down for the remainder of the day." On stormy days many meals were left untouched, which left an abundance of food for those who were not ill. Brandenburg felt queasy as he watched a man devour his portion and that of five others, who were too sick to eat and lay prostrate on the deck around the hungry man.[39] But nourishment was needed, and the sailors would anticipate a demand for fresh fruit—the only food a seasick victim could hold down—by purchasing a large supply while in port. Each piece of fruit cost one dollar. Those who had the money paid; those who did not turned their faces to the bulkhead and suffered.[40]

Many of the officers and crews that served on the emigrant ships were either corrupt or less than enthusiastic about conforming to shipboard regulations. The questionable activities that Brandenburg observed on board his ship were equally prevalent on other vessels. The theft of foodstuffs from the ship's stores for sale to those passengers with ready cash was common practice among crew members. They even hoarded toilet paper to be sold to passengers when the need became critical (when Iannace entered the steerage toilet and found no paper, he suddenly understood why the dock boys in Naples had been selling month-old newspapers). The regulations required the ship's doctor to conduct a daily health inspection of the passengers, but such inspections were often superficial if they were undertaken at all. Brandenburg noted that days would elapse without an inspection; when one did take place, the previous days were punched out on the health card each emigrant carried.[41]

The emigrants themselves contributed to the low standards of hygiene and sanitation on board ship. Even though bathing and washing facilities were inadequate, there was noticeable underutilization of those that did exist. Little effort was made to clean eating implements after meals, apart from perhaps hurriedly rinsing them with cold sea water. The technique for cleaning a food bowl on Iannace's ship was to eat the bread ration after it had been used to wipe the grease from the bowl. When passengers did not follow this procedure, their bowls accumulated layers of grease from successive meals. This led to the theft of unattended clean bowls; to prevent such loss, some passengers carried their bowls on a string around their necks. The slovenly habits of the emigrants and the high incidence of seasickness (bulkheads were stained with vomit), particularly during high seas, made steerage compartments resemble dung heaps, despite the periodic efforts of the stewards to apply hoses, brooms, and sand buckets to the problem.

When Totonno returned to Italy in 1910, he dreaded the thought of having to cross the Atlantic once again below decks, but since his friends were going in steerage, he decided to billet with them. Once the *Berlin* left New York harbor and began to roll in the swells of the open ocean, however, Totonno changed his mind.

I could not get out of my bunk all day. Here we go again, I thought. I got seasick coming over in 1906 and I will be miserable again this time. There is no cure for this *mal di mare*. That others are in the same condition gives me slight satisfaction. I made a momentous decision: I decided I could not and would not take this anymore. I was not going to submit to ten more days of this torture. I had to get out of this stifling, wretched, stinking third-class berth and move up to second class. My declaration produced much criticism from my friends. I closed my ears to their imprecations, scraped together the 163 *lire* difference, gathered my things, and headed for the stairs. As soon as the fresh air hit my face I felt better. Down below they are all bunched together in their bunks, breathing the same stale air again and again and feeling gloomy. Second class, by contrast, exposed as it is to the fresh sea breezes, is clean smelling and with only two persons to a cabin. We have all the comforts: mattresses, sheets, cushions, mirror, sofa, sink, soap. The dining room is plush and the passengers are elegant. When I think about the incredible differences between the two classes, I can only conclude that our present social structure needs to be drastically reformed.

Moving into second class was the equivalent for Totonno of moving into the main current of American society. During his four years in America, he had had minimal contact with anyone but other immigrants. Now he was associating with "real" Americans on an equal basis, and he was being treated very nicely because they were all quite anxious to hear from him about Italy. To Totonno, it was a new and fascinating world. The Americans comported themselves with style and sophistication, and they carried themselves with a casual sense of quiet self-assurance. He was impressed by their easy ways, their social graces, and their apparent lack of class snobbery. Totonno had intended to remain in Italy, but "now that I see the America of money and leisure, the America of success, the America that I had only up to this time read and heard about, my ideas are beginning to change. I want what they have."

Anticipating America

Apart from eating and sleeping, there was nothing for the emigrants to do but spend the hours on deck grouped together on the basis of family, village, or agent affiliation and think about their destination. The passengers were hungry for any scrap of information about America and unceasing in their efforts to pump those persons who had been there. They would grasp at any item or detail, and were not reluctant to pass on what they knew, or thought they knew, to others. The solidarity on board ship was a product of the knowledge that they were all sharing the same destiny; because of this they also shared the same

hopes, fears, and doubts. And doubt and apprehension made them unusually susceptible to any rumor and eager for any proffered advice
that promised to make their transition from emigrant to immigrant less
troublesome. Bernardy closely observed the interaction of the emigrants on deck:

> Every small occurrence reverberates about the ship like a cannon
> blast. What begins at one end of the ship as a small matter achieves
> universal significance and becomes worthy of extended attention
> by the time it has gone from one Italian to another as they stand
> and sit crowded elbow to elbow on the deck. The humdrum at-
> mosphere of shipboard life contributes to the intensity of the
> interchanges.[42]

The agents were as anxious as their charges that everyone be able to
pass through American customs without incident. Each rejected individual reflected on the agent's reputation and affected his right to
claim his fee. The agent was careful, therefore, to anticipate every potential problem and to work out a scheme to avoid trouble with whatever ingenuity he had at his command. When Iannace was ready to
board his ship in Naples, the agent took him aside and told him that
Abbasino, the person who was to be his official guardian, had an eye
infection that might prevent him from leaving. "If that happens," the
agent said, "you cannot leave either. Get in line, and if you see
Abbasino being pushed out, place this paper that consigns you to
Varricchio in your passport and show it to the officials." As it turned
out, Abbasino was passed through and Varricchio was rejected.[43]

　　Before the 1890s, it was easy to leave Italy and relatively easy to
get into the United States. With the passage of stricter legislation in
the United States, there were official complaints to Italy and to the
ship companies, requesting more thorough examination of intending
emigrants. The Italian government responded by initiating even tighter
procedures at the Italian ports than those found at the American processing centers. For those Italians bound for South America, the medical inspection was cursory; unless an individual had a repulsive physical condition or an obvious contagious illness, he or she was allowed
to leave. But the medical examiners took care to ascertain that a person going to the United States did not have a condition that could pre-

vent entrance. The American consulates in the port cities regulated many of the examining physicians, advising them to look for evidence of such contagious diseases as favus and trachoma. Favus is a fungus skin disease characterized by pinhead- to pea-sized, saucer-shaped, yellowish crusts over hair follicles and accompanied by a musty odor and itching. Trachoma is a viral infection, an acute, contagious, inflammatory conjunctivitis with granular elevations on the eyelids that ulcerate and cicatrize. Trachoma was especially frequent; in 1906, of the more than 25,000 intending emigrants turned away for medical reasons by Italian examiners, 8,000 had trachoma and another 7,000 were suspected carriers.[44] In 1907, those not admitted on board ship at Italian ports for disease and other reasons numbered 35,196.[45]

By comparison, few Italians were rejected at Ellis Island; in 1904 and 1905 the total number forced to return to Italy was 4,707.[46] Brandenburg was much more impressed with the examination in Naples than that which he witnessed at Ellis Island. In Naples, "our eyelids were turned up for trachoma; our heads were rubbed over for favus; any defective-looking parts of the body were touched for hidden disease."[47] In New York, he and his friends were looked at but not handled. Once on board, the agent made a point of rehearsing his charges in how to conduct themselves upon reaching Ellis Island. Were their vaccination certificates in order? Did they know their destinations in the United States? Each person had to have a card indicating name and destination. If they were going beyond New York, had they purchased their railroad tickets in Italy? If not, that would have to be done at Ellis Island. Bags could not exceed 100 kilos in weight and one-half metric cube in size. Money was needed to get into the United States; America did not want the refuse from foreign shores. In 1907, that sum was a minimum of $20 for those under 40 years of age and $40 for those older; the older Italians also had to prove that they had relatives who could provide for them.[48] When the money was lacking, the amount would be borrowed or passed from hand to hand as each person reached that stage in the processing. The officials probably will not ask to see your money; you need only declare you have a certain amount, the Italians were told, but if they do ask, you had better have it.

Each of the questions that would be asked by the American inspectors was carefully reviewed by the agents, and stock answers were rehearsed time and again until the emigrants had them memorized.

Because the contract labor laws forbade prior employment arrangements, the agent would tell any men who already had been promised jobs to answer that they had no work waiting for them and that they had paid for their own steamship tickets. "But I do have a job waiting," protested one emigrant. "You are an idiot, Giorgio," was the agent's reply. "Shut up, and do what I tell you." [49]

The intensity with which the agents reviewed these instructions added to the emigrants' feeling of apprehension. They had not come all this distance to be denied entrance to America, but the entire processing experience loomed ahead like a foreboding roadblock that would be overcome only by the most delicate kind of diplomacy. As the ship sailed into the lower bay, the men rehearsed one final time for the examination. Brandenburg wandered from group to group and listened as "hundreds of useless lies" were prepared to cover any and every contingency. Brandenburg considered many of the precautions a waste of time and was offended when he realized that some of the American immigration laws were about to be bent or broken. He favored migration but not at the expense of violating the laws of his country. All sorts of advice was being volunteered. One woman, who suspected that her child had trachoma, was told to stuff the youngster with bread in the hope that it would be fast asleep at inspection time and the doctor would not bother to awaken it for the eye examination. (Some of the Italians, accustomed to extortion by Italian authorities, set aside sums of money to palm off on the American doctors. To them, this was standard practice, for authority and corruption were one and the same thing. Anything could be had for a price in Italy; why should America be any different? After all, for a modest sum there were doctors in Naples who could disguise the stigmata of an ailment long enough for someone to pass the medical inspections in Italy and America.) [50]

The agents also conducted lessons in speech. Many returning emigrants had brought back to their native villages the language spoken by the Italians in America; that was the initial exposure of most intending emigrants to the American immigrant idiom. It was complemented by more explicit instruction on the ship. One of the first "American" words every emigrant learned was *grignoni*. That is what he was soon to become—a greenhorn, the lowest of the low on the social hierarchy among both Americans and Italian immigrants. Other practical phrases were memorized, most of them pertaining to the most crucial areas of immigrant life: food and work. Brandenburg watched as three men were taught to say *Ghifami bret* (Give me some bread), *Ghifami mitta* (Give me some meat), and *Eu wansa man?* (Do you need an employee?). The men strolled around the deck practicing on all who would listen.[51]

Illegal Migrants

A large number of Italians bypassed the well-trodden emigration path from an Italian port to an American immigration processing center. Those Italians who for one reason or another did not want to disclose to the local authorities that they wished to leave the country or did not have papers or were carrying forged ones often preferred more clandestine routes. From 1902 through 1906 the difference between the number of Italians entering America from Europe and the official Italian outmigration statistics was about 30,000 persons.[52] As many as 15 to 25 percent of these Italians had lived in other countries before coming to the United States. Others could not emigrate legally for civil, criminal, or medical reasons.

During the early emigration years, when the Italian government sought actively to discourage outmigration, tens of thousands of Italians left from foreign ports. The traffic of Italians into France and Switzerland at border towns like Basilea and Chiasso was notable. Crossing the border involved relatively few risks. Security was for the most part not strict; border guards on both sides, not always overzealous in their duties, could be bribed. In exchange for a bottle of cognac or a few packs of cigarettes, exceptions were made to the regulations or papers not scrutinized too closely.[53] Another method was to find a ship captain willing to take aboard an anonymous person in exchange for a sum of money or as a hand for the less desirable labor below decks. Rocco Corresca decided to leave for America after he had been convinced by a friendly stranger that he could cross the Atlantic free of cost. He was taken to Naples and put aboard a steamer, where he worked for the next three weeks as a coaler in the suffocating boiler room. Later Corresca learned that the man had received payment for recruiting him.[54] Another young man deserted from the Ital-

ian army, made his way from Rome to Palermo, was smuggled onto a
ship to Portugal, and from there embarked for New York.[55]

Other Italians who were not granted the right to emigrate, or
whom America did not wish to accept, kept the traffic in false or
stolen or "rented" papers heavy. There was no document or stamp essential to emigration that could not be expertly forged, including passports and health certificates. In addition, legitimate documents sometimes changed hands repeatedly. Brandenburg met a man on board
ship who had purchased in Naples the naturalization papers of an
American citizen. The man also carried a passport and a health certificate not his own. On further investigation Brandenburg discovered
that for 50 *lire* one could rent American citizenship papers that had
been brought to Italy by repatriated emigrants. Fifteen *lire* would be
refunded if the person returned them after use.[56] Bernardy, too, saw
emigration papers containing personal information that obviously did
not fit the bearer. For example, the papers would indicate that the
bearer was 55 years of age when he obviously was no more than 35, or
23 when he was clearly less than 16.[57] Such papers either were stolen
or had been forged to fit a certain emigrant "profile" intended to be
used by a number of individuals.

Any Italian who was determined to leave Italy could do so, whatever his situation or condition. There were as many methods as there
were people profiting from the illegal traffic. Every village had at least
one person who could help another leave the country undetected. Matteo was one of those who took advantage of the illegal avenues by
which Italians came to America.

When Matteo decided to emigrate, he first contacted a legitimate
travel agent and followed all the proper procedures; then, with his papers in order, he went to Palermo in July 1913 for the medical screen-
ing and embarkation. Unfortunately, he had injured an eye as a boy
and suffered from double vision. The examiner on the dock took one
look at the eye and denied Matteo passage. The agent was unconcerned. "Don't worry," he assured Matteo. "Another ship is departing
in ten days, and at that time a more lenient doctor will be present."
But it was the same doctor, and seeing Matteo, he said, "Are you here
again? Get out of line! You are not leaving now or ever!"[58]

On the train back to Trappeto, Matteo learned from one of his
seatmates that there was a person in Terrasini who for 800 *lire* could

arrange for anyone to leave Sicily without the proper documents. Matteo's father borrowed the money at 30 percent interest. In late August, Matteo went aboard a cargo ship as an ordinary seaman, shoveling coal in the boiler room. The voyage from Palermo to Brooklyn took 29 days.

Another man who found a means of illegal emigration was Antonio Margariti, who had become embittered by the downward social mobility of his family and, especially, by his life as a common laborer and soldier, experiences that remained vivid to him even in his old age. For him, Italy was not the *Madrepatria*, the Motherland that warmly embraced its children, but rather a *matrigna*, a harsh and punishing stepmother.

Margariti was born in the hamlet of Ferruzzano, Calabria, in 1891. His family's fortunes had declined steadily over the years so that by the time Margariti was a young boy, the family had been reduced to extreme poverty. His paternal grandfather had been a *massaro*, a farmer who owned some land and small herds of cows and sheep. After the grandfather's death the property was divided among his children, and most of it was eventually sold for cash. Margariti's father took his patrimony and moved into the village to open a small shoemaker's shop, where he made footwear for the *signori* of the village although he never wore shoes himself. The income from the shop was modest but enough for the parents to afford the luxury of sending their sons to school. Margariti was learning the fundamentals of reading and writing when the father died suddenly, leaving behind a wife and five sons between the ages of 2 and 12. When the wife attempted to assume operation of the shop, her suppliers took advantage of her inexperience in worldly affairs; within a few months the business was bankrupt.

There followed an intense period of extreme dislocation and privation for the family. The mother, mourning her husband's passing day and night, was incapable of a leadership role. Even though the boys left school and looked for work, the family sometimes went for days without as much as a piece of bread on the table. "Mama cried often," Margariti recalled. "She would send my younger brother out to search for food and he always returned with empty hands. The others in the village had little to spare. I remember one morning when we burst into tears from hunger pangs while playing in the square. A woman took pity on us and came out to our house carrying a fistful of dried figs. Those figs were like manna from heaven. The only person who helped us at that time was a maternal aunt who had a heart of gold despite the fact that she was married to a cruel, arrogant man who constantly maltreated her." [59]

Shortly after Margariti's ninth birthday, his mother arranged for him to work for a *padrone* for one year as a *servo* in exchange for a small amount of cash (six *lire*), some grain, and two dresses. The *servo* boys came from families that could not afford the expense of an additional child in the house. They were the refuse of a society with a high birth rate and a static economy. The boy would be given to someone as either a young apprentice or a servant. Once the arrangement was made, the parents had no say in the treatment of the child. The *servo* lived with the *padrone*, was at his beck and call, and satisfied his every command. He had no rights, and the *padrone* had few obligations to him apart from providing basic necessities, and even these could be withheld without fear of retribution. The *padrone* could also avoid honoring the contract with the parents if an appropriate pretext were found. In Margariti's case the *padrone* accused him of stealing his underwear and declared the contract null and void, despite Margariti's protests of innocence and his mother's attempts to seek justice. The boy had worked an entire year for nothing.

For the next five years Margariti lived with other *padroni*, working in their fields and grazing their animals, living primitively for months away from all human contact. He bitterly recalled those years as the bleakest and most depressing of his life, but he learned to rely on his own resources and even cared for himself when he was struck down by several serious bouts of malaria. He worked every day from sunup to sundown; consumed an unvaried diet of tomatoes, onions, bread, and dried olives; and slept in the fields, often in a haystack, or in a sack on the floor of his *padrone*'s house.

At the age of 14 he returned to the village to work as a *manovale*, or laborer, which allowed him to live with his family in comfort and independence. Once back in association with the villagers, he began, like others, to think about emigrating. Many men wanted to spread their wings and fly from their wretched lives: "Our hopes turned to the promised land, America." His oldest brother, Peppino, was the first in the family to go. A relative had suggested to the mother that her son could better support the family in America than he could in Italy, and Peppino needed little encouragement. In 1903, at age 16, he left with the promise that he would send money to his mother. He never wrote, never sent a penny, and was not heard from again until 1914, when Margariti met him in Pennsylvania.

Margariti's application for a passport was denied because he was of draft age, and the following year, 1911, his age class was called to duty for 24 months. Before going to Genoa to join an infantry regiment, he decided to marry—an impulsive and foolish gesture, as he later acknowledged; he could not support a family and had to leave his wife and child behind when he did emigrate. His army experience helped to alienate him further and cut any remaining emotional ties with Italy. After his discharge he hurried home, more determined than ever to leave Italy permanently before a war broke out and he was summoned back into the military. War clouds were gathering in Europe and men of draft age could not emigrate without exceptional reason.

Others in the village were in a similar situation. Their salvation came in the form of Giovanni Gullace, a villager who had worked in America. Gullace had detailed knowledge of an "escape route" and was willing to escort Margariti and three others to the United States. But Margariti had no money and was unsuccessful in borrowing from his friends the amount required by Gullace. Margariti was deep in despair. Then one evening a few days before the departure date, during a *passeggiata* around the town square, he was approached by a man whom he scarcely knew. As the man passed his hand over Margariti's chest as if to greet him, he stuffed 500 *lire* into the young man's jacket pocket. "Here is the money, *compare*," he whispered. "Go to America. The only thing I want from you is that you never forget that I earned that money, every penny of it, during the time I labored over there." Margariti stood there stunned, his eyes welling with tears, as the man continued his walk. "I was so moved by those simple words, by his generosity, by his total trust in me," Margariti wrote 65 years later, "that I did not know what to say." [60]

Early the next week Gullace confirmed that the English liner *Olympic* would be at Southhampton. The group of five men left the village late at night to avoid detection, but as they detrained at Milan, two policemen stopped and questioned them at length. The escape route they were using was heavily traveled, and the Milan police were stopping all men of draft age. At first Margariti suspected that the village authorities had discovered their absence and had sounded the alarm. However, the series of questions was routine, and Gullace had prepared them well. Each told the police a well-rehearsed lie to justify his presence in Milan, with Gullace summing up by stating, "We are here to see the sights. That's all." Satisfied, the police released them. The men knew that they would be watched and that the police had all of the trains to Chiasso under constant surveillance. From the railroad station, Gullace led the group to a restaurant. The owner, a vital link in the clandestine route, hired a carriage for them, and that evening they rode the back roads to Como. Early the next morning they took the train across the Chiasso bridge, then traveled through France to Le Havre and from there to England, finally to board ship for America.

Of course, once in an American port, an illegal emigrant still had to find a way to get access to American soil. But doing so presented few difficulties to men who had made it that far. When Constantine Panunzio jumped ship in Boston in 1902, he simply walked out of the dock area.[61] Matteo, with two other illegal aliens, left the ship accompanied by two regular members of the crew, who told the security guards on the wharf that they were all crewmen; they were going to a nearby saloon for a few glasses of wine and would return to the ship shortly, they assured the guards. Three of the men never did. Margariti and his *paesani* passed through the dock checkpoint in the same manner.

Landing in New York

"I was disappointed with America at first. I did not know her. I was a stranger to America, and America was a stranger to me." [1]

The Immigration Station

In mid-nineteenth-century America, although there were state laws regulating immigration, the procedure for admitting the newcomers arriving in port cities on the east coast consisted of little more than a head count.[2] New York's processing center was known as the Barge Office. It was located on the Battery, at the tip of Manhattan, where an impressive circular building called Castle Garden (originally a cultural center and concert hall) had been converted for the purpose. In 1892, this office closed in favor of the federal facility at Ellis Island—until the wooden buildings there were destroyed by fire in 1897, and entering aliens were again received at Castle Garden while reconstruction was underway. Ellis Island reopened with new brick buildings and a much larger complex in 1900.[3]

CASTLE GARDEN, 1855–1900

When the Barge Office opened in 1855, there were only about 300 Italians living in New York City, and during that decade only some 8,000 to 10,000 entered the United States (compared with more than 240,000 immigrants from other countries, especially Great Britain and Germany).

Among the first of these was Antonio Arrighi, who arrived in July 1855. Arrighi was born in Florence, and in 1849 enlisted in Garibaldi's army as a drummer boy. Wounded and captured during the battle for Rome, he was taken prisoner by the Bourbons, jailed at Civitavecchia, and later escaped to Leghorn, where he went to sea on a ship bound for America. From the Brooklyn pier where his ship had docked, Arrighi arranged for one of his shipmates to rent a small boat and row him over to Castle Garden. There, the procedure was so lax that no one took notice of his entrance, and he was completely ignored as he sat waiting on one of the wooden benches. That evening after dark, as Castle Garden was closing its doors, a sweeper chased Arrighi out into the street, where he found himself on his own—and in America.[4]

The system was still casual when Adolfo Rossi arrived, one of about 6,000 Italians who entered the United States in 1879. The cabin passengers were the first to disembark after the ship docked at a Manhattan pier, followed by those in third class, who were loaded on a steamboat for the short trip to Castle Garden. Entering the large rotunda, Rossi looked up at the ceiling 75 feet above him and around at the 2,000 or more immigrants milling about the floor. Rossi tried to identify the several nationalities by their picturesque native costumes and their "white, brown, yellow and copper colored faces." Individual workers and farmers outnumbered the family groups. In one part of the hall, clusters of German and Irish agricultural families were waiting to entrain for the Middle West that same evening. Rossi also noticed the booths where agents sold railroad tickets or offered hotel rooms, and a Labor Exchange office that listed available jobs.

The immigrants were processed quickly and quietly, with few formalities. After Rossi gave his name to the official at the desk, he and his companion Giuseppi walked over to the Labor Exchange to glance at the job board. Rossi had left home carrying a reserve of funds, planning to see New York as a tourist for a few weeks before settling down to earn his living. But his money had been stolen during the crossing, so he was now compelled to seek work right away.

The Exchange was divided into two sections, one for men and one for women, and a large chalkboard on the wall listed the daily requests for workers. Standing in front of the board, Rossi read:

29 August, 1879
Fifty miners wanted for the West, and 200 laborers for work on
the Denver and Rio Grande R.R.
Some good farmers needed in Pennsylvania.
Some good domestics needed for city families.

Rossi turned to Giuseppi and remarked, "There is nothing for us today"—little imagining how wrong he would prove to be.[5]
   When the two men left Castle Garden, they wandered aimlessly
through the streets, not knowing what to do with themselves or where
to find lodging. A reasonable alternative seemed to be to spend the
night stretched out on a park bench, which they saw others doing, but
after being molested and threatened by the thieves and vagabonds who
swarmed through the area looking for easy victims, they soon retreated back to Castle Garden. A friendly and competent immigration
official who spoke excellent Italian allowed them and other newcomers with no place to go to sleep on the wooden platform benches
for two nights. Later, this same official directed them to an Italian
hotel at 59 Rose Street. The hotel owner, who, like Rossi and Giuseppi, was from North Italy, granted the men the credit they needed for
food and lodging and gave them advice about work opportunities in
the lower Manhattan Italian colony.
   Had Rossi and Giuseppi landed in New York before 1855, they
would have experienced a very different reception. Each immigrant
ship that docked in those days was immediately beset by "runners"
from boardinghouses and travel agencies. There was a fierce competition among the boardinghouse runners. Low rates would be quoted at
dockside, but once they moved in, the immigrants were charged much
more; if they did not pay, their baggage was held in custody. The travel
agents, too, misrepresented their services and charged extravagantly.
   The opening of the Barge Office reduced many of these abuses by
bringing the services into Castle Garden and regulating costs. Fixed
rates were established for railroad tickets, handling and delivery of
luggage, money exchange, and food. Only licensed boardinghouse
keepers were admitted into the Garden to solicit business.[6] The regulations did not eliminate immigrant exploitation, however; the immigrants continued to be victimized at every opportunity. One newcomer
described the boardinghouse agents at Castle Garden as a mob that
was "let loose on us, frightening us half out of our senses and completely out of our change."[7]
   During the 1880s the Barge Office began to process more and
more persons as the numbers of immigrants rose dramatically year by
year and New York became the chief port of entry for Europeans. Both
the increased numbers and the passage of a second round of restrictive

immigration legislation began to burden the processing system. In 1875 the first immigration exclusion act passed by Congress had barred convicts and prostitutes. Those who were deemed likely to become public charges or a menace to the public health or morals were added to this list in 1882, 1891, and 1903. The acts of 1885 and 1887 sought to prohibit from our shores those who had signed work contracts in their home countries.

As soon as Rosa Cristoforo's ship docked at a Manhattan pier in 1884, the doctors came on board and checked the passengers' eyes and their vaccination certificates. Three of Rosa's companions, a lame old man and two girls with "sore eyes," were told that they could not leave the ship. The others took a boat to Castle Garden and entered by way of a boardwalk and a narrow door. "The inside was a big, dark room full of dust, with fingers of light coming down from the ceiling," Rosa recalled. "The room was already crowded with poor people from earlier boats sitting on benches and railings and on the floor. To one side were a few tables where food was being sold." Rosa was asked three questions—name, origin, destination—and she replied, "Cristoforo, Rosa. From Lombardy. To the iron mine in Missouri." She was impressed by the inspectors, who sat elevated on high stools. They spoke several languages and seemed to recognize at a glance an applicant's nationality.[8]

The newcomers' experience with the immigration officials varied widely. If the immigrant's papers were in order and he knew beforehand what to expect, or if he had a lie to tell and told it convincingly, then the processing could be completed briefly and effortlessly. So Francesco Ventresca, despite the fact that he had come to the United States as a contract laborer, went through customs without difficulty in May 1890. "We passed through a gate where our passports were examined by an Italian interpreter—there was little else to examine. We were retained a few hours in a large barracks, a new building with fresh, undressed boards lying all about, called the Battery." By the next day he was on his way to his first job.[9]

Others, less fortunate, got entangled in the web of Barge Office bureaucracy when their answers to questions were not straightforward or when an official suspected that they might be undesirable candidates for admission. Gaetano Conte, an Italian Protestant clergyman, spent a few days at the Barge Office in 1890, observing the operation

of the system and attending to the problems of some of his conationals. His description is rare both in detail and insight.

A few months after our arrival I visited the Barge Office,
where the immigrants disembark. Alongside was anchored a ship
that had just arrived from Italy, and it was evident from the extreme disorder of the sleeping quarters that the passengers had
suffered much during their interminable fifteen-day voyage.

It was a variegated, pathetic, fretful group that descended
from the ship: men, women, and children, all of them wearing
the unhealthy pallor of steerage passengers. One cried, another
laughed, while still another prayed and yet another swore. I was
repelled by the sight of these people and saddened at the thought
of those who would cheerfully follow in the coming months and
years.

I asked some well-dressed persons, standing nearby, whether
I could be of assistance. Thinking that I was speaking of myself
and my wife, they offered to help us. "No, not us," I responded.
"We are Italians but not like them." "Oh," one said, "you want
to help THEM. . . . Well, we are too busy to be concerned with
that." Before I could react, they had walked away, no doubt to
attend a music recital or to visit a museum.

The immigrants were queued for the medical inspection.
"We don't want to harm you," the doctor assured each nervous
and timid Italian while he carried out his examination, focusing
particularly on the head and eyes. Each immigrant anxiously
awaited the decision of the doctor, a decision that would either
allow him to advance one step closer to the coveted prize, America, or push him thousands of miles back to his village of origin.

Then came the exam before the government inspector. The
immigrants were separated into six lines, each line formed inside
a fenced enclosure. As each immigrant stood before the inspector's
desk, he responded to several questions. How old are you? Are you
married? Where does your family live? How much money do you
have? Who is waiting for you? What is your job skill? Are you certain you will find employment? Have you been in America previously? Can you read?

How many illusions were shattered by those questions! How

many tears were shed! Delinquents, immoral persons, potential beggars, contract workers, the elderly and infirm, women with illegitimate children, returning immigrants who came to work for a short period only (birds of passage): these people are not welcome in America. The inspector would direct Italian phrases to the frightened and defensive immigrant. "Avete monito? Avete monito? [Do you have any money?] The Italian does not know what to say. Is it better to have or not have money? He does not know so he mumbles something, says nothing, or contradicts himself. Often the immigrant will be held for a second or third exam because the officials suspect that he may be deliberately attempting to conceal his past by acting naive and confused.

One unkempt woman, with a babe in arms and two little ones clinging to her skirts, was asked by the inspector whether she had an address to go to. The inspector spoke to her in immigrant Italian. Not understanding what was being asked, she replied: "Yes, sir," and showed him her money and her vaccination certificate. The inspector became increasingly irritated as he continued to repeat himself and she attempted to push the money into his hand. Finally, she was put into detention, sobbing uncontrollably. I saw her the next day and resolved the matter.

One day another woman, after having passed through the trial of several examinations, was told that she was free to leave and that her husband awaited her outside the fenced area. Wild with joy, she mistakenly hurried out the wrong exit and, perhaps because it had been some time since she had seen her husband, mistook me for him and with shouts of sheer delight threw her arms tightly around me. It was with great effort that I detached myself from her.[10]

ELLIS ISLAND, 1892–1914

The reopening of Ellis Island in 1900 coincided with the onset of mass migration to the United States. The huge complex, certainly the largest immigrant receiving center in the world, was a marvel of bureaucratic efficiency. A rigidly structured system, operated by an experienced and multilingual staff, permitted the vast majority of immigrants, (those who had their papers in order and were not given additional examinations) to pass through and be on their way to their final destinations within 90 minutes. Even at the high tide of immigration in 1905–7, as many as 5,000 steerage passengers were cleared through customs in a single day.

One reason for this speed was that the procedures tended to be lenient, and those immigrants with entry problems were allowed every opportunity to correct them so that they could enter. Had the standards been stiffer and the rejection rate higher, the system would have become hopelessly clogged with rejectees and the cost would have become prohibitive. But with hospital, dormitory, and dining hall space at a premium on the island, only the most urgent problem cases could be detained longer than overnight.[11]

There was still considerable confusion from the immigrants' point of view, however. In October 1902, when Broughton Brandenburg landed in New York and was processed as an "Italian immigrant," his ship stopped briefly in the harbor for a health inspection and then steamed up the North River to Hoboken. The customs officials came aboard to check the cabin-class passengers while those in steerage waited. After a substantial delay the immigrants were notified to prepare for debarkation. By this time the Italians were more than anxious to leave the ship. Brandenburg watched as everyone pushed forward.

> One torrent of humanity poured up each companionway to the hurricane deck and aft, while a third stream went through the main deck alleyway, all lugging the preposterous bundles. The children, seeing sufficient excitement on foot to invite them to cry, and being by this time very hungry, began to yell with vigor. A frenzy seemed to possess some of the people as groups became separated.[12]

And the frenzy did not subside when the Italians reached the pier warehouse, a large enclosed place. They were confused, frightened, fearful that they would commit some error of judgment or insult an official, and thus be turned back. Some of the women were on the verge of hysteria, so concerned were they that they would lose sight of their children or their husbands in the milling crowd. The warehouse was a bedlam of recently debarked passengers from several ships as well as inspectors, stevedores, sailors, detectives and watchmen, and vendors of fruit and sweets, all vying for space among the large piles of immigrant luggage, which had to be painstakingly sorted out and inspected.

While the immigrants, bunched together in small groups, spent the morning and early afternoon on the pier awaiting an inspector, the vendors moved among them, offering their wares at inflated prices to those who had not eaten since the previous evening. One-cent apples went for a nickel, and a yellow cake, which Brandenburg described as a totally indigestible chalky mess not fit for human consumption— "Even the Neapolitan boys would not eat it"—for ten cents a slice.

A number of ships were being unloaded, the harbor facilities were fully utilized, and the Ellis Island barges had more traffic than could be reasonably handled with dispatch and passenger comfort. At two o'clock in the afternoon Brandenburg's group was finally jammed aboard two of the barges. There was no place to sit: "We had either to squat on the floor or sit on our bags, already mashed and crushed till the point of utter dissolution seemed not far away, so we stood up." [13] An hour later the barge entered the Ellis Island slip, but not until sundown were planks lowered and the immigrants allowed to step into the main building.

As soon as they entered, they came under the scrutiny of the officials and were not allowed to interrupt, even for a moment, the steady flow of persons from one checkpoint to another.

Half-way up the stairs an interpreter stood telling the immigrants to get their health tickets ready, and so I knew that Ellis Island was having a "long day" and we were to be passed upon even if it took half the night. The majority of the people, having their hands full of bags, boxes, bundles, and children, carried their tickets in their teeth, and just at the head of the stairs stood a young doctor in the Marine Hospital Service uniform, who took them, and stamped them with the Ellis Island stamp. Passing straight east from the head of the stairs, we turned into the south half of the great registry floor, which is divided, like the human body, into two great parts nearly alike, so that one ship's load can be handled on one side and another ship's load on the other. Turning into a narrow railed-off lane, we encountered another doctor in uniform, who lifted hats or pushed back shawls to look for favus heads, keenly scrutinized the face and body for signs of disease or deformity, and passed us on. An old man who limped in front of me, he marked with a bit of chalk on the coat lapel. At the end of the railed lane was a third doctor, a towel hanging beside him, a small instrument over which to turn up eyelids in his hand, and back of him basins of disinfectants. As we approached he was examining a woman and her two children looking for trachoma or purulent ophthalmia. He marked the woman with a bit of chalk and led her and the children to the left into the rooms for special medical examination.[14]

The next step was the customs inspection. Brandenburg's group sat in the waiting room until nine o'clock before lining up in front of a customs desk. Since they had been carefully briefed in Italy and on board ship, there were no problems; their papers were in order, each had sufficient money, and they were passed through in less than a minute. Because Brandenburg took responsibility for his group of immigrants, they were classed as "New York Outsides," free to go, as distinguished from those in the "New York Detained" category, who had to await the arrival of friends or sponsors. Other classifications were "Railroads," those who were destined for places outside metropolitan New York, and the "S.I.'s," who had to await the decision of the Special Inquiry Court and could be sent back.

Amy Bernardy, visiting Ellis Island in 1910, followed a few Italians who had been marked with chalk on the arm or the back. These "suspected" individuals were directed to lateral compartments for additional examination. The process gave Bernardy the impression of a herd of animals passing along chutes. The faces of the immigrants wore signs of "poverty and ignorance," in glaring contrast to the official, premeditated, almost haughty demeanor of the superbly confident American inspectors, who stood erect and resplendent in their well-tailored uniforms.

Bernardy went to the Special Inquiry room, a kind of court of appeals where the "suspected" immigrant cases were reviewed for final judgment. Spacious and well illuminated, the room was divided by a wooden railing; on one side was a raised platform with a large table where the judges sat. These men, Bernardy wrote in her notebook, "look capable, and are austere, resolute, and laconic. They utter only those words necessary to their tasks. The interpreter, a southern Italian, who speaks English and Italian with equal facility, stands at the railing."[15]

Each person was interrogated. One was asked the size of his family. When he declared "nine children," one of the judges smiled as if to say, no wonder you emigrated. An old woman presented herself and her three small nephews. Their relatives were waiting for them, the woman explained. The smallest nephew would be living with a brother, the other with an uncle. They would be provided for, she assured the judges. But one of the judges persisted: "Maternal or paternal uncle? Is he married? Where? When?" he wanted to know. After a brief consultation the men decided the case in her favor, and she hurried out, her face glowing.

Others who came before the railing had no one waiting for them and no place to go: no relatives, no friends, no prospects for work, no money. Some were in failing health. One was denied entry by a unanimous vote; he would have to go back to Italy, the expense most likely to be borne by the ship company that brought him over. The court assigned him to detention status on the island until he could be transferred to a returning ship. Bernardy watched as the man was escorted out of the room: "I could not tell from his face what effect this decision had on him, because he left without a clear understanding of what had taken place. The decision will be communicated to him later." [16]

Those who cleared customs and were free to proceed took one of three stairways, appropriately called "The Stairs of Separation": relatives and friends with different destinations were routed to different staircases and, before they had time to ponder the significance of the action, were abruptly separated. Many never met again. (The procedure was judged necessary and practical, for without it the immigrants would have lingered over their goodbyes, creating a blockage that would have disrupted the entire system.) "Railroads" took the stairs to the right, purchased their tickets, and were loaded on ferries bound for the Hoboken railroad terminal. The "New York Detained" went down the central staircase to fenced pens where they would await their sponsors. "New York Outsides" descended the left-hand stairs to the Battery ferry. Brandenburg had heard many reports about rampant corruption among the Ellis Island officials and was fully prepared to find fault. Instead, he was impressed by the diligence of the officials and their effectiveness in detecting "suspect" immigrants. "The more I saw of the inside of the great system on the Island the more I was struck with its thoroughness and the kindly, efficient manner in which the law was enforced." He did not want any "leakage"; the laws must be enforced to the letter, he felt, and no unwanted person should be allowed to slip through. Consequently, Brandenburg looked favorably upon the Italian-speaking female official who walked about the Great Hall aggressively challenging any woman who she felt might have emigrated for immoral purposes.[17]

If Brandenburg had taken a closer look, however, he would have located many "leakages" in the system. Any prostitute coming in could avoid that female official by traveling in first or second class, where the customs check was not as strict. Persons over 40 years of age, too, or those fearful of failing the medical exam, were told by agents in Italy that it would be to their advantage to buy the more expensive ticket.[18] And some employees at Ellis Island did use their positions and authority for private gain. Everyone knew that the money changers were less than honest and that the concessions were managed by irresponsible people who stole from the immigrants and from each other. Edward Steiner tested a money changer by giving him a twenty-mark piece. He received in exchange a bunch of bright, new pennies worth only 25 percent of his money. He was also approached by an inspector who offered to expedite his processing for a liberal consideration. Another inspector made the same promise to a comely girl, provided she would agree to meet him at a designated hotel.[19]

Many of the regulations were never rigidly enforced. At one point, attempts were made to weed out the prostitutes from the first-class passengers, but this proved to be so inconvenient to wealthy travelers that it was roundly criticized by the New York press and subsequently discontinued. The law requiring that each immigrant have a certain minimal amount of money upon debarkation was not systematically adhered to; if it had been, the rate of rejection for indigence would have been much higher. As it was, from 1900 to 1904 fewer than 1 percent of the 747,916 Italians who landed were returned home.[20]

Periodic enforcement to satisfy the demands of a political pressure group was responsible for most of those who were rejected. In October 1903 a crackdown at the Boston processing center resulted in the detention of 300 Italians from one ship.[21] And during the summer of 1909, when the commissioner of immigration decided that the restrictions should be strictly applied, 700 persons were in detention at Ellis Island within a few weeks. The Italian colony newspapers were almost unanimous in their condemnation of such practices.[22]

If an immigrant without money was young and healthy, and readily confessed his impecunious state, he was usually allowed to proceed. Fortune Gallo, having gambled away his funds on board ship, tried to enter the United States in 1895 with 12 cents in his pocket. The review board liked his spunk, decided that he was a "good risk," and put him into the hands of a priest. The priest escorted Gallo to a Bowery flophouse, handed him three dollar bills, and said, "You're on your own." [23]

It was the immigrant who appeared devious who was most likely to be detained. "How much money do you have?" one man was asked. He did not reply to the question.

"Do you have $20?"

"A little less."

"Do you have $15?"

"A little more."

At this point he was pulled out of line to be examined more closely. [24]

There is no reason to believe that the Ellis Island experience made any lasting imprint on the majority of the immigrants. It did not stand out as more profound or more inhumane or more symbolic than what had already occurred or would soon occur in their lives. Rather, it was part of a seamless continuity that began in Italy and ended somewhere in America. Their lack of worldly sophistication led many immigrants to accept things as they existed without rendering any judgments. Some had little comprehension of what was happening, or would believe any fanciful tale. Pietro Greco overheard a fellow immigrant telling his friend that Columbus had employed Indian bricklayers to build the "Batteria" in order to make the landing more convenient for the Italians who would soon follow. [25]

Some immigrants, though, sharply criticized the inhumanity of the system. For Gherardo Ferreri, who arrived in 1906, Ellis Island was another in a series of demeaning and depersonalizing experiences to which the poverty-stricken, powerless migrant had to submit in order to gain access to the American "paradise"—a paradise that then completed the process of degradation: American capitalists had need of many a strong back to realize their plans for profit, but only if the rest of the body were faceless and mindless. To Ferreri, Ellis Island symbolized this attitude toward the immigrant. He found the procedures morally and physically repulsive. The medical exam was humiliating, a violation of the person; the interrogation, in his eyes, was a direct affront to the inviolate right of every individual to privacy. Ellis Island, Ferreri concluded, "is a true market of human animals, where the immigrants are herded into compartments that look like those at the famous Chicago Stock Yards." [26]

A more famous immigrant held similar sentiments. Bartolomeo Vanzetti's memory of arriving at Ellis Island in June 1908 became for him a symbol of the heartless attitude of Americans toward the newcomers:

> In the immigration station I had my first great surprise. I saw the steerage passengers handled by the officials like so many animals. Not a word of kindness, of encouragement, to lighten the burden of fears that rests heavily upon the newly arrived on American shores. Hope, which lured these immigrants to the new land, withers under the touch of harsh officials. Little children, who should be alert with expectancy, cling instead to their mothers' skirts, weeping with fright. Such is the unfriendly spirit that exists in the immigration barracks. [27]

For Ferreri and Vanzetti, Ellis Island was the "Island of Tears," marking a turning point in the life of the Italian immigrant. He would now never again be the same person; he could neither regain fully what he had lost nor gain fully what he sought. For others, Ellis Island did not have this kind of profound meaning. Many would have agreed with Pasquale D'Angelo, who arrived in 1910 expecting a kind of Devil's Island but concluded that much of what had been said and written was mere fancy. "We went to Ellis Island where we were inspected and examined. I really did not find any of the bad treatment and manhandling that some tender-skinned immigrants complain about." [28]

Were the Italian immigrants too thin-skinned? Like any group of inexperienced travelers, they sometimes overreacted—to the extent of creating unnecessary problems for themselves as well as for those they encountered along the emigration path. The movement of hundreds of thousands of culturally circumscribed individuals across the turbulent Atlantic to a strange land could not realistically have been accomplished without some fracturing dislocations: frustration, doubt, mental confusion, rudeness, blatant malice, and extensive personal discomfort. The fact that the mass emigration was accomplished at all is a tribute both to the pertinacity of the Italians and the perseverance of institutions and emigration officials on both sides of the Atlantic. The work was not pleasant and seldom rewarding. It would be surprising *not* to find a degree of disrespect for the Italian emigrant among those who served continuously on emigration ships that plied the ocean loaded to the bulkheads with peasants from Abruzzi, Puglia, and Calabria—especially given the prevalent ethnic attitudes of the period.

The literature of the emigration era is replete with examples of unacceptable actions on the part of ship stewards, dockworkers, officials, and others, all of whom had preset attitudes about the Italians — attitudes dictating that the Italians did not need to be approached as individuals with rights and prerogatives of their own but could be bullied and intimidated without fear of reprisal. The recipients would have needed a very thick skin indeed to endure without complaint the verbal and physical battering from all quarters to which they were subjected. The Italians were herded about with utter disdain on the ships and docks. They were pushed, shoved, prodded with clubs, cursed, and openly despised. And this behavior was not restricted to the "roughers" of limited education and refinement. An Italian journalist from the *Corriere della Sera* wrote that even the doctors handled the immigrants in a rude fashion, "pushing and turning them this way and that like so many marionettes." [29]

From the sanctuary of her first-class berth, Bernardy was appalled at the "atrocious" handling of the steerage passengers: "I saw women kicked and slapped, men knocked about and blasphemed, and crying babies trampled on." [30] Brandenburg, debarking with the steerage Italians, became one of the victims. When his ship reached the Hoboken pier, he noted that the steerage stewards, who appeared throughout the voyage to enjoy goading the Italians, kept up their brutality to the very last.

> One woman was trying to get up the companionway with a child in one arm, her deck chair brought from home hung on the other, which also supported a large bundle. She blocked the passage for a moment. One of the stewards stationed by it reached up, dragged her down, tore the chair off of her arm, splitting her sleeve as he did so and scraping the skin off her wrist, and in his rage he broke the chair into a dozen pieces. The woman passed on sobbing, but cowed and without a threat. [31]

The Hoboken dock employees, tough, rough, and profane, were no better. All were Germans, some spoke a little English, none spoke Italian, and they harbored an intense hatred for those small, swarthy people from southern Europe. Brandenburg found that this hatred was compounded by the excitability of the debarking immigrants and the inability of the two groups to communicate effectively.

When the dockmen had herded the off-coming immigrants in a mass along the south side of the pier with an overflow meeting forward of the gangway on the north, it was the natural thing for the parties to begin to hunt for each other, and for the leaders of groups to endeavor to assemble the baggage. Women ran about crying, seeking their children. Men with bunches of keys hurried hither and thither searching for the trunks to match in order to open them for customs inspection, and children fearsomely huddled in the heaps of baggage, their eyes wide with alarm. The dockmen exhorted the people in German and English to remain where they were, and when the eager Italians did not understand, pushed them about, belabored them with sticks, or seized them and thrust them forcibly back into the places they were trying to leave.[32]

Individual encounters were occurring all over the dock area, and Brandenburg intervened at a number of points. In one episode, his friend Camela broke away from the group to retrieve her trunk.

"Get back there, get back there!" shouted a German dockman, speaking his own immigrant English.

"I must go unlock my trunks," pleaded Camela in Sicilian.

The dockman was not impressed. "I'll knock the brains out of a few of you dirty sons of bitches with this club. God damn your god damn souls to hell anyway. I'll break your neck if you leave that line again." To emphasize his statement, he pushed Camela in the face, and she fell backward.

Brandenburg stepped between Camela and the German and turned to face him. He told the man (in the English of good manners) to cease and desist.

"Wot!" the German shouted menacingly. "I'll fix you for buttin' in, you damn dago." But as he raised his club with the intention of producing a large bump on Brandenburg's skull, another dockman grabbed his arm. "Hold on, Herman. That fellow may be a Secret Service man. He's no dago. You can tell. He speaks too good English."

At the possibility that Brandenburg, in spite of his Sicilian countryman's attire, might be a figure of authority, the German's attitude softened abruptly. He apologized to Brandenburg (not to Camela) but hastened to add, "These bastards would make anybody mad; they ain't got no sense at all."[33]

Totonno was pushed and prodded and humiliated as well. But the ocean voyage, his seasickness, the lack of adequate nourishment, and his cramped and airless quarters had so exhausted him that he was determined to do whatever he had to do in order to reach solid ground. I do not care how they treat me, was the main thought of this 19-year-old young man, as long as I know that the end of this torture is in sight. These excerpts translated from his diary entries for May 15 to May 17, 1906, describe his arrival:

> By straining our eyes, we could distinguish a thin thread of land on the horizon. In a few hours a string of communities and farms could clearly be seen spread along the coast in one continuous line of habitation. We caught our first glimpse of the Statue of Liberty when, at five o'clock, the ship entered the bay. The ship sailed into the river that separates Brooklyn from New York. Directly before us loomed a very large bridge spanning the river. The Public Health officials briskly came aboard, and we passed before them like sheep. With the inspection at an end, the ship moved over to the other river, which is much wider, perhaps two or three miles across, and separates New York from Hoboken. All of us crowded along the railing to watch the constant traffic of ships, barges, and ferryboats. Some of the barges are large enough to carry entire trains from one shore to the other.
>
> It was announced that we would be debarking early in the morning, so we tried to get some sleep. But our excitement and the noise and frenzy of activity on board made sleep impossible. Shortly after midnight we arose to join the others in preparation. At dawn everyone assembled on deck. I was given a number—224—and at eight o'clock we left the ship. It was the beginning of a very long day of utter confusion. We stood around waiting for something to happen. Nothing did. At sunset we were directed aboard ship to spend the night. I thought I had seen the last of that

damn compartment, and here I am again, cramped in my little bunk and totally exhausted, with pains down to my toenails. I slept badly and was only too happy to heed the early morning call. Filing off again, this time we were stuffed into two barges, which were standing nearby. Our barge moved slowly across to Ellis Island and moored in the ferry slip, where we waited for our numbers to be called. Finally, at two o'clock my turn came to leave the barge and go through customs. The customs house is a magnificent building. Once inside, I climbed a long, wide staircase to a huge hall where there were many officials and an even larger number of immigrants. Benches and desks filled the hall and a balcony ran all the way around. Pushed here, pushed there. Get in this line; no, that line; get in that line; no, over there, rush over there, and wait. After answering a few questions, I was given a ticket. Show that ticket to everyone you see, they said. I did. Holding my ticket in front of me, I walked and walked down long, narrow hallways until I arrived at a small room where my eyes were examined. Some people were not passed through, but I was released and continued on always with my ticket showing. Ascending a small staircase, I reached a desk where I had to declare my money. I came here to make money, but you first have to have money to get into America. I showed the man the three *napoleoni* coins I had borrowed, and he allowed me to proceed.

Another set of stairs took me outside where I passed through more gates, turning left then right then left then right, until I found myself in a large, crowded room divided by a steel fence, which ran up to a high ceiling. The newcomers were on one side like birds in a cage and on the other, with their noses pressed up against the wire, were those persons waiting to declare us their charges. I went from one face to the next. The faces looked at me and I looked at them. Finally, with great relief, I recognized the face of my *compare*, Turiangelo. He is the one responsible for me, and his name is on my declaration of entry. De Carlo, who arrived last week, was with him. They had been there for three days waiting for me to come out. And they had not eaten since the day before. Turiangelo showed the gatekeeper his ticket, and I was given permission to pass through. We took the ferry to the Battery. My first impression was the noise. Noise is everywhere! The din is constant and it completely fills my head.

We rode the subway to 149th Street in the Bronx. Concetta
fed us macaroni, and we stuffed ourselves. My stomach is still
very sensitive from the sea voyage and I know that I will be sorry
tomorrow for eating so much. But I don't care. It does not matter.
Nothing matters now. I am here and I am happy. After twenty-two
days of waiting, standing, walking, vomiting, and being treated
like cattle, I am now free to do whatever I wish.

More Rogues and Thieves—American Style

The steamboat shuttled back and forth between Ellis Island and the
Battery several times each day, dumping boatloads of greenhorns out
of the western end of the migrant pipeline into the American version
of "The City of Thieves."

One warm June evening in 1905, Angelo Mosso strolled down to
the Battery to watch the Ellis Island ferry tie up. He was curious about
these countrymen of his and wanted to see for himself if what the
Americans had been saying about these people was true.

The ferryboat was full of migrants, all of them with a look of
apprehension. I had read many terrible things about the Italians.
Here in America they are called "those dirty Italians" and "undesirable people," so I was expecting the worst. They were workers . . . some dressed in festive clothes, others in everyday wear.
They did not look dirty at all. While disembarking, many smiled
and laughed as if happy to be on solid earth again. Each carried a
sack or a battered suitcase held together with cord. Others carried
large bundles containing blankets and mattresses. All of them
wore a yellow numbered card attached to a jacket button. The
clerks from the Society of Italian Immigrants were waiting to lead
them away.[34]

Most of these Italians were bound for New York City and its surrounding communities. (Of the more than 34,000 Italians who landed at the
Battery in 1894–95, 20,000 were planning to reside in the metropolitan area.) The others, who were in transit to New England or north
toward Albany, would linger in Manhattan only a few hours or a few
days, but even that was time enough to be plucked clean by thieves.

All the greenhorns, not only the naive and uneducated, were the targets of shoddy treatment and false representation. Rossi, an urbane Italian, received his first lessons as a greenhorn immigrant as soon as he stepped out of Castle Garden. He and Giuseppi went to a Manhattan bakery to buy a loaf of bread, which cost no more than ten cents. The woman behind the counter took his proffered quarter, placed it in her apron pocket, and went back to her chair in the corner of the shop. Rossi wanted his change, but all attempts to arouse the woman from her chair failed. She knew better than Rossi that he was a greenhorn; she knew it as soon as he walked into the shop—by his clothes, his deportment, his hesitant movements, and his facial expression. Now she knew it by his fumbling attempts to compose a sentence from his few words of English: "Oh, I do not speak English, but *io voglio il resto altrimenti chiamo un* policeman." Since she did not respond to the threat, Rossi did summon a policeman, but the officer brushed aside his complaint. Rossi was soon to discover that it was accepted practice for the Americans to cheat the greenhorns at every opportunity—they were fair game. The greenhorn not only lacked knowledge of the American language, money, and customs, he was not privy to the many subtleties of American society, subtleties that only natives could comprehend. Without this insider's view, the greenhorn could not protect himself from manipulation and exploitation.

Rossi knew no one in America. He had to make his own way. There were no *paesani* to meet him, so each move he made was a gamble, a step into the unknown. The immigrants who came with an address in their hands or a friend waiting were fortunate. They had a place to go, a home away from home, and someone to protect and assist them until they were able to stand on their own. Those with no contacts, who arrived only with a desire to work, put their pocketbooks and often their lives at risk as soon as they left the sanctuary of the immigration offices. A horde of exploiters were ready to take advantage of their greenness and innocence. These "speculators," to use Rossi's word, operated free of interference from the authorities, if not with their tacit agreement.

> Despite constant police surveillance, Castle Garden is surrounded by a small army of thieves and scoundrels of every genre, ready to give chase to the new arrivals. The techniques

used to systematically fleece the unsuspecting immigrants are innumerable and often ingenious.

At the exits these persons are perched like birds of prey, surmising at a glance the nationality and financial status of a person. With glib persuasiveness, they go about gaining the person's confidence and trust.[35]

One of these persons might volunteer to serve as an interpreter or a guide and then, once the relationship deepened, as a friend or job agent or employer. The New York newspapers frequently reported the discovery in hotel rooms of alleged victims of suicide, many of them Europeans who had arrived only days earlier. Rossi wondered if some of these persons had in fact been killed by another's hand, if they were the victims not of their own remorse but of someone else's greed. The prime targets for this sort of violence were departing immigrants, who often carried with them substantial savings accrued during several years of labor. Homebound Italians who stayed at the Campidiglio Hotel on Mulberry Street were at grave risk; several deaths took place there. The men were murdered by asphyxiation the night before their departure and stripped of their valuables. Their deaths were reported to the police as suicides.[36]

The "speculators" continued to operate unimpeded for decades. Conte, in 1890, expressed disgust at the unwillingness of the City of New York to take anything more than qualified action to protect the rights of immigrants, many of whom one day would become American citizens. What he saw indicated that the "speculators" had become, in the decade since Rossi first arrived, even more proficient in their trade.

The bloodsuckers and the greedy vampires were waiting outside the Barge Office, seeking to take advantage of the immigrants' misery and ignorance, ready to attach themselves to the first unsuspecting greenhorn. There are several types. There is the pseudolawyer who offers you his unnecessary services with payment in advance. There are those who will send telegrams to relatives and friends in Italy; the telegrams are never received. Money exchangers are ready to give you dollars for your *lire* at a rate many times the actual one. Once away from the docks, a second wave of bloodsuckers descends on the immigrant. Porters, hotel owners, common thieves, railroad agents, those who sell the "mandatory" railroad box lunch: all of these vampires work the crowd with the aim of relieving the wretched new arrivals of their remaining ready cash.[37]

Rosa and her friends were unwitting victims of one of these vampires. As they were leaving Castle Garden, a number of well-dressed men wearing badges approached the newcomers. One elegant man introduced himself and welcomed them to America: "I heard your talk and knew you were my *paesani*. I came to help you," he said. "You have the railroad tickets and the American money?"

Taken in by his elegance and his apparent sincerity, the immigrants were soon confiding in this man and accepted as fact that the train for Missouri, their destination, was not leaving for three days. "But don't worry," he assured them, "I will take care of everything— food and a room in my hotel—and I will escort you to the train." He did these things, but not before cleaning their pockets of every penny they possessed. They had nothing to eat until they reached St. Louis.[38]

The "*paesano* approach" was a favorite tactic because the "speculators" understood intimately the strong tie of the *contadino* to his *paese* and to his *compaesani*. It was a "weakness," a point of entree exploited time and again—a trap that the Italian gladly set for himself. In the *paesano* culture, loyalty and trust are reserved for those with traits similar to one's own, particularly those with a common geographic origin. On the basis of the in-group/out-group principle, those persons not *paesani* are automatically considered outsiders; when dealing with such people one is formal and guarded, less open and less accepting. Oh, the relief felt by the Italian caught in a foreign land, surrounded by unyielding elements, who suddenly hears the dialect of his hometown. *Paesani* ties were strong enough to weather a number of challenges, particularly when the Italian had to make a choice in loyalty. As one immigrant rationalized after being defrauded by the son of a friend of his, "Better to be cheated by a *paesano* than by an American."[39] The money is no longer mine, he could have added, but at least it has not left the "family."

Another common ploy was the "interrupted service" technique practiced by baggage carriers, cabbies, and other service workers. The worker would agree to perform a service for a greenhorn for a negotiated price. Once the greenhorn was committed and the service partly performed, the exploiter would ask for additional remuneration. If the immigrant did not comply, the service would not be completed; he would often have to empty his pockets before the job was done. One such episode described by Brandenburg was typical. Antonio, a veteran immigrant, had picked up Giuseppe, a newcomer, at the South Ferry. Antonio bargained with a cabman until an agreement was reached to take Giuseppe and his baggage to the railroad station for $1.50 (a day's wage for a ditchdigger). As soon as the cabman had turned the corner and was out of Antonio's sight, he stopped the cab and demanded an additional dollar from Giuseppe. It was either that, the cabman made clear through sign language and rough English, or he would dump the luggage on the street. Giuseppe's response in sign language and angry Italian made no impression on the cabbie, so he paid the dollar. Two blocks later the cabbie asked for two more dollars and—after a ten-minute argument—received the money. His next demand was for three dollars, but Giuseppe did not have any more money. Physical threats were exchanged. When the cabbie struck at him with the butt of his whip, Giuseppe climbed out, shouldered his bags, and walked the few remaining blocks to the station.[40]

Fortunately, not all immigrants fell into the clutches of the Battery thieves. There were individuals who sought to help the newcomer, and Gabriel Iamurri was lucky enough to meet such people. At the Barge Office, this very young boy was separated from his guardian when the immigrants were grouped alphabetically. Iamurri never forgot the tenseness of the adult Italians in his group. Because of their fear that they might be sent back, every move made and every word uttered by the officials was interpreted in the most negative way. When they were told to get on the ferry to go to Ellis Island to get their money exchanged, most were sure that it was a ruse to get them on board a ship bound for Italy. Back at the Battery, Iamurri stood on the street not knowing which way to turn. What to do? Where to go? He finally walked up to a man and asked for assistance. "I accosted him and by the way he was dressed I knew that he was an Italian. I asked him where he was going. He told me that he was on his way to Mulberry Street, the rendezvous or the headquarters of most Italians." Iamurri followed the man to one of the Italian banks where, with the help of a youthful clerk, and much to his relief, he located his guardian.[41]

Not all the immigrants were naively unaware of the dangers that awaited them on the streets of New York. Some knew from talk at home and on board ship that they were susceptible to any kind of deceit or fraud. They had heard tales of children and immigrant women who were kidnapped and forced to live as slaves or prostitutes; of unsuspecting men who had been beaten and robbed of their possessions or life savings and then received nothing but the back of a policeman's hand when they sought justice.

As a result, many immigrants hesitated to speak to *any* stranger, convinced as they were that everyone was out to get them. Mosso, seeing a group of recent arrivals sitting on the ground, watching the turbulent city life swirl about them, tried to strike up a conversation, but his words of greeting were ignored. They would not even look at him. Mosso later learned that before landing in New York, these immigrants had been warned repeatedly not to trust anyone, not even the police or other officials. "Be careful of someone who approaches you," they had been told. "Once you fall into his trap, you will be deceived and robbed of all you possess. Rely on no one for direction or advice. Whoever attempts to speak to you will certainly be a scoundrel with a foolproof plan to snare you." [42]

But how could the immigrants avoid all contact with the very society upon which they must depend? They needed advice, they needed aid, they needed housing, they needed jobs. How were they to obtain these things? Even those who had friends or kinfolk were still little more than innocents in a hostile environment. Frederico Garlanda described the plight of Italians who were now essentially people without a country:

> It is a sad sight to see these poor peasants washed up on our side of the Atlantic like so many bales of coal. Here they are without resources, abandoned by everyone, ignorant of the language, the localities, the customs, and exposed to all the extortions and the most odious robberies that rascals can inflict upon them.
>
> Nothing any longer exists for them. The mother country has been left behind. Their consul makes no sign of life. The last link, the last root, which held them to their native soil, has been destroyed. And this before they are in a condition to assimilate the life of this new land, to which hunger has driven them. [43]

One very early attempt to assist such immigrants was the formation of benevolent associations, or mutual aid groups. The Societa' Italiana di Mutua Beneficenza, the oldest continuing Italian institution in the United States, was founded by the San Francisco Italians in the 1850s. Many of these associations were modest in size and scope and were organized on the basis of region, province, or village affiliations. The Circolo Abruzzese di Mutuo Soccorso, founded in New York in 1903, and the Società Pugliese di Utica, founded in 1911, are two examples of regional mutual aid associations. Often the closer-knit village-based associations would evolve from the larger region-based groups. Those Italians in Utica from the village of Alberobello who belonged to the Società Pugliese also formed their own Alberobellese Club. And those Alberobellesi who moved from Utica to join their *paesani* in Endicott, New York, formed in 1934 the Federazione Alberobellese, an association that continues to the present day.

Several organizations in the large cities also served a general population and tried to reduce the more obvious abuses suffered by the newcomers. By 1907, Boston had Denison House and the Benevolent Aid Society for Italian Immigrants; New York had the Settlement Italiano di Richmond Hill, the Italian Benevolent Institute, and the Società di San Raffaelo. In San Francisco there was the Comitato Soccorso della Italiana e Patronato di Protezione degli Emigranti Italiani. The organizations received funding from many sources, including the Italian government, to render such services as protecting the newcomer until he reached his relatives or friends. In 1906 the Society for the Protection of Italian Immigrants, with the blessings of the American authorities, inaugurated an escort service: clerks from the society would take the Italians from Ellis Island to their destinations in New York or to the railroad station for a fee much less than that charged by the enterprising teamsters. Protective services were also offered to those who were returning to Italy.[44] Two Italian officers from the New York Police Department regulated the process.

The number served by these government-sponsored associations was a minuscule percentage of the total number of immigrants to be served, however. And unlike the all-embracing nature of the *paesani* associations, the services they offered were short-termed.

THREE

Working in America

> My job was my *via crucia*, my misery, my
> hatred, and yet I lived in continuous fear of
> losing the bloody thing. THE JOB that damna-
> ble affair, THE JOB. Nightmare of the hunted,
> THE JOB, this misery, this anxiety, this kind of
> neurasthenia, this ungrateful, this blood-
> sucking thing. THE JOB, this piecemeal death,
> this fear that grips you in the stomach, this
> sovereign lady who leaks terror, who eats the
> very heart out of man.[1]

The Job Market

"The Americans," wrote Napoleone Colajanni in 1909, "consider the
Italians as unclean, small foreigners who play the accordion, operate
fruit stands, sweep the streets, work in the mines or tunnels, on the
railroad or as bricklayers."[2] Because the Italians were restricted to
"immigrant work" and a few other jobs that they came to monopolize,
the American community, not surprisingly, did develop a stereotyped
portrait of the Italian as an individual who could fit into the social structure only at the lower levels and therefore was capable of contributing to
society in limited ways. This portrait was incorporated into a variety of
jokes about Italians. In one of these, circa 1890, an American speaker
discussing the immigration problem before an anti-immigration audience, notes matter-of-factly that the Italians are the cleanest people in
the country. His listeners utter a collective gasp of disbelief. "But it is
a fact," the speaker insists. "I ask you, who cleans the shoes? Who
digs the sewer ditches? Who shaves our faces? Who collects the garbage? Who washes the dishes? They are all Italians. They cannot suffer seeing humanity wallowing in its own filth."[3] He got his laugh.

It was true that the Italians virtually dominated some jobs. By the

1880s in New York City, they controlled the macaroni market, sold plaster figurines of famous religious and secular leaders, operated candy stores, and made and sold artificial flowers. The retail fruit trade was in their hands; apparently every village or city on the east coast had an Italian fruit peddler or an Italian fruit stand. In winter the fruit merchants sold roasted chestnuts and peanuts, and in summer dispersed slices of watermelon and soda water to the children. The organ grinders were older men who were physically incapacitated or who could get no other work. They would walk the streets all day until 9:00 P.M. (a curfew set by law).[4] The shoeshine boys in the large cities were mostly Italian; 80 percent of the emigrants from the village of Laurenzana, Potenza, shined shoes in America. The shoemaking and repairing business in New Haven, Connecticut, was wholly in the hands of the Italians, as was trash and garbage removal in Philadelphia and San Francisco. By 1910, Italians were a significant factor in the New York City barber trade, and much of the import commerce between Italy and the United States was controlled by New York Italians. And the Italians had moved into the factories, including the cotton and woolen mills of Lawrence, Massachusetts, and the silk mills of Paterson, New Jersey.[5] There, as a contemporary local poet recognized, hard work may have been the most there was to look forward to in immigrant life:

> Let us weave the silk and gold:
> Our lot, our misery, our pain it
>   will lighten:
> Let us weave, let us weave until
>   death arrives;
> And on the cold weaving frame we
>   are extended.[6]

The United States economy at least offered the Italians a greater variety of jobs and greater potential for occupational mobility than had existed for them in Italy. Most were deadend jobs, but even the deadend job could be turned into an opportunity by an enterprising immigrant, an opportunity that would have not been possible had he not emigrated. There were those who opened small retail shops or purchased a piece of income-producing property after years of scrupulous saving while digging ditches. A peddler could buy his own business, a laborer could work his way up to foreman, a construction helper could become a skilled bricklayer, and so on. An immigrant with no training could also achieve occupational mobility through the skills brought over by other Italians. Those who emigrated with transferable trades such as tailoring, butchering, or shoemaking, which could be taken directly from the Italian village to the Italian colony in America, opened opportunities for their unskilled *compaesani*. Thus an Italian barber, once established in the Italian colony, could take on apprentices as his business expanded to two, three, and four chairs. These opportunities, products of a growing American economy, were not present in the stagnant economy of South Italy.

Some eight out of every ten Italians who came to the United States between 1871 and 1910 were from the rural and urban laboring classes, and had no job specialties. The others had practiced a small number of trades and professions. Between 1899 and 1910, for every 1,000 Italian laborers who emigrated to America, there was only 1 barber, 35 skilled artisans (carpenters, cabinetmakers, painters, masons, plasterers), 5 stonecutters, 34 shoemakers, and 23 tailors. When we compare this distribution with the jobs that the Italians held in America, it is immediately evident that there was a greater proportion in the trades and professions. Thus, in 1900, for every 1,000 Italian immigrant laborers, there were 140 Italian immigrant railroad employees, 120 skilled artisans, 40 stonecutters, 110 shoemakers, 90 mill workers, 100 tailors, 50 hucksters and peddlers, 150 merchants and dealers, and 20 professional men.[7]

Yet though the job opportunities in America exceeded those in Italy, both in quantity and quality, they did not compare favorably with those available either to the native-born Americans or to some of the other immigrant groups. For the most part the Italians were restricted to a very narrow occupational stratum near the bottom of the job prestige and salary hierarchy. Even the Italian professionals and tradesmen were forced to operate largely in the Italian colonies. The Italians were overrepresented in the precarious and peripheral types of employment and were markedly underrepresented in the more secure, better-paying jobs. Before 1920, of the five major groups of unskilled Italian laborers in New York City, only two—the hod carriers and the New York tunnel workers—had attained labor union representation;

workers in the construction gangs, maintenance-of-way men, and longshoremen were almost completely unorganized. According to Alberto Pecorini, in 1909, when 1.5 million Italians were residing in the United States, there were among them only 800 Italian physicians and 500 Italian lawyers.[8] An analysis of the 1900 federal census manuscripts for New York State shows that such "career" jobs as insurance men, railroad engineer, postal clerk, machinist, lithographer, and the like were overwhelmingly monopolized by native-born Americans.

The most common occupation for the greenhorn was that of outdoor laborer, a man who worked with a pick or shovel or sledge or axe or wheelbarrow. The railroad companies first employed Italians during the 1870s, and within a decade the Italians had monopolized the labor force on most lines in the United States and Canada, particularly in the northern states. It was grinding labor that consumed the men at a high rate—as one Italian poet has expressed it, a system without pity:

Here in the land of far famed liberty
Men are treated as part of a machine;
Hired and fired without necessity
According to set rule, and set routine.
By younger men the old were soon replaced,
Because they had outlived their usefulness;
Cast off like some worn part in discard placed,
Without regard to those it brought distress.[9]

The Italians were valued as laborers, however, because they cheerfully performed even the most demanding and routine work. For example, although comparatively few Italians engaged in coal and ore mining in America (there were colonies in Longacre and Boomer in West Virginia, and several small ones west of the Mississippi), some mine owners preferred the Italian worker and would pay premium wages to attract and keep him. The Thurber colony, at a coal mine in Texas, was composed of 500 Sicilian workers and one priest. As each new pit was opened, the owner would encourage his men to write home to tell friends that work could be had in Texas. New workers received $1.00 a day, but as their skills improved, their wages rose accordingly; the experienced Sicilians earned a minimum of $2.00 to $3.00. Because food and lodging were cheap, these miners were able to send home as much as two-thirds of their earnings.[10]

Such an operation was the exception, however. If the Italian new-comer was valued for his industriousness, he was no less valued for his willingness to work for low wages. When the pay was high and the working conditions acceptable, the Irish were hired before the Italians. It was when an employer was looking for cheap labor that the call went out for Italians. In a contemporary novel, a businessman explains his labor problems:

"The place is just overrun with Irish," Brother Pierce began again. ". . . I know 'em! I've had 'em in my quarries for years, an' they ain't got no idee of decency or fair dealin'. Every time the price of stone went up, every man of 'em would jine to screw more wages out o' me. . . . I've got Eyetalians in the quarries now. They're sensible fellows: they know when they're well off; a dollar a day, an' they're satisfied, an' everything goes smooth. . . . I grant ye, the Eyetalians are some given to jabbin' knives into each other, but they never git up strikes, an' they don't grumble about wages. Why, look at the way they live,—just some weeds an' yarbs dug up on the roadside, an' stewed in a kettle with a piece o' fat the size o' your finger, an' a loaf o' bread, an' they're happy as a king." [11]

The Italians in effect contributed untold millions to American industry by accepting low wages and inferior working conditions. Prior to 1910, Italians were instrumental in constructing 25,000 miles of railroad track at a total cost much lower to the companies than had Irish labor been used. In general, Italians were hired if they agreed to work for at least one-third less than the Americans or the Irish. Nevertheless, they seized whatever work they could get:

You gave me sorrow for my daily bread.
You threw cheap words at me.
And I found what scant nourishment was in them,
and bit into them like a rabid dog. [12]

In 1906, unskilled Italians were paid $1.46 for a ten-hour day (as were Slavs and Hungarians), while the Irish commanded $2.00. Italian tunnel workers in New York received daily from $1.75 to $3.00; Irish wages for the same work ranged from $3.00 to $5.00. [13] Some work for

Italians during this period paid substantially more, but the labor was so physically demanding that only a few immigrants had the capacity for it, and then only for a short period. The Italians would take these jobs if they wanted to collect quickly a small *gruzzolo* (hoard of money) for passage back to Italy or to make an investment. Totonno worked at one of these backbreaking jobs in a midtown Manhattan warehouse. After an exhausting four weeks he had $100 in his pocket, which he then used to buy a partnership in a retail food shop.[14]

Because of their initial willingness to work for less, the Italians invariably came into conflict with other immigrant groups that were competing for the same jobs. Once the employers began to hire the Italians, the other workers responded with threats and violence; the first Italians to join work gangs often feared for their lives. Much of the ill-feeling was fostered by the employers. For example, greenhorn Italians who accepted jobs at "good wages" had no way of knowing that they were being brought into town to serve as strikebreakers or as a means of depressing the wage scale.

The outstanding feature of immigrant work, particularly common labor, was its temporary nature. A typical pattern for the worker who came over without his family was to move several times, seeking work as he went along. Using immigrant labor allowed employers to hire a man, put him to work immediately, and fire him shortly thereafter. Workers would be let go if they became troublesome, or for the slightest infraction, or to make room for someone else: either a person who would work for less, or a friend or relative of the employer. Emanuel Carnevali bounced from one job to another, never remaining in one place for more than a few weeks. An acquaintance first found him a place in an Italian restaurant as a waiter-helper: "It was a table d'hote on Eighth Street and there I worked seventeen hours a day and came back to my room at night to dream of plates, plates, plates."[15] Carnevali lasted one month but went from there to work in dozens of other restaurants, large and small, being fired from most of them for one minor reason or another.

Turnover in pick-and-shovel work, railroad labor, lumbering, mining, road construction, and factory work was constant as the Italian workers arrived in America and left again in large numbers, and shifted from one job to another because of economic fluctuations, inadequate pay, contract terminations, hiring preferences, and the like.

Outdoor work was determined by the weather as well as the economy. Contract work was always temporary; once the job was completed, the workers moved on. Sometimes construction projects would be started and never finished for lack of financing; in such a case, when the workers were not paid on time or when wage agreements were not honored, they walked off the job. The difference of five or ten cents per day, when each penny counted and savings were measured in pennies, was also sufficient motivation to quit one job for another. The Italian's allegiance was not to the employer or to the job but to his own kind, his own family and his own conscience: some workers would quit their jobs and risk privation and debt rather than do what they did not wish to do. On the other hand, some found the American Work Ethic very agreeable. They had come from a background where hard work was valued but employment was scarce. They liked to work hard, took pride in their physical abilities, and remained loyal both to job and Boss as long as they were kept occupied and minimally fed, clothed, and housed.

Outside labor was the most exploitative form of immigrant work and the least desirable. Factory work, by contrast, was less demanding physically but more difficult for the greenhorn to obtain if he had no connections in the Italian colony. (Once an Italian entered a factory and became established, he was in a position to know of job openings and—out of obligation or for a consideration—to select *paesani* to apply for them; the *paesani* network always took care of its own people first.) While factory work could continue through the winter months, outside work rarely did. The winter period of unemployment could last as long as four or five months. If the worker had no family in America, he had to shift for himself, relying on *paesani* to tide him over; as a consequence he was forced into debt, which would be paid off when new jobs opened in the spring. If the worker had a family, his wife and children would be expected to take up the slack by making whatever kind of contribution they could to the household. To people who had never known full employment in Italy, forced inactivity was not necessarily a tragedy. It was *Il Destino*, the fixed order of things, and one made do with what one had. The miracle was that in this kind of uncertain economy no one starved, debts were settled, and money was saved and remitted to Italy.

Bartolomeo Vanzetti's job history is a dramatic example of the *millemestieri* (thousand jobs) pattern. From his arrival in 1908 until his arrest in 1920, he held countless jobs in New England and New York state, interspersed by periods of unemployment. A few days after Vanzetti stepped off the Ellis Island ferry, he got his first job as a dishwasher with the assistance of a compatriot who was a cook. After three months he left to work at another restaurant for eight months. There, he stood at a sink in a windowless room for 12 hours one day and 14 the next; he got five hours off every other Sunday. "The vapor of the boiling water where the plates, pans and silver were washed formed great drops of water on the ceiling, took up all the dust and grime there, then fell slowly one by one upon my head, as I worked below. The heat was terrific. The table leavings amassed in barrels near the pantry gave out nauseating exhalations. The sinks had no direct sewage connection. Instead, the water was permitted to overrun to the floor. In the center of the room was a drain. Every night the pipe was clogged and the greasy water rose higher and higher and we trudged in the slime." [16]

He did not want to take another restaurant job; it was too reminiscent of his work as a pastry cook in Italy, and he had a fear of contracting consumption. After walking the streets of New York for three months with no success, he met a young man at an employment agency one morning who suggested that they go to a small town in Connecticut where the man had lived previously. Thus began an odyssey for Vanzetti that took him through much of Connecticut and Massachusetts. The two men worked at a farm for two weeks and then wandered about the countryside giving their labor in return for dinner. They earned no money, and some days no food: "We were literally without a penny between the two of us, with hunger gnawing at our insides. We were lucky when we found an abandoned stable where we could pass the night." [17]

In Springfield they lived in a colony of northern Italians and worked in a brick factory. The ten-hour day at the furnace face was, for Vanzetti, "one of the most exacting jobs I know," but he stayed with it for ten months, although his friend lasted only two weeks. The next stop was the Meriden stone pits, where he broke and chiseled and sawed rock for two years. It was raw, demanding labor, and his co-workers finally persuaded him that the quarries were a place only for those who could do nothing else. The life of a granite cutter was often

short: the fine stone dust that hung in the air was a frequent cause of
respiratory ailments; flying stone chips caused daily injuries; and occasionally a man would crush a leg. You are fortunate, they said to
him. You have a profession as a pastry cook. Go back to it. You can
get respect and earn a decent wage. All you can get here is a sore
back, disablement, or death.

Returning to New York, Vanzetti worked in two restaurants—one
for eight months, the other for five months—and was discharged without explanation from both positions. Later he realized that the chefs
purposely kept workers only a few months because they received a
commission from the employment agency for every man hired.

After five months of looking halfheartedly for another restaurant
job, he decided to try outdoor labor, despite his friends' argument that
his baker's skills would eventually give him job stability and a better
future. An agency on Mulberry Street was advertising for pick-and-
shovel men. Vanzetti was transported with others to a barracks in the
woods in Massachusetts to construct a railroad. He worked there long
enough to repay his debts and then moved on to Worcester to live in
another barracks for a year and do factory work. In 1913 he transferred to a factory in Plymouth. Two years later Vanzetti participated
in a strike, was consequently blacklisted, and could no longer apply
for factory employment. He remained in Plymouth for the next five
years as a casual day laborer, taking any work that came his way, including ditch-digging, fish vending, ice cutting, snow shoveling, and
clam digging. During these years he continued to participate in labor
union activities. It was on May 5, 1920, while preparing a meeting,
that he was taken into custody and thus catapulted from the mass of
faceless Italian workers to the spotlight of worldwide attention in the
Sacco-Vanzetti case.

The Boss System

By the end of the Civil War, American industrialists were proclaiming
a shortage of unskilled labor. The problem was addressed by President
Lincoln in 1864 when he authorized a commissioner of immigration
and allowed the free entrance of migrant contract labor. The labor
agents ranged far and wide for recruits. Their subagents in Italy orga-

nized groups of workers and brought them to the United States for a stay of two or three years. The system, with all of its abuses, was similar to that which was then attracting Italians to Brazil and Argentina. The Italian Boss System evolved from contract labor and continued to bring Italian workers to American jobs long after the Congress approved the Anti-Contract Labor Act: the Foran law, which forbade the entrance into the United States of foreign workers who had accepted work contracts before emigrating. The Foran law was passed in 1885 and went into effect in 1887.

The implementation of the Foran law impeded but did not stop the flow of contract laborers into the United States. Daily violations occurred because enforcement was extremely difficult and evidence almost impossible to obtain. The contract laborers did not wish to reveal their status, and the inspectors at the immigration stations had no means of detecting them.[18] Many of the emigrants on Broughton Brandenburg's ship in 1902 were there because they had been promised work. One group had been hired for the Lackawanna mines by two agents who had been sent to Italy to recruit workers. (These same agents had been in the province of Potenza, Basilicata, the year before on instructions of their Boss, an Italian banker in Scranton, to recruit 300 men to work in the anthracite mines.) Beginning in the early spring of 1902, the men were dispatched in small parties on successive steamers to New York and Boston, where they were met by travel agents who escorted them to Pennsylvania.[19]

The Boss System was complex, and its configurations changed over the years, but it endured in one form or another until the end of the First World War. State regulation did not begin to affect the system until after 1900. In 1904, State Representative Giorgio Scigliano introduced a bill in the Massachusetts legislature to abolish the exploitative system of the "*padrone o bosso di campagna*" (non-urban work bosses). He was vehement in his denunciation of the Boss System, as were the newspapers in the Italian colonies. Scigliano documented for his political colleagues the excesses of the system and noted that the workers, robbed of their earnings by the bosses and the company store, would return to Boston during the winter—unemployed and forced to go on public relief.[20] In the same year a new law went into effect in New York state to regulate the employment agencies. A license to operate cost $25 per year, and a $250 fine was imposed for noncompliance.[21]

The Boss System was composed of layers of functionaries per-forming different tasks, with some of the individuals operating through institutions in the Italian colonies.[22] Many of the procedures were in-formal: some hiring bosses worked out of shoeboxes on street cor-ners, while others had offices. Some entered the system only on oc-casion to make a few dollars, since turnover in personnel was high and the prospect of making much money in a brief time was great. At the top of the hierarchy was the Boss, the man who could lead the workers to the jobs. Other roles in the system included clerks, run-ners (called *comari*), bankers, "enforcement" people, work camp em-ployees, hiring agents, travel agents, crew bosses, factory foremen, and finally—on the job site—the American foremen and employers. One person could occupy more than one role and profit from each, because the worker paid from his pocket or from promised wages at each step in the process. The network extended from the Italian vil-lages to agents in Italy (who could facilitate legal and illegal emigra-tion) to the Italian employment agencies, banks, boarding houses, and *paesani* groups in America. Workers—both greenhorns and veteran immigrants—were recruited in Italy, at the American immigration stations as immigration officials stood by, and from the Italian colo-nies. The large cities served regional areas: Chicago was a recruitment depot for the western states, New Orleans for the South, and Boston for New England.

When Rossi lived in the Bleecker Street Italian colony for a short period in 1879, he discovered that the immigrant job market in New York City was under the tight control of a handful of Italian bosses who made their headquarters in the local bars and gambling dens. Rossi saw larger sums of money wagered by the bosses at the turn of a card than a worker could earn in months of hard labor. In the fashion of the traditional Italian *padroni*, they provided jobs, granted favors, meted out punishments. The bosses were powerful and ambitious, with a bent for violence. They mediated between the immigrant and the American community, selling their countrymen's cheap, efficient labor to American employers and profiting from both parties. A man could become a Boss by recruiting 30 or 40 men in Italy, paying their passage, using his previously acquired knowledge of the American job market to get work for them—and then living in grand style from their sweat.

The American employers knew that the bosses were corrupt and were dealing in what amounted to a slave market. They were even aware that many of the bosses had originated from the Neapolitan *Camòrra*, a criminal organization, and had followed the Italian workers across the Atlantic because America was more fertile ground for their nefarious activities. Yet like many Americans—who looked upon Italians and other ethnic groups as inferior beings—the employers accepted the common wisdom of the day that a strong *padrone* was necessary to guide and herd the Italian workers, who could not care for themselves because they had the instincts of animals. Without a strong leader, who would get the Italians to the work site and see to it that they were not laggard in their duties? The Boss was handsomely rewarded for his efforts; as much as two-thirds of the worker's pay went into his pockets. Disturbed by what he saw as a system of servitude, Rossi asked one of the men why he and the other workers did not do for themselves and send "the bosses to the devil." "Sir," the immigrant responded, with a weak smile, "we are ignorant and we don't know English. The Boss brought us here; he is the one who knows where there is work and how work contracts are made. He takes care of everything for us. What would we do without him?" [23]

The Boss System provided opportunities for rapid wealth and advancement. As the immigrant worker stream widened, the ranks of those who profited from this trade in Italian muscle grew dramatically. Any Italian who knew basic English, who had some literacy, and who could move between the American and the Italian worlds with confidence and ease could make a living from the Boss System. Some of these persons were little more than opportunistic thugs; others were basically decent folk, but they were all to a degree ambitious, shrewd, and avaricious men who found capitalistic America a place where self-improvement was limitless. Cianfarra had little opportunity to make good wages until he took a job with a Boss who furnished men for the railroads and mines and constructed Shanties (company stores and sleeping quarters) for the men. Cianfarra operated the Shanties and did the office work for $30 a month, plus food and lodging. The Boss earned from $600 to $800 a month. [24]

Some swindlers represented themselves as agents just long enough to defraud a group of greenhorns. Carmine Morante landed in New York in 1895 and got a room with other immigrants on Mulberry Street for ten cents a day. During the first few weeks the men were hired on a daily basis, at the morning "shape up," a gathering of men seeking work to collect garbage. One evening they were approached by a "man of affairs" who offered them work at a dollar a day, with a paid train ticket to the job site. Each man had to give him a $5.00 *bossatura* or *senseria*, the job fee, before boarding the train. Once the man had collected their money, he escorted the group of 40 greenhorns to the depot—and disappeared.[25] Occasionally, the arrest of one of these racketeers would be reported in the Italian newspapers.[26] More likely, however, they eluded capture by moving from city to city until they had a substantial amount of money with which to return to Italy or invest in a legitimate business. "I knew him fifteen years ago, in 1880," Cianfarra's friend said, pointing to a man on the street. "He opened an office and placed an ad in two newspapers asking for men to work in West Virginia. Eight hundred men were gathered together in ten days. After he got the $2.00 *bossatura* from each, he fled to Chicago, where he changed his name and did the same thing. After three years he returned to New York and opened up a food store. Now he is a pillar of the community." [27]

Who exploited the Italian worker more, the Americans or his own compatriots? Many felt that the true exploiter was the Italian Boss. He was more likely to take advantage of and to profit from such immigrant limitations as the language barrier. A factory foreman, for example, could pocket pay increases that his workers were not aware of because they could not understand English.[28]

> It is painful to say this, but the conditions of employment are also terrible when the Boss is an Italian. The worst enemy of the Italian, and of Italy, in America is much too often a compatriate. There is one Boss in Somerville, Massachusetts, to cite one of thousands of examples, in a bicycle factory. He extracts five dollars from every unfortunate immigrant he can grab and put to work. And that is not all. After two or three weeks he gets them fired so that new ones can be hired. The victims do not dare complain for fear of the worst kind of retaliation.[29]

Most of the Italians were fatalistic about the Boss System. They took whatever pennies dribbled down to them, minded their own affairs, and kept their mouths shut. But not all the workers were puppets, nor were they fools. Sometimes they would seek work elsewhere or confront the Boss directly; occasionally, workers suddenly rose up and killed a particularly dishonest or brutal Boss.[30] When one work gang Boss was firing men after one week on the job, so that he could collect the $2.00 *bossatura* from each new person he hired, he made the error of discharging four Anzanesi when there were 20 other Anzanesi present. These men immediately laid down their shovels in support of their *compaesani* and demanded the return of their *bossature*. The Boss and his "enforcers" were no match for the 24 men. The job fees were returned.[31]

Most of the bosses were what Colajanni called Small Bosses; by 1900 there were over 2,000 of these in New York City alone.[32] The occupation was precarious, and the turnover must have been high. The Small Boss usually worked among his own *paesani*, procuring jobs for individuals and small work parties. Many owned retail stores or were speculating in any number of business ventures at one time. Others would recruit a few men in Italy or in America to work for American employers on construction projects. When business was good, the Small Boss might hire a person to assist him for a specific task. Totonno supplemented his modest income as a butcher on one or two occasions when he shepherded a group of recent arrivals, bound for Scranton, from the Battery to Grand Central Station. "These simple people," he wrote in his diary in 1909, "seemed so completely confused and bewildered. They do not know where they are or where they are going. I had to coax them onto the train." Seventeen-year-old Fortune Gallo got a job as a runner for $3.00 a week in 1895. He ran errands all over the city and wrote letters for immigrant clients. Later on, when he had developed a modest command of spoken English, he met greenhorns at the Battery and gave them their first introduction to the wonders of immigrant life.[33]

One day Brandenburg watched a group of more than 20 greenhorns boarding a train in New York under the direction of a Small Boss:

> one short, black, thick-set prosperous looking man who spoke Italian to the left and broken English to the right. [The immigrants] were tagged for Boston and other New England towns, bearing their heavy burdens of luggage and bundles, with faces

drawn and weary, eyes dull with too much gazing at the wonders of the new land, with scarce a smile among them except on the faces of the unreasoning children. They were herded together, counted off as they passed through the gate and taken aboard the train, much as if they had been some sort of animals worth more than ordinary care, instead of human beings. Here they were in charge of the conductor, who grouped them in seats according to the towns to which they were destined.[34]

The Italian factory foreman could also be called a Small Boss. The employer usually gave the foreman the authority to hire his own *paesani*, to be responsible for them, and to do as he pleased as long as he got work out of his men. Certainly, the employer did not want to deal directly with the greenhorns nor, in most cases, could he. Because there were more workers than jobs, the foreman could pick and choose. His *paesani* always came first, and relatives were given preference; the others had to wait their turns. It took Totonno several weeks to get his first job in 1906 in a piano factory through a *paesano* Boss, and then only after much begging and some subtle threats of retaliation back home by his older brother. And once on the job, an employee had to keep the foreman happy both for the worker's own sake and that of others whom the Boss might be persuaded to employ at a later date. Pietro Greco arrived in Brooklyn with a promise, through his brother, that the factory Boss would hire him. Immigrants in Greco's circumstances usually brought from Italy a load of *paesano* delicacies for the Boss. It was a form of tribute. Unfortunately, Greco did not bring his cheese and salami with him. His brother, who had gotten the *Bosso*'s gastric juices flowing in anticipation, exploded with anger when Greco appeared with empty hands. The brother had planned to make *una bella figura* (a nice gesture) with the gift. Now the Boss would be disappointed, and that was not good.[35]

With perseverance and luck a Small Boss could evolve into a Big Boss by expanding his business until it included at least one employment agency and contracts from employers who were in need of large numbers of workers. There was also a third category, the Boss Employer. The work bosses who were successful in accumulating capital and experience in the construction trade were free to form their own independent firms. They would then hire only Italian laborers and bid on the open market for work contracts. Before the First World War there were very few Italian construction companies, perhaps a dozen small ones in New York City and six each in Philadelphia and Boston.[36] A natural byproduct of the domination of the construction trade by Italians, these were forerunners of the much larger and successful Italian construction firms that by the 1930s existed in every city with an Italian colony.

Individual Immigrant Work Experiences

CONTRACT LABOR AND THE BOSS SYSTEM

Immigrant labor continued to be contracted for in Italy long after the passage of the Anti-Contract Labor Act. Two basic techniques were employed. In the first, the recruitment would occur in Italy, and the workers would be escorted over with their passages prepaid; in the second, a Boss would use the *paesani* network to call for workers, whom he would then meet at the docks in America.

Francesco Ventresca's experience was of the first type. A villager named Paradiso, who had returned from America in 1890 after a ten-year stay, put his knowledge of America to good use by becoming a Boss for those *paesani* who wished to emigrate because they could not find work in Italy. Since most of the men were penniless, Paradiso agreed to pay their transatlantic fare ($26), to be paid back in six months at an interest rate of 100 percent. He extolled the virtues of the American economy and convinced many of his *paesani* not only that repayment of the loan would entail no hardship but that they would be able to send money home to their families, as well. During the 1890s Paradiso returned to the village at the beginning of each year to form another group.

Many of the villagers who migrated with Paradiso found that jobs were not as easy to secure as they had thought, and what money they did earn went mostly for living expenses and repayment of the debt. But Ventresca's father had worked out a loan with a wealthy village lawyer, rather than fall into the clutches of Paradiso; the lawyer charged only 6 percent for six months. Moreover, Ventresca was a scrupulous saver in America. Never spending a penny unless compelled to, he managed to live on $6.00 a month, and when work was steady, he saved close to $30 a month. It took him only three months to retire his debt to the lawyer, whereas most of the other workers realized very little personal profit from their ventures.[37]

Pasquale D'Angelo, his father, and a few other men left Italy in 1910 after a *paesano* in America had promised them jobs on a state road crew. This man, their Boss, met them at the Battery and after a hurried greeting, led them to a train that proceeded to Hillsdale, where the pick-and-shovel job was located. With the exception of D'Angelo, who was a boy of 15, the crew members were married men of 30 or 40. They were all quiet, unassuming, and accustomed to the most taxing kind of hand labor, and they had one objective in mind—to earn money to send home. The crew lived together as a family in a shack in the forest and worked from dawn to dusk. Even though their daily routine was monotonous and laborious, involving the continual movement of large quantities of dirt from one place to another, the men were content. The Boss was kind and reasonable; the work was steady and profitable; and the comradeship among the men, who shared equally the vagaries of the worker immigrant experience, was comforting and satisfying. There was little friction. These were men who would have been working together at home, if fortune had not gone against them, rather than in a foreign country.

For their first few years in America, work was plentiful. The crew moved from one location to another—in New York, New Jersey, and Maryland—rarely missing a day's pay. Then the Boss decided to return to Italy and left the men to fend for themselves. They decided to stay together and sell their labor as a unit, but it became increasingly difficult to find work for eight. They spent weeks in New York City unsuccessfully looking for any kind of job. Once their meager savings were exhausted, they took their meals on credit from a generous *paesano* who owned an Abruzzese restaurant on Mulberry Street.

They had purposely avoided the Italian employment agencies, which had a notorious reputation among the immigrants, but now one of the men suggested going to one of the "job giving" places, for they had nowhere else to turn.

We presented ourselves in front of the door half an hour before the appointed time, and began to walk back and forth in order to keep warm, for it was a cold, raw day. As soon as the door was flung open we timidly approached it and entered. A young man was putting out some glaring signs in Italian calling for *braccianti* or laborers. Inside, a pompous gentlemen loomed in back of a wooden counter. Majestically, the man put on a pair of eye glasses and scanned us. Other laborers were crowding into the place. "It is like this," uttered the almost obese-looking man in a sonorous Neapolitan dialect, "you can start tomorrow if you want. The place is in West Virginia, which you may know, though I doubt it."[38]

The men standing there listening to the agent had already heard on the streets that this proposition was a gamble: the railroad fares to get to the job sites were high, and there was no certainty either that the promised wage would be honored or that the Boss would not be one of those greedy and brutish slavedrivers. Their forced idleness over the weeks had depressed their spirits, however, and they were ready to take any job. When D'Angelo and his *paesani* presented themselves as a work crew of eight, the Neapolitan responded that the train fare would be only $5.00 apiece if they could persuade three others to join them. So the eight men set out into the streets to find three willing recruits. Most of those to whom they spoke either had no money for the fare or did not allow them to complete their sales pitch. "You'll never get me to go down to that '*casa du li diavel*' in West Virginia," one man replied, "even if they give me five dollars a day." But by the end of the afternoon there were 11 men.

The next night the group arrived at a small station in a wooded area near the Potomac River and walked several miles through a freezing snowstorm along the tracks to the work site. They were shown to their Shanty by Mike, the commissary man, who sold various necessities to the laborers at exorbitant prices. D'Angelo soon learned that Mike was the Italian Boss, an influential and powerful individual who stood in the railroad crew hierarchy between the workers and the American foreman and profited from each relationship. He furnished the company with laborers and in return was given the privilege of a store monopoly. Mike's dominance was felt by the workers in many ways. The Americans never interfered in his relationships with the Italian workers; he could fire or hire or keep a man on the job at his will. His word was law. He had put some of the workers on his own private payroll and used these persons to encourage their friends to spend their wages on drink and other commodities, thereby increasing their debt to the commissary. If a worker refused to spend money in Mike's store, the man was cheated by adding nonexistent debts to his passbook. If this technique met with complaints, Mike would discharge the man. After a few days, the men realized that they had committed a grave error. Not only was the work oppressive and dangerous, but there was no way they could profit from their labor. Nonetheless, they remained on the job for several weeks, helping to cut a new railroad line through solid rock, until one man was crushed to death before their eyes in a grotesque accident. Disheartened, the others quit and returned to New York. What had they accomplished during their four years in America? They had left their families for an adventure that had turned into a nightmare. America in the abstract had promised them much; immigrant America had done little but sap their spirit and energy. There was drudgery to look back on and more drudgery to look forward to, apparently without limit. The men decided to disperse as a group. D'Angelo, at age 19, took his own path when his father and two others decided to return to their former lives in Introdacqua.

That winter D'Angelo lived in a boxcar and worked on the Erie Railroad for only $1.13 a day. In the spring of 1916, he was lured to a road job in New Jersey by the $2.25 wage. The work consisted of pushing a wheelbarrow filled with wet concrete for ten hours a day under the watchful gaze of a demanding Boss. The wheelbarrows were purposely overloaded, and the men complained that they were unstable, especially on an incline. The Boss cursed the workers and told them to put their backs to it. When D'Angelo pushed his wheelbarrow onto the plank leading to the wooden forms, he lost his balance; the wheelbarrow tipped over, and as he reached out to break his fall, his hand was run through by a nail. The Boss chased him off the job. It was several days before he could manage his hand well enough to work for another crew, and at the end of two weeks that crew was told that the contractor had gone bankrupt. No one got paid. Before walking back toward New York, D'Angelo talked about his wounded hand and his feelings of hopelessness with an older *paesano*, who finally said to him, "Boy, a stupid world drove nails through other hands—other hands." [39]

WORK CAMPS AND THE BOSS SYSTEM

D'Angelo's experiences in West Virginia with Mike the commissary man and the working conditions he encountered were repeated in virtually every immigrant work camp across the country. The Italian worker predominated in these camps. According to the 1900 federal census more than 33,000 unskilled Italian laborers worked in New York state, the majority on rural railroad, mining, quarrying, and lumbering crews.

The work camp immigrants came close to becoming the new American slave class of the post–Civil War era. In some camps the workers were held prisoners—if they wished to leave, they had to escape—and performed labor that weakened the constitution of even the strongest. The men were regarded as so many interchangeable producing units in the work camp system; as the units broke down or refused to function, they were replaced. The work camp laborer did not come under the protection of any national jurisdiction. Only the laws of the camp applied, and the Boss was God. The workers were so totally isolated from everyday American life that a camp culture independent of the outside world developed. They were neither Italians or Americans, but merely camp inmates. Those immigrants who knew only the work camp environment were ill-equipped to fit into conventional American society or even be accepted by their compatriots in the urban Italian colonies because of their "peculiarities" of dress, language, appearance, and comportment.[40]

Tens of thousands of Italians were transported directly from the ports of debarkation to work camp sites. In two or three years, after the system had taken from the men what it wanted, they returned to Italy, never having spent any time in an American city or village or having associated with anyone but camp workers. To them America was a place to work and Americans fanatics about work; nothing else seemed to matter except work and money. What is America like? the men would be asked upon their return home. Well, America is an axe, a shovel, a marble quarry, a railroad track, a wilderness, they would explain. One repatriated Italian said of America after a six-month sojourn, "For women and cows, America is Heaven. For men and horses, it is the other place."[41]

The company store (called the *Storo*, *Spaccio*, or *Shantee* by the Italians) was a fixture in the work camps. It served two purposes.

First, it was a necessary institution because the camps were usually far away from legitimate retail outlets. The immigrants had to rely on the *Spaccio* for basic necessities, including food and tools. The second purpose was purely exploitative. The man who acquired the concession was given the inalienable right to extort from the powerless camp worker, in a blatant fashion and by a variety of means, whatever portion of his wages would otherwise have been sent home to his family or saved for a future investment.

The *Spaccio* prices were never less than two to four times the prevailing market prices. Macaroni that would sell for 3 cents a pound at a legitimate retail outlet would cost the camp worker 10 cents at the *Spaccio*. Wine, 30 cents a gallon outside, would be 80 cents; meat at 5 cents a pound would cost 15 cents. *Spaccio* debts were settled at the end of a pay period. Each time an item was purchased, the clerk noted the cost both in the worker's paybook and on the store ledger. This system provided the clerk with every opportunity to falsify the record, so that the amount owed by the worker was often well in excess of his actual debt—and debt carried over to the next pay period had an interest penalty. Sunday, the day of rest, provided yet another chance to fleece the weak-willed workers and those starved for diversion by involving them in card games and tempting them with strong drink and prostitutes. No one could stay in the camp and avoid escalating debt. It was the rare worker who did not end up "owing his soul to the company store."

Survivors of the work camps brought out with them tales of corruption and consummate greed, and complaints about the camps became so commonplace that by the 1880s the Italian government was filing official protests in Washington. Despite the protests and the publication of reports documenting cases of outrageous exploitation, the work camps continued to thrive into the early 1900s. Agents continued to collect job fees from greenhorns and then send them off by train to the midst of some desolate wood where living and working conditions were probably the most primitive and oppressive that any immigrant group endured in America during this period. Most camp Bosses were American or Irish, brutal and violent men who maintained work discipline with their fists and clubs and would threaten the workers with their revolvers if orders were not carried out immediately. As part of his labor organizing activities, Carlo Tresca worked for five

days as a laborer on the Lackawanna Railroad. He was so shaken by
the experience that he helped to establish a free employment agency in
New York under the supervision of an honest agent.[42]

At most employment agencies—called Lions' Mouths by the
Italians—potential camp recruits would be given a rosy picture of the
job and told what they wanted to hear—that they would be close to a
sizable town where Italians resided and Italian retail establishments
existed, that the foremen were Italians, and the like. One evening on
Mulberry Street, Cianfarra listened to a hiring agent giving his sales
pitch to a group of newcomers. In a mixture of Italian dialects he told
the men:

> Don't concern yourselves. I assure you that the job will last for
> three years. The *Bosso* is a *compare* of mine. Why, he treats his
> workers as if they were his own sons. You get paid once a month.
> You need no money. The Company pays for the voyage to the job
> site. And if you have money at the end of the first month to pay
> for your *spesa* [expenses], you can pay, otherwise the *Bosso*, my
> *compare*, will give you *credenza* [credit]. The air is marvelous
> there. We will house you in shanties where you will live like *si-*
> *gnori*. The Company is financially secure. There is no chance it
> will go bankrupt.[43]

Regardless of the promises made, conditions were particularly harsh
for the Italian worker in the South. There were several documented
cases of Italian farm laborers on cotton plantations in Mississippi and
other states who were forbidden to leave; they were arrested and
brought back in chains if they did so. The railroad construction companies in the South would entice the workers by offering a free railroad ticket to a terrestrial paradise, rich in fruit, with a mild, tropical
climate. They found instead unbearable heat and humidity, clouds of
mosquitoes, disease. In 1907 the East Coast Florida Railroad Company hired a large number of Italians to build the 153-mile line from
Miami to Key West. Once the workers reached the camps on the coral
islands, they realized that they had been trapped into a system of in-
voluntary servitude. Some managed to escape to the mainland and
make their way back to New York, but others who tried to leave were
apprehended, by order of the company, for vagabondage and were
transported back to the camps.[44]

BOSTON'S NORTH SQUARE

One of the most active recruiting centers for work camp laborers was located in North Square, in the heart of the Boston Italian colony. Workers would be collected there and sent to any one of a number of construction projects as well as lumber and logging camps near the Canadian border. Supplying immigrant manpower to New England's bustling economy was a profitable business, and competition among the agencies was keen. Notices would be tacked up outside their offices: "The Bank M. T. & Co. needs for immediate employment 300 men. For Gravel Train work. 200 men for shop work. We need 250 men. Weekly pay at $1.50 per day," [45] and small boys would be sent out into the streets to distribute flyers. One of these was acquired by Bernardy in 1909, when she visited North Square. Its message, translated below, stresses the agent's integrity and compassion—traits that were in short supply, to say the least, among those who were trafficking in immigrant muscle.

Fellow countrymen:
        The acceptance, the trust, the gratitude of my large clientele, accumulated in a very brief period, have encouraged me to continue in my modest work as banker and contractor.
        The long years I have spent assiduously at the side of the workers (I was a worker myself) have served to give me an uncommon insight into the life of the laborer. So I am able to furnish you with reliable information about the benefits of such work.
        Almost every day I send men out to construction sites, and the work I have procured for them is always satisfying and the conditions humane.
        Never have I received any complaints in regard to prompt payment of wages, work conditions, or board. Never has anyone had to pay a penny for the so-called bossatura or anything resembling a payment of cash to obtain work.
        The constant demands for money and the continuing threats perpetrated on the poor workers by bosses should be sufficiently obvious to open anyone's eyes. How often does one witness a swindler who with honeyed words and all sorts of engaging promises takes your one or two dollars and then disappears from sight.

Workers should turn to a well-known person with a good reputation. Only in this way can you be sure that you will earn enough money to send remittances to your families back in Italy. To those in the past months whom I have helped to find work and to others who wish to use my office, I am at your service.

Let me also note that we offer other conveniences. Money orders will be mailed any place, steamship tickets are available for any ship company, and we do notary work.[46]

TWO WORK CAMP EXPERIENCES

After a brief stay in New York in April 1895, Gabriel Iamurri and his guardian took the Boston train and from the station made directly for North Square. For weeks they remained idle, and it was during this period that the young Iamurri had his first contact with the Italian labor agents called *Bordanti*, because they provided their immigrant workers with room and board in boarding establishments. These men, Iamurri observed, controlled the Italian immigrant labor market. Once in their clutches, a worker was squeezed for every penny that could be extracted from him. Iamurri learned to loathe the *Bordanti*; he found them rapacious, vicious, vengeful, with a lust for money that knew no bounds. "They were," Iamurri writes, "the very SCUM of the Italian race: Liars, cut-throats, ruffians and what not. They lied to you so much that they did not know when they were telling the truth. They were a very small group of willful people left to racketeer you without a check."[47]

The money Iamurri had brought from Italy, given to him by his father, was gone when he was hired along with several others to work on a job outside the city. The men slept in shacks and ate unpalatable food for two months, each day increasing their debt to the *Bordante*, who had purposely brought the workers to the site before the work was scheduled to begin so that they would become indebted to him. Once on the job, Iamurri realized that he was not fit for pick-and-shovel labor. The men were expected to work at a steady pace for "ten solid hours every day throughout the week, and sometimes even on Sunday, not to say anything about the time we were being cheated in the morning, in our noon hour, and at night on the job." Iamurri was too young and too slight of build to be able to endure the demanding regimen. He could not even assume the task of waterboy, because that required knowing English well enough to convey messages and run errands for the American employer. But Iamurri had to work, to earn his way like everybody else. He was finally given the job of assisting the clerk of the *Bordante*, helping him bottle beer to be sold in the evenings to the workers. This task placed Iamurri in a position to observe the clerk's practice of cheating the workers. Each time someone purchased one or more items in the *Spaccio*, the clerk wrote only the total cost in his ledger and in the man's paybook, and did so in such a way as to make it easy to change the number at the time of the next purchase. Iamurri describes the technique as follows: "For instance, you bought a bottle of soda for five cents, he put down in his book and in your passbook merely the digit 5 without a cipher before it .05 as it should be. He could easily insert before it whenever he saw fit sometime after, any digit he wished and so raise the amount from five cents to .45¢ or to $1.45 if he so desired." If a worker contested the accuracy of the numbers, the clerk would argue him down. "You don't remember what you bought three weeks ago," the clerk would say. If the worker persisted, the clerk would respond angrily, "Are you calling me a liar?" And if the worker threatened to retaliate, the clerk had only to report him to the company as a radical agitator, and he would be summarily dismissed. Those few who had the courage to pursue their grievances were ambushed by the *Bordante*'s "enforcers" and severely thrashed. The workers knew that they were being systematically cheated; the techniques were crude and obvious, and worked only because the immigrants had no recourse. To whom would one complain? They deliberately chose to ignore what they saw, or to swallow their pride and remain quiet.

Iamurri decided to earn a few extra pennies by becoming a secretary for those men who could not read or write. One day he read a letter to one of the men from an uncle in New York, a Boss, who suggested that the man join a crew that he was taking to work in Maine. Because the Boss promised a good wage and because Iamurri had yet to earn a full day's pay after several months in America, he decided to join the new crew as well. The Boss advanced the train fare to each of the men and gave them money for incidental expenses as they occurred. Once on the job, the loans were to be paid back at an interest rate of 50 percent.

The crew was halfway to Ashland, Maine, when the Boss took a good look at Iamurri and realized that he was little more than a boy who would be unable to perform to the exacting standards set by the contractor. The Boss's first thought was, "I bought the ticket for this puny kid; how can I get my money back?" He pondered the possibilities and decided to disguise Iamurri's youthful appearance with a man's cap and a long coat. As the train ground to a halt at the Ashland station, the Boss instructed Iamurri, who looked so ridiculous that he and his compatriates could barely keep their faces straight, what to do: "After we get off the train and go before the contractor, don't look in his face, so he won't see yours and see that you are nothing but a boy; for if he does he won't let you work at all on the job." Once Iamurri had worked off his debt, the Boss explained, he would be free to reveal himself and quit the job. The next morning when the workers were reviewed, Iamurri stood on his toes with his hat pulled down over his ears. The contractor walked by with no reaction.

The men worked steadily and quietly with shovels and pickaxes. The only sounds were made by the tools and by the foreman, who barked incessantly at them, urging each worker to dig faster and faster. "Hurry up, hurry up, move on, move on you . . . you . . . ." Within an hour's time Iamurri's hands were blistered and bleeding. His Boss, who was close by, became agitated at the sight of the blood and told Iamurri not to let anyone else see his hands.

With each passing day the pace of the work quickened as the Americans sought to extract every ounce of energy from the immigrants: "They worked us like horses and treated us like slaves." Iamurri was so spent after a day of moving tons of dirt that he had to be lifted bodily onto a flatcar to return to his boxcar residence. For the first week "it seemed, and, indeed, I felt as if my back was broken in two parts, since I couldn't straighten up at all." [48]

The work also took its toll in sapping the spirit and morale of the men. They had come to America with promises of decent and rewarding opportunities, even riches. The harsh reality of the work camp, the constant fatigue, the seeming hopelessness of their situation far from loved ones and familiar surroundings drove some over the brink into a deep, dark despair. Iamurri witnessed attempted suicides by two totally despondent men who wanted death to rescue them from this inextricable labyrinth. One, a *ciociaro* fresh from the Roman countryside, placed his head on a rail to await an oncoming train. As his *paesani* dragged him from the track, he cried out, *"Lascitami, lascitami stare per carità. Voglio morire. Non vale la pena di vivere più"* (Leave me be, for God's sake. I want to die. Life is no longer worth living). Iamurri was appalled by the inhuman treatment inflicted on the immigrants. They were men who sought only to make a modest living, yet they were not allowed even to do that without losing their dignity. Today "the human mind can never conceive or grasp how hard they worked us or how beastly we were treated and how much we suffered unless he himself lives through it." [49]

Constantine Panunzio landed in Boston in 1902 and within a few days had drifted toward North Square. He and his French sailor friend Lewis stayed at an Italian boardinghouse, where they were informed about the job market by the older immigrants. "We were given to understand by our fellow boarders that pick and shovel was practically the only work available to the Italians." Hearing this, Panunzio made a mental note to practice "peek" and "shuvle"—which became his first English words—as much as possible. He was vague as to the exact meaning of this phrase; it was probably some kind of office work, he concluded.

Each morning the two men would present themselves in North Square with others to be looked over by the hiring bosses, and one day an unshaven, dirty, and shabbily dressed Sicilian expressed an interest in hiring 20 men.

> We listened intently when this padrone came up to our group and began to wax eloquent and to gesticulate about the advantages of a particular job. It is only twelve miles from Boston, he said, and you can come back anytime to visit your friends and family. The company had a "shantee" in which you can sleep, and a "storo" where you can buy your "grosserie" all very cheap. "Buona paga," he continued, $1.25 a day, and you only have to pay me fifty cents a week for having gotten you this "gooda jobba." I only do it to help you because you are my countrymen. If you come back here at six o'clock tonight with your bundles, I myself will take you out.[50]

The men who had gathered to listen were impressed by the magnanimity of the Boss, and Panunzio was excited at the prospect of accumulating in a few weeks enough money to buy passage back home.

The discussion was brief and the decision unanimous: Let's go. After the first day on the job site, however, Panunzio realized that he had been naive. The work was heavy and monotonous, and the Boss turned out to be a crook. The men were working for nothing; once the Boss had deducted the cost of the bunk beds and groceries from their daily wages, there was nothing left but "sore arms and backs." The laborers began to grumble and tempers flared, but most remained on the job.

To Panunzio, however, the situation was intolerable, and Lewis agreed. On the afternoon of the third day, they dropped their tools on the ground, walked away, and kept walking until they reached a village. There they secured jobs in a woolen mill, sorting rags and carrying them in wheelbarrows to a hot oven: "Every time a person went in it he was obliged to run out as quickly as possible, for the heat was unbearable." The other workers, all Russians, despised the two foreigners and felt that these two "dagoes" were a vanguard of others who would take their jobs from them. The word "dago" was new to Panunzio, and he was mystified about its meaning, but not for long. Threats from the Russians and pushing and shoving occurred throughout the work day; in one encounter Panunzio suffered a nasty cut on his hand. At this point the Russian Boss intervened and discharged the two dagoes to avoid more serious bloodshed.

They had worked on two jobs and were penniless. Not knowing where else to find employment, disheartened and embittered by their initial encounters with America, Panunzio and Lewis walked back to the filthy Italian boardinghouse in Boston to begin anew. This time they had no intention of chancing the "shape up" at North Square. While strolling around the streets one afternoon they noticed a sign in the window of the Stobham Employment Agency, where lumbermen were being recruited. Inside, the clerk explained that the job "was out in the country, in the woods of Maine. A good, healthy job." Panunzio did not know what "woods" meant and had no notion as to the meaning of the designation "Maine." But the clerk struck both of the men as a decent chap, and anyway, they needed to earn money.

The night train to Maine was crowded with workers recruited through the agency. When the men left the hot and stuffy railroad car several hours later, they walked through a wilderness to a large lake, where a steamer ferried them across to the work site. There was nothing to see but thick forest. You are here to construct a new lumber camp, the men were told. Trees had to be felled, buildings raised, and roads constructed before the lumbering operation could commence. Panunzio became an axeman, even though he knew nothing about wielding an axe and was not anxious to learn. The Boss pushed the men at a killing pace. When Panunzio realized that the guards stationed around the camp were there to prevent the workers from leaving, he decided that he had to escape if he were to survive. He and Lewis crawled out of the camp late one night and headed for the lake.

At the lake they could not convince the steamer captain to take them across. They argued and pleaded with him but to no avail; he had his orders. It is a one-way trip, he kept repeating. Fearing that the guards might be following their trail, Panunzio and Lewis spent the night deep in the woods. The next morning they met a Russian who had also escaped, and the three men constructed a raft of logs to cross the lake. They hiked through the woods for a number of days. One morning the Russian disappeared, and the next day Panunzio and Lewis walked into a French Canadian lumber camp. The Canadians were decent, humane individuals and did not hesitate to accept the two men. Lewis found a home among his conationals, but Panunzio, dissatisfied with the life of a backwoodsman, decided to move on.

After what seemed an interminable walk, Panunzio finally trudged out of the woods and met a farmer who, upon being asked if he needed a man for the day, offered Panunzio a very liberal $15 per month with room, board, and washing if he would stay on. Panunzio, touched by this obvious decency, accepted. He was once again optimistic: in a short while he would have his passage money to Italy. Panunzio was a loyal employee for six months, during which time he received only $5.00 in cash from the farmer. When he told the farmer that he was ready to leave and asked for the remaining $85, the man "laughed me out of court, and with a sneer upon his lips which I remember to this very day, he handed me a five-dollar bill and said that that was all he could pay me." Panunzio boiled over with anger and threatened to go into town and engage a lawyer. The farmer laughed again, louder this time, and dismissed him with a gesture of contempt. They both knew it was an empty threat. Panunzio had come to learn one thing about the Italian in America: he had no civil rights; he could be cheated by his employers and treated with less respect than a beast of burden, and no one cared. Panunzio took his few belongings and walked down the road toward town, so full of rage that he was shaking uncontrollably.

WORK ACCIDENTS

> Many were broken by the crushing load,
> And perished in the evil of the hour!
> We buried them where they fell by the road,
> The poor victims of greed and scheming power.
> We saw the evil, and we knew the sin
> Of those who ruled with insolent disdain,
> But we had faith, my son, and will to win—
> Against this *Rock* the world shall storm in vain.[51]

One fate that Italians shared with other worker immigrants was injury and death on the job without compensation. The Italians were the "I" in Michael Novak's acronym, PIGS (Poles, Italians, Greeks, Slavs).[52]

A. Dosch was visiting a railroad construction site in New Jersey along the Hudson River shore. Dosch asked a young assistant whether any workers had been killed on the job. The young man smiled. "There wasn't any one killed except wops," he replied.

"Except what?"

"Wops. Don't you know what wops are? Dagos, niggers, and Hungarians—the fellows that did the work. They don't know anything, and they don't count."[53]

The Italian colony newspapers were filled with reports of the injuries and deaths of immigrant workers. Iamurri was witness to daily accidents that were forgotten by the employers as soon as they occurred. The Bosses were more upset by a broken shovel than by the broken body of a laborer.

> Di Angelis was shoveling gravel on the flatcar of a train one day, in the gravel-pit, when the train started to go without warning. The gravel-bank caved in. . . . Di Angelis tried to run . . . but was pushed under the moving train by the avalanche of gravel and killed instantly. No one ever paid anything. . . . The engine all of a sudden gave an unexpected hard push making all of us fall in all directions. Two men fell between the cars and were there and

then killed. . . . The very next day, a friend of mine carrying a case of dynamite and caps together on his shoulders, as he was told, fell down and the case of dynamite with the caps exploded and my poor friend, Jimmie, poor Jimmie, was torn to pieces—died. No one of the concern ever shed a tear over him. The list of casualties here of like nature could be made almost unending if I didn't try to be brief.[54]

Sometimes the tragedies assumed larger proportions. Guido Sella described to Angelo Pellegrini his first work experience in America as a laborer building a new track line along the lower Columbia River.

> I remember the first day we went to work. At six in the morning, with pick and shovel on our shoulders, we marched off to work. . . . There were men of all colors, all races, all sizes—Chinese, Hindus, Mexicans, Spaniards, Italians, Slavs. All hungry. All with families to support in faraway lands. All miserable. . . . We walked about half a mile and stopped in front of a mountain. . . . It was a mountain of solid rock. . . . The mountain had to come down.
>
> Our interpreter explained that we should have to dig tunnels fifty feet long, four feet in diameter, and fill them with dynamite. . . .
>
> Well, it was bound to happen. And it was a massacre! It came in the middle of the day when the sun burned like fire. Pro-to-to-to—ton! Rigid with fear, I stood there clutching the shovel. Down from the blackened sky came dirt and stones and the crushed bodies of men. The turbaned head of a Hindu fell on my shoulder and covered me with blood. Twenty-one men were killed. There were many wounded.[55]

Although precise statistics are not available, there can be little doubt that immigrant labor was being consumed by the United States industrial machine at a rapid rate. And a significant proportion of those immigrants were Italians, for they usually were to be found in the most dangerous work. Bernardy estimated that at least one-fifth of the Italians who came to the United States to labor in the mines, on the roads, and in building construction were victims of work accidents and work conditions [56] and that up to 25 percent of the industrial casualties were Italians. As Enrico Sartorio said to an America whose industrial infrastructure had been built by Italian labor, "Your railroads, your public buildings, your coal are wet with Italian sweat and blood." [57] Dr. Antonio Stella, one of the first prominent Italian physicians in New York City, concluded after an investigation of the city's Italian mortality and morbidity that the official statistics were seriously inadequate.

> The Italian immigrant may be maimed and killed in his industrial occupation without a cry and without indemnity. He may die from the bends working in the caissons under the river without protest; he can be slowly asphyxiated in crowded tenements, smothered in dangerous trades and occupations (which only the ignorant immigrant pursues—not the native American); he can contract tuberculosis in unsanitary factories and sweatshops without a murmur, and then do this country an additional favor when, disabled and weak, he goes back to his mother country to die, thus giving the American city the credit for having a low death rate. [58]

Dangerous work was made even more dangerous by the casual attitude with which men would be hired. If a man looked healthy enough and expressed a desire to work, he would be given the appropriate tool and placed on the payroll. Although these jobs were considered "unskilled," a background of experience was essential in order to work intelligently with other men and to do the job efficiently and safely. Conte noted that he met many Italians in America who were bending their backs for their daily bread for the first time in their lives; in Italy they had been priests, lawyers, and journalists. He even met a count and a baron working in a sewer ditch. These men actually constituted a danger to themselves and to others because of their inexperience. [59]

There was collusion among coroners, lawyers, undertakers, and the police to cover up an accident and to profit from work-related tragedies. The immigrant's ignorance of his rights and the nature of most immigrant work hindered full investigations and contributed to a conspiracy of silence. The turnover in Italian labor was high. Most construction jobs were temporary; they did not last beyond a specific contract or a work season. Italian superstition also contributed to the problem: it was believed that an accident was part of the *destina* of the work crew and that other accidents would soon follow if the workers remained—especially if someone had been killed on the job. That was a signal for the Italian gang (railroad workers, for example) to quit that section and move to another section or to a new job. A new gang would replace the old one. Given the mobility of the workers, the men who had been on the job at the time of the accident were often not available months later to testify at legal hearings. They had moved on without leaving forwarding addresses, or even returned to Italy.

The matter would often be settled without litigation by offering the victims a modest cash settlement to prevent any future suits or claims. One of Iannace's friends was seriously injured when his leg went into a vat of caustic acid. The railroad company offered $100 in compensation if the man would sign a form lifting the responsibility for the accident from the railroad. Being no longer employable, he took the money and went back home.[60] In 1904, a fifteen-year-old boy lost a hand in a factory accident. The firm offered to settle for $500, but the parents refused the money and sought a lawyer. A spokesman for the firm told them, "Go to court if you wish. For the Italians, there is no justice!" The court case dragged on for years; and in 1910 there was still no settlement. But there were immigrants who did receive justice. In a similar case, which occurred a few years later, the accident victim was awarded $10,000 by the court for the loss of a limb.[61]

Some of the larger companies had accident insurance (the premiums were paid by the workers), but it served more as protection for the company than as a means of adequate compensation for the worker. To get the coverage, which paid a lump sum for illness or death, the worker had to sign a release exempting the company from any responsibility for accidents.

Most immigrants were reluctant to get caught up in the legalities of a court case. They lost time from the job, and there was realistic fear that to take the side of the worker against the company would result in being blacklisted from further employment. They were in a foreign land where the legal system and the language of the courtroom were incomprehensible. The immigrants knew that the Americans held all the cards, and they felt inferior to and intimidated by lawyers and judges. How were they to discern whether justice was being served? We do not know how to defend ourselves, the immigrants would say. The American creed of justice for all meant little to them. Acutely aware of their second-class status, the immigrants learned to distinguish between equity at the abstract level and equity as practiced in everyday life. The law is equal for all, the immigrants would say, but justice is something else. The Italians would take what they could and be satisfied with it. They saw no other alternative. Even when indemnities were paid to injured parties, the Italians were not at all surprised to receive less than others. They knew that they were at the bottom of the pecking order. One instance, among many, of unequal compensation occurred in Black Diamond, California, in the early 1900s. A number of men had been killed or injured in an explosion. The non-Italian workers were awarded $1,200 each in compensation, the Italians only $150.[62]

The immigrant who could not work was of no use to anyone. America wanted cheap labor, not charity cases. Industry wanted no responsibility beyond replacing the diseased, injured, or worn-out worker with a healthy one. Moreover, the man who could not support himself and his family became a burden to his *paesani*, and if he had a family in Italy dependent on his regular remittances, they would become destitute. The sick or injured immigrant often had little choice but to return home with little or nothing to show for his years in America.

City and county officials encouraged such repatriation because they did not want these people to become burdens to the community. As the charity service reports for Cook County, Illinois specified in 1908, any immigrants "becoming dependent in whole or in part within twelve months after landing, excepting, *perhaps*, such as become dependent through injury by industrial accidents, should be considered as being here in violation of the law and should be deported to their home country."[63] The audacity of the qualifier "perhaps" revealed the true position of the worker immigrant in America as a cog in the industrial machine, a cog that when broken could be cast aside and replaced. There was no sense of obligation to this individual.

Even a just settlement of a deceased worker's own property was unlikely, particularly if his wife lived in Italy; if compensated at all, a widow would have to accept whatever she received. Yet many of the men who had been working in America for years and who intended to return to their families in Italy had substantial savings in American banks. Giacomo Musso, a miner, was crushed by an enormous block of coal. He had worked in the mine for ten years and had planned to return to Italy the following week. Everyone knew that he had accumulated a "nice pile of savings." [64] In most cases, however, the spoils would be distributed by the court to the undertaker and others to pay for burial and debts, some real and some contrived. Undertakers in particular were known for their insatiable greed. If the deceased had saved $75, that is what his funeral would cost. If he left behind $175, the undertaker would present his bill for that amount.

These forgotten victims were commemorated by the poetess Rosina Vieni in an Italian sonnet:

The bricklayers came by the hundreds,
an entire gang with calloused hands
to create a building of forty stories
without counting the roof and the basement.

It seems that they challenge the heavens
to the honor and glory of the Americans;
but who cares about the greenhorns, the paesani
struck dead, without the sacraments?
What's it worth, if by misfortune or by accident
your body falls and smashes to the floor below—
poor Guinea, poor Dago?

Sitting in front of a half-pound of steak
the Boss sneers and shows his teeth of gold:
—who got killed is dead . . . I'm alive and that's all that
    counts. [65]

THE TRADITIONAL PADRONE SYSTEM

Existing side by side with the Boss System in America was the Padrone System, a form of indentured servitude or quasi-slavery that had flourished in the Italian peninsula for some time. The Padrone System was an answer to chronic poverty, unemployment, and over-population. It became acceptable practice, both in the cities and in the countryside, to give or sell or contract the children that a poverty-stricken family could not feed to a man who would use them as his chattel. Antonio Margariti's experience in Calabria as a child *servo* to a farmer was a typical example from his part of Italy.

Immigrant *padroni* were found in the nineteenth century wherever Italians lived abroad—in England, South America, and—after the Civil War—in the United States. By promising economic security and material comfort, Italians who had lived in America persuaded men, women, and children to come to America to work under their guidance and protection. The contracts were usually for two or three years; a few were for seven years. Once in America the men were placed in pick-and-shovel work or similar unskilled labor; the boys were sent out on the streets as newsboys, bootblacks, thieves, and beggars; and the women went into the brothels. At the end of each day the money earned was consigned to the *padrone*, and he, in turn, would provide his workers with the basic necessities. The traditional Padrone System began to fade from the American scene with the expansion of immigrant work opportunities and the increased sophistication of the Italian emigrant. Those who had been ensnared by *padroni* would return to their villages and enjoin their relatives who were about to emigrate to avoid a similar trap.

Rocco Corresca's life in Italy and his first year in New York were unique in that he was a victim of the Padrone System in both countries. Corresca was one of a group of illegitimate children being raised by nuns in an orphanage near Naples when a man appeared claiming to be his grandfather. Satisfied that the documents he presented were legitimate, the nuns released Corresca to his custody. The man expressed relief to the nuns that he had finally tracked down his grandson; now, he assured the nuns, little Rocco could lay claim to the heritage that was rightly his and live a comfortable life on the spacious family estate.

Corresca was never able to ascertain whether or not the man actually was a relative. Whatever the case, the man was a traditional *padrone* for beggar children. The eight-year-old Corresca was taken to Naples to live in a hovel with several other child beggars. The *padrone* controlled every aspect of their lives, forcing the children to go out each day to beg at the churches and every evening in front of the theaters. Corresca lost little time in learning the many tricks and deceptions of the begging trade, for to return from the streets with an insufficient number of coins was to invite a painful beating from the *padrone* and to receive no supper.

The children had few comforts and no amusement. They were deliberately kept in a ragged, barefoot, malnourished state in order to incite the sympathies of passersby, especially American and English tourists, who were shocked by the sight of children begging on the streets. The boys ate black bread rubbed with garlic or accompanied by a herring and slept on the bare floors.

Corresca lived this life for three years. One night he overheard the *padrone* plotting with some other men to deliberately maim him; the boy was recalcitrant, he said, and must be taught a lesson. The plan was to have the men reduce Corresca to a crawling, crippled church beggar, the kind of pathetic, deformed creature that would make people shudder to look at him. In that state, the *padrone* was convinced, he would arouse much more sympathy and earn plenty of money.

The next evening Corresca and his best friend, Francesco, did not return to the *padrone*'s house. Instead, the two boys walked aimlessly along a road, begging as they went, until they reached a small seacoast town, and there they lived for five years with a generous and compassionate fisherman and his family. While earning their living as fishermen, the boys heard stories about America from the returning emigrants. This was in the late 1890s, and America was being described as a country with a magnificent and modern vision, a place where Italians could earn enough money to enable them to live in Italy in splendid comfort, like gentlemen of leisure.

Corresca and Francesco landed at Ellis Island in 1900 with empty pockets. When they were taken before the review board, the decision was to deny them admission. But as the boys' names were being placed on a list of those to be sent back to Italy, a man calling himself Bartolo stepped forward and announced that the boys were brothers and he was the uncle who had been for the past two days patiently awaiting their arrival.

Corresca and Francesco said nothing. When they were asked, through a translator, whether Bartolo had spoken the truth, they merely nodded their heads. They did not want to return to Italy under any conditions, and Bartolo, whoever he was, was making it possible for them to enter the country. "Uncle" Bartolo took the two "brothers" to his boardinghouse on Adams Street in Brooklyn. As soon as Corresca walked into the house, he knew that for the second time in his life he had fallen into the clutches of a *padrone*. In a single room on the third floor lived several boys and men, each of whom had met Bartolo either

at Ellis Island or at the Battery. Bartolo expected gratitude; he had
"rescued" the two boys and was now giving them a place to sleep and
their meals, which he prepared on a small stove in the center of the
room. In return, they would work for him.

Bartolo was a junkman. Each morning he furnished his workers
with large burlap bags and sent them far and wide throughout the
streets of Brooklyn to pick up any discarded items that were salvag-
able and salable: rags, bottles, mattresses, hats, boots, bones, um-
brellas. Bartolo repaired and sold whatever he could. The rags were
washed in the back yard and hung to dry in the room; the bones were
stored under the beds until Bartolo could strike a good bargain with
the bone merchant. He also secured pick-and-shovel jobs for the men
at a weekly fee of 25 percent. Corresca rarely saw any cash. After
Bartolo had summed the costs of housing, food, and clothing for each
worker and subtracted the total from the wage, only a few pennies
were left, if anything. When anyone complained, Bartolo would assume a look of personal hurt and anguish, and say, "See what I do for
you and yet you are not glad. I am too kind a man. That is why I am so
poor." [66]

Like Bartolo, most *padroni* saw themselves as both Father and
Boss to their men, as *Padre Padrone*. They were greedy persons, self-
centered and egomaniacal, who devoted their energies to profiting
from the cheap labor of their fellow countrymen. But they also func-
tioned to ease the passage of many Italians from a post-medieval Italy
to a modern, industrial society. The immigrants with whom Corresca
lived were like himself: naive, young, insecure, ignorant individuals
fresh from the Old Country, where many had depended on the Padrone
System for their sustenance. They had arrived in America on their
own, alone, not part of a kinship network that could aid them in making an adequate adjustment. There were no *paesani* or brothers or
cousins waiting for them at the docks to get them a job and a household to live in, to teach them the ropes. Without the protection and
guidance of such primary relationships, the greenhorn immigrant had
to face a hostile society head on. More than one Italian newcomer,
stunned and paralyzed by the shock of culture change, turned on his
heel and returned to more familiar surroundings. Men like Bartolo
filled the void by acting as a substitute father. Not only did they provide work; they also provided a home of sorts, where psychological

needs could be satisfied and the greenhorn could practice his first steps before venturing out alone into the new society. Bartolo's reaction when Corresca and Francesco spread their wings and flew the nest was predictable. He was outraged. They were his boys; he had trained them, he had succored them, and now they were leaving. But after one year with Bartolo, the boys had learned that they need not depend on the *Padre Padrone* anymore. There were better work opportunities available for Italians. For a $5.00 fee Francesco and Corresca secured pick-and-shovel jobs with an Irish Boss. Bartolo followed them to Newark and made a great deal of noise. You are ingrates, he told the two boys, and you owe me your labor. He retreated only after the Irish Boss, a soft-spoken and kind but firm man, went for the police.

THE PAESANI NETWORK

The Italian relied on his *paesani* in Italy for information about jobs in America, and once in America, he was most likely to get work through a *paesano* and to work with his *paesani*. The typical Italian would enter the American Paesani Network, an extension of the same network in Italy, as soon as he cleared customs. Immigration officials claimed in 1897 that most of the Italians who arrived in New York were met at Ellis Island by about five people. Those who were not carried the addresses of their *paesani* in their pockets. Because communication flowed freely between the home village and America, it was necessary to protect one's reputation in both communities. Here is a letter from an immigrant to his father, who told him that his returning friends had been slandering him.

> Dear Father . . . I would like to know who has been gossiping about me. Do not believe them. It is all lies. I will give some thought to those disgusting people. Tell those gravediggers who are now back in Italy that I would like to be there right now to defend myself.[67]

The Boss preferred his *paesani* as employees because he knew that they would give him respect and would be easier to command. The workers preferred a *paesano* Boss because he could more easily earn their respect and they could expect, if not demand, that he be honest and fair with them. Work crews were almost always homogeneous. "In this country immigrants of the same town stick together like a swarm of bees from the same hive, and work wherever the foreman or boss finds a job for the gang."[68] Italians from North and South Italy had little contact and rarely worked together; the ethnic differences were too great. And southern Italians tended, at least at first, to group themselves according to their village, province, and region. If a Sicilian and a Pugliese asked a Sicilian Boss for a job, the Boss would select his *compaesano*; he would feel no obligation to the Pugliese and would be roundly criticized by his Sicilian employees if he did not look after "his own" first. When Cianfarra landed in New York, he went to a pasta and oil wholesale house to seek a job. As soon as he opened his mouth the clerk told him that he was wasting his time, for the Boss only hired *compaesani*.[69] What Cianfarra needed was a relative or friend who could vouch for him and ask the Boss, as a personal favor, to take him on. A favor demanded reciprocation, and the Boss would keep that in mind.

There was safety in numbers. The Paesani Network offered job security; it engendered a feeling of mutual trust; and it gave its members the comfort of sharing familiar tastes and customs, especially among crews that worked, cooked, and slept together in constant daily interaction. There were also disadvantages. The Paesani Network was confining and provincial; it stifled ambition and deterred any desire or attempt to move into American society; it limited the immigrant to low-wage jobs; and it often made him vulnerable to exploitation because his guard was down with his *paesani*, whom he felt would not endanger his interests in order to promote their own. Moreover, because personal criteria were paramount, questions of hiring and firing were related not to job performance but to *paesani* loyalties. And such loyalties died hard. Regardless of the actual facts, choices were made consistently in terms of one's own people—a "consciousness of kind" that could reappear even after years of disuse.

The work experiences of Margariti, Ventresca, Iannace, and Totonno illustrate both the advantages and disadvantages of the American Paesani Network.[70] Margariti and his four companions had a precise destination in mind when they entered America illegally in 1914. Their *paesani* in the village of Pittsford, near Rochester, New York, had been alerted through the network that they were on their way. The day after their arrival a *paesano* took them to a German road gang that needed men. At first Margariti and his friends could not grasp from the German Boss and their German coworkers what was expected of them. After much gesticulation and yelling in English, German, Italian, and Calabrese, Margariti recognized the word "stone" from a conversation he had had aboard ship with a returnee who had described his roadbuilding work. The Italians picked up their sledgehammers and went to the task of making "smaller stones out of big ones." For ten hours a day Margariti received $1.98—which, since it far exceeded his brother's railroad wage of $1.40, gave him a heady feeling of affluence.

With the winter months, outside work became increasingly scarce. In January 1915, Margariti and his brother moved to a very remote and wooded area near Clearfield, Pennsylvania, to join a *paesani* crew of railroad laborers. For two years Margariti lived communally under very crude and primitive conditions. The tarpaper shacks afforded few comforts. Clothes were washed in a brook, and wood had to be chopped daily for cooking and heating. One day Margariti heard from his oldest brother, Peppino, for the first time since Peppino's departure from the village in 1903. Peppino had discovered that his brothers were in America after he had written home (at the urging of his Boss) to ask them to join him. When they met, Margariti was impressed by how much Peppino had changed: he could speak English, he had American friends, he had money in his pocket, he was well dressed and looked confident. By comparison, Margariti and his coworkers knew next to nothing about America; they were thin and haggard, and wore rags.

The vivid contrast made Margariti think about a number of things. Working on a *paesani* crew was getting him no place. It offered him nothing but the same relentless labor day after day. He promised himself that at the first opportunity he would go off on his own. Margariti moved to Clearfield, worked for a few weeks in a terra-cotta foundry, and then returned to Pittsford to board with other Calabresi and to work in a factory. He later moved to Philadelphia with two of his friends to work for the Victor Talking Machine Co. Dissatisfied by his association with other Italians (he had become ashamed of his *paesani*), he tried to break out on his own by taking a job in a bakery staffed by non-Italians. The experience was very nearly disastrous, as were his attempts to live away from other Calabresi, and he retreated back to the sanctuary of the Italian community. Margariti did not succeed in breaking away until he found a job at the Budd Automobile Company, which he held until his retirement in 1956.

When Ventresca landed at the Battery, friends from his Abruzzi village were waiting and took him to their apartment on Mulberry Street, where he enjoyed his first "American" meal of spaghetti with *braciola* and Romano cheese. He was initiated to American customs when one of the "enriched neighbors" treated him to a nickel stein of beer at the local tavern.

Two days later Ventresca changed his remaining 43 *lire* into $8.00 and followed his *paesani* to the Hudson River night boat for the trip to Albany. They were startled by the cold, snowy weather and shivered (no one had an overcoat) while waiting for transportation to Saratoga Springs, where they were to work on a railroad section gang at $1.25 for a ten-hour day. Compared to his life as a railway laborer in Italy, Ventresca found the job light and easy. He was disappointed that it did not require any competence or give him any new satisfaction. Ambitious men, he thought, would not stay at this long. He had expected that America would give him something different, not more of the same. To earn additional money (his goal was to earn and save as much as possible) and to prove he could do it, he once worked 30 hours in succession—day-night-day—for $3.75. In July several men from the crew took jobs at a gravel pit outside of Ithaca for $1.50 a day.

By early fall Ventresca was at Forestport, New York, removing trees, stumps, and boulders, with the help of horses and scrapers, to clear the ground for a railroad right-of-way. Each worker was given a metal number plate—Ventresca's number was 94—also inscribed with the names of the Italian Boss and the American foreman. The plate was attached to the worker's jacket so that he could be identified by number rather than name. (On some jobs, the numbers were painted directly on the jacket.) The maximum wage was $1.25; it was usually less. Cold, numbed hands and feet were accepted as part of the job. The immigrants were happy to have a job at all during the winter months.

With the coming of spring, Ventresca's group packed their few belongings and hiked 30 miles along narrow forest paths to catch a train for Bradford, Pennsylvania. On arrival, the Italians discovered that the jobs they had expected to get did not exist. The men remained there until they heard through some countrymen that day laborers were earning $1.50 in Niagara Falls. Ventresca spent a sweaty and dusty summer on the streets of that city, breaking rock and living in a Calabrese boardinghouse. It was his first opportunity to see city life and to observe Americans at close range. He was becoming good friends with the boardinghouse owner and more than good friends with his pretty brunette daughter when the job ended, and one of the group suggested that they move on to Chicago where, it was rumored, wages were $1.75.

Chicago was a bitter disappointment. Jobs were scarce in the city; the streets and bars along South Clark Street were filled with idle men. The congestion, the apathy and poverty of the Chicago Italians, and the filthy streets so depressed the men that they sought to leave as soon as possible. Workers were in great demand on construction projects throughout the West, and Italian newspapers contained ads for hundreds and thousands of jobs: "500 Italian workers needed for Iowa, Michigan, Illinois, Texas and Arkansas. Good pay and low railroad rates. Go quickly to: R. F. Christian, 284 So. Water St." [71] There was also an opportunity to go to Colorado, but the men were reluctant to venture that far from their *paesani* epicenter. To them Chicago was the outer limit, beyond which lay all sorts of hazards. The problem seemed solved when they heard that a Boss named Jim, a *paesano*, needed men to dig sewers in nearby Western Springs. An older immigrant, Jim spoke some English and served as an interpreter. His ability to communicate with the "world of Americans" gave him an "exalted position" both among the Italians and with the American contractor, who paid him an enviable $2.50 daily. The significance of all this was not lost on Ventresca. He admired Jim, wanted to be like him, and realized that the key was the language. If he continued to follow his *paesani* around from job to job, he would eventually return to Italy, as others had done, with only a pair of shiny patent leather shoes, a bowler hat, a collection of tall tales, a handful of cash, and memories that would grow stale over the years. Encouraged by his friends, Ventresca at age 20 quit work and enrolled in elementary school.

Iannace, another immigrant from Abruzzi, was bound for Meadville, Pennsylvania, in 1906, where he was to live and work with relatives who had settled there a few years previously. From Ellis Island,

Iannace took the ferry to the Hoboken railroad terminal. Before boarding the train, each immigrant was constrained to pay a dollar for a box lunch of bread, moldy salami, an apple, and a banana. Iannace did not eat again until 21 hours later, when he was met at the Meadville station and taken to an Italian boardinghouse, where his aunt fed him spaghetti.

The next day Cavuoto, his cousin, who worked 12 hours a day as a crane operator at the sprawling railroad complex, took Iannace to the office manager to ask that his relative be hired. The manager glanced at the slightly built 16-year-old and remarked that the company did not hire schoolboys. "This is a worker," Cavuoto insisted. "He arrived yesterday from Italy; he is not a student." Glancing at Iannace again, the manager said in a neutral voice that the railroad took on only men between the ages of 21 and 45; "that is the law." However, he added, an exception could be made if the man were just short of his twenty-first birthday. "Well," Cavuoto interjected, "he is 20 years and some days old. I am sure an exception can be made." The manager looked skeptically at Iannace once again, shrugged and told them if the foreman agreed, it was fine with him. Iannace filled out the work form, on which he noted that he was 21, and received a metal tag stamped with the number 2067. He was now part of the American work force.

The manager violated the law by hiring a worker who was obviously underage. He did so, however, as a result of pressure from Cavuoto and a realization that Iannace, even though a boy, had to earn his way like any other immigrant. The manager was responding to an attitude brought over by the Italian immigrants: namely, that children had an obligation to contribute to the household as soon as possible. The *contadini*, in particular, saw the child as an instrument of labor and consequently felt that schooling for children was wasted effort. Thus the Italians actively sought to circumvent the American laws that excluded children from working in adult jobs. Iannace's case was commonplace. The Italian child, arriving in America with his family at the age of 11 or 12, was sent directly to work instead of to school as the law dictated. Parents or relatives would exaggerate the child's age so that he could qualify for work. Pecorini, visiting factories in the New York metropolitan area in 1908, saw many children at work on the machines: "In the New Jersey glass works one finds everywhere

Italian children who are little more than ten years of age. They give the money they earn to the family." [72]

In the months that followed, Iannace performed a number of unskilled tasks as a railroad employee. For example, during the frigid winter of 1906–7,

> our job involved emptying the ashes from the furnace of the locomotive, filling the boiler with water and seeing to it that sufficient coal and sand were loaded on board. Each locomotive would move under the coal chute. We stood on a wooden structure about fifty feet above the ground. The cars containing the coal and sand were backed into the locomotive waiting below. We were completely exposed to the weather. The wind and cold were so intense that by spitting on the chute I could form instantly a small ball of ice, which would go rolling down like a marble. The day crew was composed of six men and the night crew had five. Once positioned, the coal car would be inclined toward the chute. We would climb on top of the coal with our pickaxes to dislodge and break the frozen mass of coal into pieces and then push them down the chute. Our footing was precarious, and more than once a worker lost his footing and slid down the chute with the coal into the locomotive coal bin. [73]

Work occupied the entire day. There was little time for anything else besides eating and sleeping. Iannace was paid for ten hours but usually worked 12, from eight in the morning until eight at night. The walk back to the boardinghouse took another hour, so he rarely ate dinner before ten o'clock.

The workers knew that they were being exploited. Discontentment smoldered just below the surface and occasionally erupted in wildcat strikes. Iannace lost one job when there was a general shutdown by the workers. Management immediately replaced the strikers with greenhorns. Fresh from Italy, these newcomers, unlike the older immigrants who had had exposure to the American radical notions of "workers' rights," had little trouble adjusting to a work system similar to the one they had left.

The Italian Boss, in particular, was not interested in the concept of workers' rights. He was accustomed to treating his workers in a paternalistic manner and making decisions for them, even in regard to their actual worth on the job and what their wages should be after the job was completed. To the Italian Boss, a promised wage meant nothing. Everything was negotiable, and the Boss had no intention of committing himself to a certain wage until he had evaluated what the worker accomplished. The Boss carried in his head the model of the *padrone* (literally, "big father"), who, as head of his "family," could act as he wished.

Iannace experienced a striking example of how the Old Country tradition was interpreted in America. To earn money for his return to Italy, he dug ditches for an Italian contractor, Caravella, for two weeks. Caravella had promised his 20-man crew $1.60 apiece per day. At the end of the first week, no one was paid because Caravella claimed that he had not been paid. When the job was completed, Caravella took the men to a bar for a drink (a typical gesture of noblesse oblige) while he distributed their wages. Without a word of explanation, he had subtracted five cents per day from Iannace's pay envelope. The others were paid according to their height, or so it seemed to Iannace; Isitano the Calabrese, who was the runt of the group, received only $1.25 for each day's work.

The other men remained quiet, but Isitano, his face red with anger, shouted that he was being cheated. Caravella replied calmly that the biggest man had excavated four and one-half meters of dirt per day while Isitano had succeeded in moving only two and one-half. "You're stupid and blind," Isitano retorted. "Didn't you see that where I was digging was all rocks?" "What rocks?" Caravella said. "I saw no rocks." "What rocks!" Isitano yelled all the more. "One even fell on my head. Look here at the bump." Caravella brushed the evidence aside and said in a tone more paternal than critical, "You complain like an old lady. A rock fell on Romano's head, and he isn't saying anything." Isitano was silent for a moment as he pondered Romano's head, and then said, "If I am Calabrese and I felt it, and Romano did not . . . well, all I can say is he must have the skull of an elephant." Everyone roared with laughter and then turned back to the beer. But as they were leaving the bar, Iannace overheard one of the men mutter, "And I thought it would be different here. I had the same thing happen to me in Italy—what they tell you in the morning they don't honor in the evening." [74]

Caravella was carrying forward a practice of long standing. One Italian recalled the former system of work for fieldhands in southern Italy:

> What was it like at that time? In the morning, when it was still dark, the *braccianti* went to stand in the piazza. The *caporale* [foreman] looked at you with a sour face. There were always more men than he needed, so when he selected his workers no one ever asked either the rate of pay or the location. We understood the system; there was no need to be reminded. The job began at first light and continued through the day. On Sundays the *caporale* set up a table outside the door of the farmhouse and we would line up for our wages. "How long did you work?" he would ask. If you replied six days, he would correct you. "You are wrong—four days." "Why four?" you would ask. "Four," he would say. "You doubt my word? If you don't trust me, don't come to work." He would pay us for four days of work and would pocket the rest.[75]

Totonno landed in New York in the spring of 1906. From Ellis Island his sponsor took him to 588 Morris Avenue in the Bronx, in the midst of a very large and heterogeneous Italian population. There he found several friends of his family who were waiting to see him and eager for word from their homes in Alberobello. Totonno had a message to give to each person.

Totonno's *paesani* had formed two main colonies in America, one in the South Bronx and the other in the upstate textile city of Utica, each containing a few hundred Alberobellesi. Even though, with the passing years, new colonies of *paesani* were founded in New York, Pennsylvania, and New Jersey, the Utica and South Bronx colonies remained natural gathering places and points of reference for the Alberobellesi. Very little happened in either colony that was not known in the other and in Alberobello. The two colonies were in many respects one community linked by a five-hour train trip. Many of the men moved regularly and easily between them, either to work or to visit relatives.

The colonies provided living quarters, friendships, food, a familiar dialect, and a place to which one could return if a job or a business venture elsewhere failed. The young immigrants seldom wandered far outside their confines; in his first years, Totonno's America was composed almost exclusively of his South Bronx/Utica Paesani Network. He never strayed from it except in the care of friends who could translate for him the world of native America.

Totonno's family members had very carefully cultivated their emigrant friends; such contacts were essential, it was felt. Favors had been done in Alberobello, and now these were favors to be returned in the New World. Totonno arrived in America confident that a job would be waiting for him. He had come to make money, and he could not wait to begin. The first evening, he visited a family friend, an older man who owned a wine and oil import company and who, Totonno had been led to believe, was under an obligation to find him employment. The man was cordial but noncommittal, and did nothing to help.

In the weeks that followed, Totonno came to learn that few of his *paesani* were willing to go out of their way for him. *Paesano* loyalties did not mean as much in America as they did in Italy. Nor did a man's word. It was a topsy-turvy world. Men who in Italy had not been worth a "goddam penny," and whom Totonno had safely snubbed, now snubbed him. It became agonizingly clear that the reputation his family had so painstakingly earned in their hometown over the years meant nothing to some of the immigrants. Italian rules did not always apply in America. Here, money was the measure of a man's worth. To get money, one had to get employment; to get employment, one had to stand in line and remain patient.

A very narrow range of jobs was available to the Alberobellesi in the South Bronx. The few barbers and cabinetmakers, most of whom learned their skills in Italy, were considered fortunate. Their wages exceeded those of the factory laborer, the work was steady, and they could carry their skills with them wherever they went. The majority of the others were sporadically employed as polishers at the many piano factories in the city (by 1914 about half of the pianos made in the United States came from New York City factories), where they generally worked a six-day week, nine hours a day. The wage scale ranged from $8 to $18 per week. After 1900, the number of Italians in the industry rose rapidly. Those *paesani* who were without jobs, and they were numerous, were supported by those who were working.

Totonno learned that the only way he would get a chance at employment was to continually badger the older immigrants who were in a position to suggest to their American employers that a friend was available to fill a vacancy. Getting these jobs sometimes required that money change hands, but more likely the new employee simply became indebted over the long term to the *paesano* who had put his name in. Four weeks after his arrival, Totonno got his first job at the piano factory. The wage was $1.50 until he acquired the necessary skills, meaning the acquisition of a rubbing technique that would not wear a man out before the end of the day. Two days later, everyone was laid off; two weeks after that, when the workers had been called back, the factory burned to the ground.

The money Totonno had earned, $7.50, did not cover what he owed. As he remained unemployed and his debt accumulated, he began to give serious consideration to returning to the meat trade. He had wanted to leave that life behind him when he left Italy; in fact, he had listed himself on the ship manifest as a common laborer rather than as a butcher. But now his friends were pressing him to take a meat-cutting job, and Totonno allowed Turiangelo, his mentor and *compare*, to convince him to take a job in a small meat shop run by a *paesano* who lived with his family above the shop. Totonno, as was the custom, left his boardinghouse to move in with the family and eat at their table. To entice a reluctant Totonno to take the position, the owner had promised him a quasi-partnership; that is, he was to share in a portion of the profits. But in predictable *padrone* style, the owner reneged on that promise and all of the others he was to make. There was no sharing of profits. All Totonno received was whatever the Boss felt like giving him: three dollars one week, four dollars the next. Several arguments took place, and Totonno finally walked out in disgust and found a factory job at $7.00 a week—which he quit three days later because the work did not suit him. The meat shop owner welcomed him back with open arms, promising $5.00 per week with additional regular increases up to $9.00. Totonno never saw that kind of money. For the few dollars he was paid, he cut meat and waited on customers from early morning until ten in the evening Monday through Saturday, and until noon on Sunday.

In April, Totonno's bondage ended with an offer from an acquaintance in Utica. Come immediately, the letter said, I have a business proposition for you. He showed the letter to his Boss (who fumed at the unfairness of it all), went upstairs to pack his bag, and then rushed about all day from one *paesano* household to another collecting money that was owed him and borrowing as much more as he could. In Utica, Totonno's partner informed him that he needed an additional $70 to buy his full share of the grocery business. Totonno sent a letter to Morris Avenue asking a friend to collect the money, and in a few weeks he had it. Without this kind of cooperation among the *paesani*, Totonno, as well as others who wished to make an investment or to become self-employed, would not have succeeded, because young immigrants did not possess sufficient assets to pursue a momentary opportunity. The answer was to pool funds and to keep money in constant circulation. Since idle money served no one, any *paesano* who had extra cash lent it out to those who needed it. The amounts usually were small, and one person could be both a creditor and debtor. At times Totonno had to keep a running list of who owed him and whom he owed.

The loans were repaid, even if it took months or years, either to the lender or to his family in Italy. And of course, some loans were not intended to be repaid, especially when the recipient was totally destitute. In those cases it was considered a form of charity, and the giver might get "repayment" by gaining himself a lifelong friend or supporter as well as considerable prestige and respect among the *paesani*. Any person who took unfair advantage of the loan system, who cheated, who did not repay his loans or who refused to lend money when asked, risked complete isolation in his own time of need—which would surely occur. A man did not lend money to persons outside his Paesani Network, however; he was under no obligation to do so, and such loans often had bad results because the borrowers could not be constrained to repay.

Totonno looked forward to the gratifications of self-employment and the promise of prosperity. Now, perhaps, he said to himself, this is really America. I am the Boss, laboring for my own interests and future, and not under the thumb of some slavedriver. But that rosy future continued to elude his grasp. He soon began to miss the excitement and diversity of New York. Utica was a small, gray factory town, and his work took on a predictable routine, with each day much like the previous one. "I get up at five in the morning, take my coffee, go to work, eat my big meal at one o'clock and then I take an afternoon nap.

We reopen the store for the evening trade, and I eat a cold dinner while working. On some days the customers are very few, and we have to count our profits in pennies."

One morning Totonno took in a grand total of eight cents. Both of the men wanted to get rich, and when this did not happen right away, the partnership began to deteriorate. Neither partner trusted the other. There were several accusations of taking money from the cash register for personal use without a proper notation in the store's books. By spring 1908 it became clear to both that one of them would have to buy the other out, and Totonno accepted his partner's offer of $292. He mailed $250 to his family in Italy and moved back to New York to his former meat-cutting job. (Totonno felt that he had received the better part of the bargain until he learned a few years later that his ex-partner had sold the business and returned to Italy with over $2,000 in his pocket.)

In 1909 Totonno bought a meat shop for $550, which he operated with two of his friends as part-time employees, but he never succeeded in establishing a loyal clientele. Success in business in the Italian colony was contingent on the ability of the tradesman to convince his *paesani* to buy from him, because unless a retail business was centrally located and large enough to attract a general Italian clientele, the *paesani* trade was all a businessman could hope for. Yet the *paesani* were the most difficult customers of all, always looking for and expecting bargains, finicky over quality and personal service, envious of success and reluctant to release their hard-earned pennies.

In 1910, homesick, discouraged, and dismayed by his failure to make his mark in America, Totonno decided to return to Italy. He sold the store to its former owner and worked in various butcher shops to earn the money for a passenger ticket. He returned to Alberobello with the same amount of money he had had at his departure.

THE INDEPENDENT

There were some immigrants who did not live in an Italian colony, did not work for an Italian Boss, and were not part of any kind of Paesani Network. Either they had broken away from their Italian contacts because of a desire to live among Americans, or they had in the first place emigrated out of a desire for adventure and to see America at firsthand. If some education and a degree of sophistication allowed them to learn new customs rapidly and to move easily among Americans, they were less likely to be regarded as "dagoes," although they could not escape the stereotypes entirely. Some had job skills that kept them out of the immigrant job market and enabled them to interact with Americans from the very first day. Being able to speak English offered the best opportunity to meet the kinds of Americans who lived in "decent" society and were often willing to help rather than oppress and exploit a newcomer. Ernest Tummolillo, for example, quickly secured a job at Ellis Island as a translator because he had studied English in Naples.[76] Often the independent immigrant cared neither for the Italian colony nor for the immigrant style of life. His ambitions transcended "immigrant work" and the confinement of immigrant culture. He did not care to identify with immigrants or to be identified as one; indeed he often went to great lengths to conceal his ethnic origins and to Americanize himself.

Initially, when Adolfo Rossi and Giuseppi arrived in New York in 1879, they drifted to the Italian colony in lower Manhattan. That is where the Italians live and work, they were told. But a few days in the neighborhood was enough to convince the two men that the people there had nothing to offer them. Rossi and Giuseppi, middle-class Italians from North Italy, had no intention of associating with the low-life forms inhabiting the tenements along Mulberry Street. Instead, Giuseppi went off to work as a baker in an American establishment, and Rossi took a job as a wine salesman. You are Italian, you should be able to sell wine, he was told. Unfortunately, although whiskey and beer were consumed in great quantities, few Americans drank wine; Rossi quit after three weeks without making a sale. His next job, which lasted a few months, was at an eyeglass factory as a $3.00-a-week apprentice. The job was not taxing. Rossi spent $1.50 a week on a room, 30 to 40 cents for laundry, and with the remaining $1.20 he ate and drank and brought tobacco and stamps. Then, after a period of unemployment, Rossi met an older Italian named Rebagliate, an unemployed waiter who was also on his own, and together they opened a high-class boardinghouse for Italian gentlemen. This venture collapsed when Rebagliate lost his life savings of $1,000, and their creditors repossessed the furnishings.

Nevertheless, Rossi's background enabled him to enter social circles closed to most immigrants. A well-to-do American woman, who had taken up the immigrant cause, befriended him. She spoke Italian and gave him lessons in English. With her influence, Rossi got his next job as a baker's apprentice. After he had spent several weeks in the cellar of the bakery kneading dough with two Germans, the owner learned of Rossi's literacy and promoted him to bookkeeper. The job was interesting, and the prospects for a comfortable future were good until five months later, when the mercurial owner fired him without giving a reason and denied him several weeks' back salary, Rossi made this entry in his diary:

> Saturday, 12 June 1880. I am again out of work, with only seven dollars, but I do have a room that is paid for until the end of the month. I still do not speak English well enough to find another job. However, courage![77]

After one week as a street vendor of hand fans (he did not sell any), Rossi interviewed for a job at the Metropolitan Concert Hall as an ice cream maker at $10 a week. Having watched ice cream being made at the bakery, he was able to convince the director, Mr. Kauffmann, that he was a master of the art. The concert hall closed for the season after two months, and Rossi went on to hold successive jobs as an Omnibus (busboy) in two New York luxury hotels. In December he assumed the editorship of a small, struggling newspaper called *Il Progresso*. This job, which he believed was finally the answer to his dream of becoming a journalist, turned into a nightmare. He was responsible for all phases of the newspaper's production and the task was too much for one person. His nerves frazzled by a long series of grueling 15-hour days, Rossi decided to quit, leave the city, and take any work as long as mental effort was not involved.

In July 1881 there was much discussion in New York of building a railroad into the Rocky Mountains that would open access to the mineral deposits. Rossi went across the river to Hoboken to talk to the hiring agent, an Italian from Genoa, for the Denver and Rio Grande Railroad. The agent assured Rossi that there were positions for foremen and timekeepers and that he could sign on without fear of having to wield a pick and shovel. The agent's brother would be waiting in Denver to meet the workers. The daily wage was $3.00, and the train was leaving the next day. At the appointed time, Rossi boarded with 70 other young immigrants, all from North Italy and all in a carefree, happy mood. There were farm workers, musicians, laborers, and artisans: men who, like Rossi, were motivated more by their desire to see the Wild West than by hunger or deprivation. Cappelli, the Italian consul in Colorado, met the men at the Denver station, directed them to a hotel, and the next morning put them on a train for Como. From Como the group set off on foot, carrying their luggage along mountain paths and through extensive forests for several hours before reaching the work camp. It was a primitive, makeshift site located 11,000 feet above sea level along the new railroad's right-of-way. The men lived in log houses, which they were given a week to construct, and cooked their meals in the open. There were two work groups: the Americans and Irish, who cut into the mountainside with explosives, and the Italians, who shoveled away the debris and leveled the track bed.

The situation was not what Rossi had been led to expect. The daily wage, out of which living costs were deducted, turned out to be much less than the promised $3.00, and the only job available to the Italians was pick-and-shovel. To Rossi and the others who had never done hand labor, this came as a great disappointment. They were soon to learn that as far as the American contractor was concerned, pick-and-shovel work *was* Italian work; the Italians were not considered capable of aspiring to better jobs. Moreover, the Italians were so good at simple and arduous hand labor, so superior to any other immigrant group, that the Americans concluded they were ideally suited for it. And so did most Italians. The work crews that had been brought over during Rossi's day were composed of men who had been conditioned from boyhood to handle a farm tool and to work with soil for long hours each day. The Italian *bracciante* could adapt perfectly to track work in America. No one was his equal—he was a hard, skillful, reliable digger, bred to pick-and-shovel work for generations; *nacqui con la vanga in mano* (I was born with a shovel in my hands) was an old saying in rural Italy. This stereotype worked against the ambitions of immigrants like Rossi, but at the same time it did establish a solid niche in the occupational structure for the Italian, and help to ensure work for him even when jobs were scarce. For pick-and-shovel labor, Italians were the first hired and the last fired.

Each Italian work crew along the road was supervised by an Italian Boss, who would stand on a nearby knoll carefully scrutinizing the deeply tanned, muscular men bent over their tools below. Bearded, fierce, arrogant-looking men bearing sidearms, these bosses were more guards than foremen; they reminded Rossi of typical Calabrese brigands who would not hesitate to take a traveler's life for a few pennies.

Some of the workers suffered intensely from the high altitude (several had to be hospitalized), and the few men who had never done physical labor had great difficulty adjusting to the steady pace of the work. Rossi was the first to quit. He had to be pulled from his bed after the first day, and by that afternoon he knew he could not continue. He drew his pay—30 cents—from the timekeeper, packed his bag, and walked to nearby Breckenridge, a miner's camp, where he won a job in a bakery-restaurant by demonstrating to the owner the skills that he had acquired in New York. Rossi was still there several weeks later when Cappelli tracked him down and accused him of cheating the company by leaving the job. But after extended discussion, impressed with Rossi's credentials, Cappelli made him an agent-translator for the railroad, a position that Rossi found much more to his liking than manual labor. As winter approached and work ceased on the line, Rossi decided to return to his New York newspaper job. Three years later, in 1884, he sailed for Italy.

FOUR

Living in America

> We were in a heated debate over the rights of
> Blacks in American society. Momma came
> into the room and said: "Stop your arguing.
> We're all Americans. It's Thanksgiving. Eat
> your spaghetti."
>
> —*Geno C. Baroni*

Housing

In the 1870s the Italian community in lower Manhattan began to spread beyond lower Mulberry Street. The Italians took over Hester and Mott Streets from the Irish, gradually replaced them on Baxter Street, and spilled over into upper Mulberry. By 1880 there were 20,000 Italians living in the Mulberry Street area, on Eleventh Street, uptown in Yorkville, and across the Hudson River in Hoboken. They occupied some of the poorest housing in the city. The notorious Five Points section of lower Manhattan was referred to jokingly as the "Boulevard des Italians," thus discrediting the Italians by associating them in the public's mind with the creation of the worst slum in New York.

The thousands of Italians who moved into Five Points, crowding others who had been there for decades, lived in filth and squalor, working as shoeshine boys, organ grinders, garbagemen, and rag collectors. These people had known the chronic poverty of the Italian countryside, but even the stark misery of the most desolate mountain village of Basilicata could barely compete with what awaited them in New York. In 1879, Adolfo Rossi wandered through these streets several times, marveling at the tenacity of the inhabitants and their ability to survive in an environment poorer than most barnyard animals enjoyed. A sense of total alienation and hopelessness so gripped the population that, whenever possible, men and women would descend to one of the many subterranean bars to drink themselves into a stupor on overpriced rotgut.[1] Angelo Mosso, in 1905, was appalled by what his countrymen had to endure as immigrants. "It is a sad spectacle seeing tens of thousands of famished people as collectors of animal and human refuse. The ugly, overcrowded tenements in which they reside must harbor every conceivable infection."[2] Marginati was shocked by the filth and misery of Mott and Mulberry Streets. The entire Italian colony, he said, was not worth "the price of the small amount of dynamite needed to blow it up."[3] Franco Ciarlantini on the other hand was entranced by the pace and style of life among the New York Italians. He found a certain exotic charm in the slum existence, describing the Italian colony as emitting "a babble of sounds, a variety of odors. The tone is set most of all by the children, who are everywhere. They dominate the streets, the squares, the parks, incontestably. The streets are full of color, of contrasts, of festivity."

Immigrant housing in other major cities was also rude and primitive. Gaetano Conte was struck most by the density of Boston's North End tenement population, where 85 percent of the Italians lived in the 1890s. Ciarlantini's "variety of odors" was for Conte an "unsupportable stench," particularly noticeable on a sweltering summer day. The smells were nauseating, the vermin omnipresent, and the cleaning facilities scanty. There was no escape from the rot and decay of the housing and the suffocating pressure of people. The poorest Italians lived huddled together in miserable apartments, covered with filth and dressed in rags. Their diet consisted largely of stale bread, stale fruit, and stale beer. The rents far exceeded the quality of the apartments. Back rooms with little or no natural light, renting for $1.75 to $2.50 a month, were occupied by whole families or by a number of male lodgers. Three or four slept to a bed.[4] To the outsider, the North End was a dusty, dirty, and mysterious place, considered dangerous after dark.

The housing available to immigrants in the United States was not always an improvement for them; even those who had lived modestly in Italy were shocked by what was considered habitable housing in urban America. Alessandro De Luca's expectations of America the Beautiful were shattered when his family moved into an apartment on Mulberry Street. "The city look to me very ugly. I never see good sky.

It is difficult for me to explain my disgust. The next day I feel to come back to Italy." [5] He had enjoyed the comforts of a large house in his homeland; now the family was squeezed into a few rooms, and the rent took most of their income. F. Paul Miceli's early years in America were spent in an unheated flat in New London, Connecticut, which was "dingy in comparison to the stonehouse which we had left behind." [6]

Only a small portion of the total number of Italians who arrived before 1900 settled in the large cities along the eastern seaboard. Many more were destined for the interior: of the 7,200 Italians who landed in New York in 1879, two-thirds of them went on to other locations. Some of these were males who would remain in America for only a few years, but others, including family groups, settled in the smaller interior industrial cities.

The development of Italian colonies in the cities of upstate New York was probably typical of similar patterns of development in other states. By the 1890s, when large Italian colonies had become firmly established in New York City, those upstate were still being formed. In 1900 only about 3 percent of the Buffalo population of 350,000 was Italian; the Italian neighborhoods, the largest with no more than 500 inhabitants, were hidden among the larger clusters of other immigrant settlements, and many Buffalo Italians lived outside the Italian sections, intermingled with the Poles and the Irish. The large Italian colony in Rochester had yet to develop; most of the Rochester Italians lived in mixed neighborhoods. There were small concentrations of Italians in many of the villages and rural towns throughout New York state. The stone quarries in western New York were dominated by Italians, as were most of the salt mines, and Italian railroad workers and their families settled in villages along the New York Central's route. Colonies began to form in many of the mill and factory villages during the 1890s when owners began to hire Italians. More than 100 immigrants arrived in the village of Geneseo in 1898 to work in the bran factory. By 1900 the factory colony in Amsterdam, New York, numbered 150 persons. [7]

Immigrant housing in the smaller industrial cities and villages was generally superior to that of the large cities. The single family home or the small apartment house, rather than the tenement, was the typical place of residence; conditions were less crowded, and rents were lower. Moreover, there were opportunities for an immigrant family to purchase a house, so property values were better maintained.

THE ITALIAN BOARDINGHOUSE

The Italians did not live alone; single-person households were very rare. One characteristic arrangement for unattached male immigrant workers was the large boardinghouse. These were sometimes found in the large cities, but more often they were established in quasi-rural locations near the work sites. Such houses were usually operated by an Italian hostler who was sometimes also the Boss of the men who lived there. They ranged from households of a dozen boarders to hotel-type arrangements with 30 to 50 residents. The Boss had either brought the men over from Italy or recruited them to work for him after their arrival, or he was acting as their hiring agent. Most of the money that such workers earned went to the Boss for food and lodging. There were few amenities: living space was at a premium, and the men did their own cooking. Rocco Corresca's first accommodations in America were in an urban boardinghouse. "We came to Brooklyn to a wooden house on Adams Street that was full of Italians from Naples. Bartolo, the Padrone, had a room on the third floor and there were fifteen men in the room, all boarding with Bartolo. He did the cooking on a stove in the middle of the room and there were beds all around the sides, one bed above another."[8] Immigrants who moved from one temporary contractual job to another were usually housed together. When Francesco Ventresca worked in Western Springs, Illinois, digging sewer lines, he and a dozen *paesani* from neighboring towns in Abruzzi were lodged in a whitewashed bunkhouse. All activities were carried out in common, including the preparation of homemade spaghetti and eggs on a stove in the middle of the room. During the winter, Ventresca lived with a large group of railroad construction workers in an armory barracks in Forestport, New York.[9]

The most common type of living arrangement in the Italian colonies was the nuclear family household: a man, his wife and their children, and frequently a few unrelated boarders—in some cases as many as ten—most of them between the ages of 15 to 40. Such an arrangement became a necessity for the large proportion of men who arrived in America alone, without their families. (The pattern had a relatively short life span, perhaps no more than three or four decades; it disappeared after the First World War with the dwindling of worker immigration and the return to Italy or the formation of their own nuclear families of those who had been boarders.) Without Italian families to take them in, there would have been few places for these worker immigrants to live. Only a handful of Italians boarded in non-Italian households. A review of the 1900 Federal census manuscripts for up-state New York reveals that there were only two Italians boarding with families not Italian in origin. Few Italians, particularly the new ar-rivals, had a desire to live with foreigners who did not speak their language or cook their food, nor were they welcome to do so. Ameri-can boardinghouses frequently made the sentiment explicit with signs reading, "We do not rent to Negroes or Italians."

The ideal arrangement was to live with one's own *paesani*, and *paesani* were usually preferred as boarders. Totonno was not suc-cessful in persuading his Boss to accept a non-*paesano* friend of his as a boarder, even though the man came from a village only a few kilo-meters from their own. There were good reasons for such a decision. Mixed Italian boardinghouses created problems: regional differences were often too glaring to be overlooked, and daily friction was predict-able. Totonno wanted to move away from his *paesani* because they were "suffocating" him, but he found that other Italians were worse. Margariti lived in a number of mixed boardinghouses; there was vio-lence in each one. He soon realized that to live a peaceful existence, he had to remain with other Calabresi like himself.

It was common practice for the head of a household to board any man who was working for him. The boarder would take part in the life of the family, its fortunes and misfortunes; he ate at the family table and was in all respects treated like a dependent member of the family. As an example, the Barbieri family (selected at random from the 1900 Federal census manuscripts) lived at 162 Hartford Street in Rochester, New York. The head of the household, Frank Barbieri, a pianomaker, was born in 1854 and emigrated in 1882 at age 28. In 1884 his wife Mary, then 27 years old, and their infant daughter joined him. The next four children, ages 14, 11, 8, and 6, were born in Canada and the last two, ages 5 and 1, in New York state. In addition, there were two single male boarders; one man worked for Frank, and the other was a day laborer.

Because taking in boarders meant additional income for the fam-ily, two or three men might be accommodated even if it meant consid-erably more housework and congested quarters. Typically, the hus-band and wife would give one or two rooms over to the boarders, while they and their children slept together in the master bedroom. The woman of the house sometimes had the responsibility of ministering to the needs of a large number of men. Not only did she wash and cook for her own boarders, but often on Sundays, a day for socializing, men who were boarding elsewhere and did not enjoy good cooking during the week would also be at the table. At large festive dinners, several women would contribute to the meal.

Arrangements between the boarder and the housekeeper varied. She might do all his housekeeping chores for a specified sum, or the boarder might pay for each service as it was rendered. In some cases, the boarders purchased their own foodstuffs, and the woman would place the goods, carefully labeled, in a cupboard or on a shelf above the stove. Then each man would let her know when he left in the morning what he wanted for dinner that evening, and she would have each dish prepared when the men arrived from work. One man would have spaghetti, another liver, a third pork ribs and cabbage or the popular sausages and peppers. Those men who were down on their luck might satisfy themselves with an inexpensive but filling vegetable stew or some other simple dish without meat.

Rosa Mondari was one of these women who spent much of her life providing for immigrant boarders. Rosa came to the American West in 1908 as a young bride of 18 years of age. She cooked and washed for dozens of miners in addition to raising her four children and caring for her husband. She would arise before dawn, prepare an early breakfast for the men, pack their lunches, and cook them a big meal in the evening. She took her job seriously and was interested in keeping the men content. "The man who works hard must eat well," she believed. "A good dinner is his only comfort." [10] Rosa, and others like her, had been raised in the Old World tradition of household servility and accepted her role as mistress of the house, a person who established high standards both for herself and her boarders. In the house, she ruled; the men would refer to her as *La Signora* or *La Bossa* or *La Padrona*.

The atmosphere of the boardinghouse was important for the men. To keep them happy, the housekeeper had to be a congenial person and provide excellent service. If the boardinghouse, the man's home away from home, did not give him a *sense* of home, he would become discontented and seek other accommodations. Carmine Iannace's conversation with a coboarder illustrates the desire of the men that the Padrona serve them as their mothers would have done.

Cavuoto: All the padrone are angels for the first month. Then the service begins to deteriorate. Your socks aren't ready when you want them. The handkerchiefs aren't ironed properly. Your shirt comes back torn, and a thousand other things. When that happens, I do not make an issue of it. I pack my bag, say politely to her, "Biona ssera Ssignoria," and leave.

Iannace: But here, at this pensione, we are well off. The Padrona is a good and intelligent woman.

Cavuoto: Yes, but the food is never on the table when I come into the house from work. I want to eat as soon as I get home. If I have to wait for dinner, then it is too late to go anyplace. One evening I explained to her how important it was for me to eat as soon as I got home. I even suggested that I would gladly eat the leftovers from the day before. Do you know what she did? She cooked a large pot of stringbeans on Monday and served them to me for the rest of the week.

Iannace: But the poor thing is up to her ears in work. She has no time to cater to you.

Cavuoto: That's not true.

Iannace: She has an infant that demands her attention.

Cavuoto: Yes, that's right. That's all she thinks about now is that kid. She wastes all of her time with him.

Another of Iannace's friends, Giulio, a quiet man who lived at a boardinghouse down the street, would voice his complaints by leaving notes in strategic locations. Noticing that the tablecloth was seldom washed, he pinned the following sentiments to the offending linen:

I was born unlucky. I do not even know my name.

If I were a table cloth, I would be washed every week.

If I were a kitchen rag, I would have to be washed every ten days.

Even if I were a doormat, I would not be so grey and dirty.

Please, someone give me a name.

The next evening a freshly laundered cloth was on the table.[11]

Not all Italian boardinghouses were inhabited by workers or were exclusively for men. Enterprising Italians seeking to establish a profitable business sometimes secured several rooms in an apartment building or a house and advertised for boarders. Some of these houses were exclusive and appealed to the middle-class immigrant of means; the majority attracted men and women whose tastes (but not necessarily incomes) exceeded those of the laboring classes. Camillo Cianfarra lived in a boardinghouse on Hester Street in New York, operated by a woman and her niece, where the boarders were mostly skilled workers or artisans from North Italy. Dinner each evening was followed by much drinking, animated discussion on the topics of the day, and, on occasion, sexual activity. Cianfarra describes one of those evenings:

> It has been two days now since I have eaten at the pensione. I have made myself as scarce as possible for fear that someone will read in my eyes the shame I feel. It is true, I should have contained myself, I should have resisted the temptation, but that night it was not possible. Perhaps the fault is not entirely mine. While my girlfriend, Maria, was with her aunt, the Milanese entered my room and acted provocatively. I almost lost my self-control. The Toscana, drunk and scantily attired, was lying on the staircase landing, throwing her nude legs into the air, while one of the Piemonte women was in the small courtyard in the arms of the waiter, who was covering her with kisses. After a while the Milanese went out and followed the waiter to his third-floor room. As soon as she left Maria ran in. Her face was flushed, her breasts were heaving, she had a wild look in her eyes. Starved for love, she took no heed of the terrible risk she was running, of the painful consequences if she were discovered. . . . Now what do I do? Do I marry her? I can't; I do not have the money nor do I want to assume the responsibility.[12]

SHANTIES AND BOXCARS

The worst living conditions were endured by the work gangs. Throughout the late 1800s and early 1900s, countless thousands of Italians were hired to labor in lumber camps, on road construction, and on the railroads in various parts of the United States. Because there were rarely any civilized amenities in these areas and because they moved frequently from one work site to another, these immigrants lived in the most primitive fashion. There were no women to take care of the domestic chores; the men labored a full day and also had to do their own cooking and cleaning, and sometimes had to construct their own living quarters. The tales that have come out of these work gangs reveal that the men were brutally exploited by these who hired and commanded them, that they were little more than chattel, and that they lived under conditions that were demonstrably worse than those they had left behind in Italy. Outside of Rome, New York, one hot July day in 1913, Totonno encountered a road gang cooking a meal outside the tumbledown shanty they had constructed. Totonno was shocked by the way these men "chose" to live. Their clothes were little more than rags, they were indescribably filthy from the ever-present road dust, their bodies were emaciated, and they were totally spiritless. It was a depressing spectacle for Totonno, who was ashamed that his countrymen would allow themselves to be reduced to so subhuman a level.

Domenick Ciolli, an Italian-born college student, volunteered to work on a railroad gang in Indiana one summer prior to the First World War. He lived with 50 men crowded into six railroad boxcars. The work day began at 4:00 A.M. and ended 12 hours later. The workers had to walk a substantial distance to and from the work site. On their return in the afternoon they prepared their dinners on perforated tin boxes that served as stoves. Everyone retired at 7:30 P.M. in order to rise at 3:00 the next morning to boil coffee for breakfast and to prepare bread and sausage lunches. Ciollo offered this description of the inside of one of the windowless boxcars.

> As I entered one car for the first time the odor choked me. I saw eight beds, if boards placed across two boxes can be dignified with so respectful a title. On these lay bags of straw, and for a covering the men used old tan coats or horse blankets. The blankets were covered with vermin. . . . Roaches and bed bugs livened the walls. . . . The tables were covered with oilcloths or newspapers, as dirty as the floor. . . . I opened the cupboard. There I discovered a can of conserves, covered with a film of vermin and green mold, a loaf of soggy bread, a few rusty forks and spoons, and three or four tin dishes.[13]

To the railroad companies, boxcars were ideal dormitories for the crews. Cars that had been abandoned or retired from active service cost nothing to maintain and, if still mobile, could be easily moved as the job progressed along the line. The men who lived in these cars never forgot the experience. Ventresca, who worked on a section gang in upstate New York, called life in the boxcars a "compact existence." [14] Along the Cumberland Railroad in West Virginia, Pasquale D'Angelo slept on boards over which dirty straw was strewn: "The creaking and cracked floor was covered with straw which had fallen from the wooden shelves where we slept. The whole inside . . . with its forlorn occupants gave a picture of moral wreck and bitterness. We were pigs in our sty." The boxcar Iannace occupied in Pennsylvania contained no straw for fear that it would ignite. The Sardinians in the car found the bare boards comfortable; they had never known a bed. Iannace awoke each morning stiff, cold, and exhausted. [15]

One of Gabriel Iamurri's first jobs took him to Ashland, Maine. The agent led the 38 men from the train to two boxcars; later, more were shoved in. "They herded us like a flock of sheep. But such were the times. We had to make the best of it. There was no other alternative. We either had to take it or leave it." [16] Much later, after Iamurri had learned to speak English, he returned to railroad work as a foreman. The 40 men who worked for him were housed in four boxcars. A fifth car was Iamurri's residence, in which he had a bedroom, a kitchen, and a storeroom. Once he became the Boss, his perspective changed; he enjoyed those later years.

The foremen, the timekeepers, and the other railway employees, most of whom were American or Americanized immigrants, kept their social distance from the laborers, whom they considered to be loafers and ingrates. The railroad companies carefully selected the toughest and meanest foremen, individuals who were willing to do the railroad's bidding for a little more pay and who could obtain from the workers their last ounce of effort. There was no desire to improve the living conditions of the men, because workers were thought not to have sensibilities. "Those workers are beasts," the foreman told Ciolli. "They must not be given a rest, otherwise they will step all over me." He sold the Italians stale and moldy bread at nine cents a loaf: "Take that, you pigs," he would tell them, "you never had better bread at home." The workers, the foreman insisted, did not deserve any better than they were getting. The American timekeeper was in full agreement; when the men complained about intolerable conditions, the timekeeper dismissed their complaints as unfounded. "These dagoes are never satisfied," he told Ciolli. "If they are given a finger they will take the entire hand. They should be starved to death. They don't belong here." [17]

The Italian Bank

The men who lived and worked under miserable conditions were frequently sent there by their own compatriots.

> The exploiter of the Italian worker was always the *prominente*, the *notabile* in the *colonia:* he was the president of many Italian benefit societies, a church member and a dispenser of charities, the owner of the local paper, the grocer and the banker. And what a banker! In the general merchandise store, where spaghetti and Italian cheeses were on display, one usually found in a corner the banker who received the savings of the immigrant, either for deposit or for transmission to Italy. Receipts were never found necessary. The business transaction was a friendly affair between fellow countrymen.[18]

The Italian Bank was one of the most significant institutions in the Italian colony. Many activities revolved around the Bank, and as the colonies grew in size and number, so did the Banks. In metropolitan New York in 1900, there were 412 chartered Italian Banks and fully as many more that operated without charters.[19]

The Banker played a central role in the recruitment of workers. Generally speaking, when the Boss received a contract from an employer for a specified number of men, he notified the Banker of the stipulations of the contract (daily wages, job fees, location). The Banker then got the workers by placing a notice in his window, by sending his runners out to "make the men," or by notifying his representative in Italy to recruit in the villages. The Banker profited from his efforts by receiving a recruitment fee from each worker and by selling railroad tickets to the work destination. In addition, when men were brought over as migrant workers, the Banker would sell them steamship tickets for their return home. Sometimes a Banker attempted to lock the worker into a full commitment: he would not provide a job unless all transactions were performed through him. The Banker would appear at the work site once a month to receive the worker's savings, either to be remitted to Italy or to be deposited in his Bank.[20]

Beyond the job picture, though, the Italian Bank was the focal point of the community, comparable to the nineteenth-century general store. The Banker could and did perform an astonishing number of services that the immigrant could not get elsewhere. As a result the Bank became a place of rendezvous—friends met and the unemployed lingered there. Mail, messages, packages, suitcases, and money were left and collected there. Money orders and tickets were purchased there. Advice, both personal and financial, was given by the Banker, and deals were consummated there. It was the Italian's newspaper: rumor and fact began and ended there. The immigrant who was on his own without contacts in America would be directed to the Italian bank. From that moment it was a point of reference to which he could always return at need.

Cianfarra's experiences as a clerk in a New York Italian Bank led him to conclude that the Banker was "the immigrants' most humble servant." The Banker was obligated "to receive the letters from Italy and forward them to the worker's new address; to furnish paper, envelopes, stamps and pencils; to send fancy cards to sweethearts and families on Easter and Christmas; to lend money; to write tickets for those who wished to join relatives in America; to pick them up at the docks; and to respond punctually to written requests." From Cianfarra's point of view, the immigrant *paesani* were persistent in their demands on their Banker to perform a variety of services and favors for little or no compensation. If the clerk hesitated to perform a service, the client would threaten to take his business elsewhere. For the princely sum of $6.00 a week, Cianfarra often had to work far into the evening to satisfy the demands of the Bank's clients; in addition, he had to submit to the same inane questions, for which there were no real answers, over and over again.

> *Worker:*   I haven't received a letter in 40 days. Why not?
> *Clerk:*   The letter is probably still "at sea."
> *Worker:*   When will it arrive?
> *Clerk:*   At any time. Shortly.

Three hours later the worker returns.

> *Worker:*   Did the letter arrive?
> *Clerk:*   What?
> *Worker:*   The letter, the one that was at sea.[21]

Totonno got his first job in America while standing in front of the Bank on Morris Avenue in the Bronx. When he was not working, he would meet his friends at the Bank. They would talk about job possibilities, the events of the day, the latest news from their native Alberobello. The Banker collected Totonno's mail, sold him his return steamship ticket, remitted his savings to Italy, and held his money. And the Banker was a father figure to the young immigrant. When Totonno had a problem (which was from his diary notations only too often) or a decision to make in regard to his future, he would talk with his Banker.

A Banker's dishonesty or ineptness did not necessarily deter the immigrant from continuing to do business with him. In one case a Banker invested an immigrant's savings and lost every penny. The immigrant forgave him, and they continued to do business. In another, the Banker absconded with the depositors' money, only to return a year later and reopened his Bank at the same location—without an incident or any threat from his former clients.[22]

Why did the immigrant willingly place himself in the hands of such men? Sometimes the immigrant had no choice. Since he could not easily go outside the Italian colony to get those services performed, he had to trust his *paesano* Banker, for there were no other alternatives. Italian officials in America had difficulty understanding the Italian *contadino*'s complete faith that the Banker had his interests at heart.

> *Consul:* Where is your money?
> *Immigrant:* I have given it to the *compare* [read: Banker].
> *Consul:* Why don't you deposit the money into a municipal savings bank?
> *Immigrant:* My *compare* will hold it.
> *Consul:* And suppose he "eats" it?

The immigrant responds to the question with a smile, indicating an unlikely event.

> *Consul:* Do you mail your own money home?
> *Immigrant:* No, the *compare* does that.
> *Consul:* How do you get your money exchanged?
> *Immigrant:* He does that too.[23]

Among other meanings, the term *compare* signifies friend; in that context the immigrant felt his money was safe. The Italian consul was looking at the situation quite differently. He regarded the immigrant as a gullible simpleton who was not aware that the Italian Bank was a pernicious, ultraparasitical institution often operated by thieves, some of whom had criminal records in Italy. The Banker had his own interests at heart, not the immigrant's interests, no matter how the immigrant himself defined the relationship. The Banker was in business to make money, lots of it, and the naiveté of the immigrants was making that possible. The Banker was a camp follower who was to be found wherever Italians toiled or settled.

Initially, the Bankers were not supervised by the state banking boards. Strict supervision probably would not have been possible, because the cultural context within which the Italian Bank operated was so very different from standard banking procedures in America. American banks were cold, impersonal, and efficient. The Italian Bank had a more familial atmosphere, where ethnic bonds predominated and business was conducted in a much more casual manner. There were no codified rules. A Banker could set up shop any place and move at a moment's notice. Whether interest was paid on deposits was a decision made for each separate account. In some cases a fee was charged to hold an immigrant's savings. There was nothing to stop the Bankers from freely speculating with their depositors' money, and large amounts were lost in risky investment or stolen outright. The *Boston Herald* reported that "within a period of a dozen years [the Italians of North Boston] have been robbed of $150,000 by the proprietors of the so-called immigrant banks." By 1905, in most states, there was legislation to protect the depositors from crooked bankers. That this legislation did much good is doubtful. A more effective approach would have been to abolish the Italian Bank, as Representative Giorgio Scigliano attempted to do in Massachusetts.[24]

A Bank failure or theft was a major tragedy for those immigrants who had slaved for years to build a nest egg. One hot and humid August morning Cianfarra arrived at the Bank to find a crowd of *paesani* milling around, crying and screaming. The Banker, Don Raffaele, had absconded with the funds. Some of the depositors had placed hundreds of dollars in the Don's care, and now he was gone. Many others who were working in various parts of the country would not know for several days. The police were called to clear the office and to keep order. Some of the men went out to seek a lawyer for advice. Why had Don Raffaele left? Maybe there was a reasonable explanation and he would soon return. Everyone had considered him an honest man, and no one had had the slightest suspicion that he might be a crook. He had done many favors for his clients for no fee. When the Don's partner arrived, the safe was opened. It was empty save for a letter stating that for the past two years Don Raffaele had been at the brink of bankruptcy. He had squandered through ill-timed investments the $20,000 that had been entrusted to him by his loyal clients. At that moment a man wielding a knife rushed in and shouted for his money: "I want it! Give it to me!" When told that not a penny remained, the depositor sank slowly to the floor in a dead faint.[25]

Social Interaction

ITALIANS WITH ITALIANS

The harsh, cold world in which the immigrant lived easily produced much quarreling and occasional acts of violence. The Italian colonies were peopled largely by young men who lacked the stabilizing tendencies often associated with family life. These men did physical work and were consequently physical in their actions and reactions. Their immigrant culture emphasized physical prowess and strength. That man who could work day in and day out without complaint was admired by his peers and, indirectly, by the host society. Moreover, many of the immigrants came from communities where one had to use threats and force to earn respect. Margariti reiterates this theme time and again in regard to his *paesani*.[26] Certain cultural imperatives that the Italians carried with them allowed for only one interpretation of events and consequently only one reaction. For instance, verbal insults were not tolerated. An insult was always met with a counterinsult, threat, or overt violence. D'Angelo relates a typical episode that occurred on board ship during a storm. One claustrophobic immigrant unbolted a porthole to look out. Water poured in, and two sailors rushed to close it. When they cursed him, the man's response was immediate: he drew his knife and lunged at them.[27]

Regional rivalries, hatreds, and stereotypes long bred in Italy were not diminished by the Atlantic voyage. On the contrary, the mixing of regional Italians in America further fueled the fire, particularly when the interaction was between the educated northern Italian and the southern Italian laborer. The consulates in the American cities were staffed largely by northern Italians. These bureaucrats took care to distinguish themselves from what was called the "dago class," made up of persons whom they felt to be both morally and intellectually inferior. The Italian immigrant often received more respect from his non-Italian neighbors than he did from these Italian officials. Ziffiro Ciuffoletti accurately described the attitudes of the latter:

> As far as the consuls and their functions are concerned, the immigrant is not an Italian citizen in a foreign country who chooses to live and work there with his family in peace, but a bureaucratic pain in the neck, a *cafone*, who, because of his boorish behavior, offends his country, brings scorn down on all Italians, and embarrasses his more urban compatriots. The mentality of the consulate employees is not far removed from the judgments prevalent among the Italian ruling class.[28]

To the educated Italian, "dirty immigrant" was one word and connoted a person of no refinement. The kind of incident that Ferdinando Maurino relates in his autobiography, *Dal cavo delle mani*, was commonplace. Maurino lived in Endicott, New York, and belonged to the Sons of Italy lodge in that upstate village. Most Italians in Endicott worked in the Endicott-Johnson factories, manufacturing shoes or pulling huge cowhides from the vats of the malodorous tannery. When a scholar of northern Italian origin was temporarily residing at the local college, he was asked by Maurino, a language professor there, to speak to the lodge members. The scholar scoffed at the suggestion that he associate with immigrants, particularly ordinary factory workers, who could never appreciate his pronouncements on "high" Italian culture.[29]

To that Italian scholar, the Italians in Endicott were *cafoni*, a term that figuratively means a boor or a simpleton. The *cafone* was more than unlettered; worse, he was unconcerned and uninvolved. He remained blissfully ignorant of his surroundings and possessed only one desire—to live a mundane existence and to make as much money as he could. The *cafone* personality and its effect on other Italians in America, especially those who desired respectability, is described by Gaspare Cusumano in his study of the Cinisi colony in New York City.

The caffoni, who were in Sicily mostly villani, are looked down upon by their own people and especially by that class of Italians who want to stay here and who feel injured whenever the Italian name is hurt. To this superior class a good name for the Italians is a requisite of their progress. The caffoni don't care. All they want is to make money and go back. So we often see the superior class preaching and speaking to the caffoni in meetings, in groups and individually, persuading them to uphold the Italian name. The caffoni listen, but then they shrug their shoulders and it is all over. "It does not give me any bread whether Italians have a good name in America or not. I am going back soon."[30]

North/South antagonisms were further divided into regional antagonisms. Every Italian child was conditioned at an early age to distrust "strangers" and to accept as immutable certain beliefs about regional differences in behavior and temperament. You trust members of your own family first, relatives second, *paesani* third, other Italians a distant fourth, and everyone else not at all. Leonardo Sciascia, a Sicilian, said of his father's generation: "All the Calabresi that my father knew were small and swarthy. My uncle said that all Calabresi have hard heads. The people of Sardinia are treacherous, the Romans rude, and the Neapolitans are a bunch of beggars."[31] Totonno, from Puglia, would have added that the Sicilians are adept with the stiletto and razor, and that they originated from the dark tribes of Africa. Totonno's experiences in America softened his ethnic attitudes significantly. He had been in New York less than a month when he left his South Bronx enclave to venture forth into the greater immigrant community. His *paesani* took him down to Greenwich Village to a *caffè concerto*, where he was introduced to a party of Sicilians at the next table. To his surprise, if not shock, the Sicilians were civil and intelligent; they even could speak "real" Italian in an elegant fashion.[32]

But there was ample opportunity to reinforce attitudes about non-*paesani*. D'Angelo, an Abruzzese, met a Calabrese who was down on his luck. Finding the man witty and engaging, D'Angelo invited him to stay at his boardinghouse. The man disappeared two days later with $60 that belonged to one of D'Angelo's friends. The Abruzzesi walked the streets for days until they spottted the crook. They dragged him to a police station, but got back only $40.[33] Iannace befriended a fellow from Salerno and lent him $25 that had taken months to save. The next morning the man was gone, and Iannace was roundly criticized by his *paesani* for having given his life savings to a total stranger. He keenly felt the outrage: being cheated by a *paesano* can be rationalized, Iannace mused, but being cheated by someone else is unacceptable.

Margariti, a Calabrese, lived among Sicilians and Neapolitans as well as his own kind. He had been thrown together with immigrants from various parts of Italy (and from various Italian social classes) by a host society that considered all Italians to be alike. But Margariti witnessed no commonality among Italians from different parts of Italy; the atmosphere in mixed groupings was always heavy with tension and potential confrontation. A gratuitous remark that would mean nothing from a *paesano* would be taken as a challenge from a relative stranger. One evening Margariti was conversing with an acquaintance when a Sicilian sitting across from them, for no apparent reason, called him a silly fool: "*Tu sei un pezzo di stupido.*" Flushed with anger, Margariti turned to the man:

> I replied that if there is a stupido at this table it is him, not me. He came at me with a large table knife. Battista, who was at the table, ran out for help. He brought back two big, tough-looking Neapolitans. One of them grabbed the Sicilian by the shirt and pushed him down on a chair. "Assettate cca, mannaggia a m...! e non ta move, si' no ta accio!" (Sit down, damn it, and don't you move, or else!). Thinking that the Neapolitans would then mal-treat me, I armed myself with a length of wood. But they came over and shook my hand, and told me to forget about it, that it would not happen again.[35]

Margariti's extensive documentation of his many negative encounters with other Italians is instructive. Trust, fidelity, and honesty were not found in great abundance in the world of the immigrants. In some respects, the Italian colony was more a jungle than a community.

Margariti was initiated to that jungle as soon as he stepped from his ship onto the New York docks.

> We were stopped by some men who spoke Italian. They wanted $3.00 for three packages of food, one for each of us. I looked inside my package and saw that it contained less than fifteen cents worth of food. I handed the package back, and said, "I am not hungry. I want my dollar back." They threatened me. "*Prendi e cammina!*" [Take it and move on!] What could I do? Well, I thought, they have *camorristi* here too.[36]

A few weeks later Margariti was almost killed when his brother, a railroad laborer, had an argument with a coworker over salting some tomatoes that they were preparing for dinner. The brother, who preferred a lot of salt, put a knife to the man's throat; the man, in turn, placed a pistol against the brother's stomach and fired. Hearing that his brother had been wounded, Margariti rushed to the bar and upon entering was promptly confronted by a one-eyed Calabrese from the province of Catanzaro. The man drew his pistol: "Your brother was first and now you're next!" Margariti responded by drawing his knife. As he did so, the police entered and took the man away in manacles. Margariti hoped that the New World would offer a better life and that the immigrants would pull together to achieve it. "It is inconceivable that two men from the same part of Italy could hate each other so much rather than liking and supporting one another in this strange land." But it was not to be. "Force settles things here as well," he concluded. "It is still the strong pressing their heels into the necks of the weak."[37]

Margariti's observations were merited: everyone quarrelled, and fighting was a common occurrence even among *paesani*. As a pick-and-shovel man, D'Angelo witnessed several brawls; Totonno participated in innumerable arguments and at least a dozen fistfights, in New York and in Utica, with *paesani* and non-*paesani* alike. He felt that he was drawn into these quarrels because others acted irrationally. One day he cornered and flattened another butcher, a competitor, because the man had squealed to the police that Totonno's business partner was illegally selling meat "through the back door" (outside of business hours) on Sundays. And in a feud that erupted between Totonno and an immigrant family, Totonno gave one of the members a public thrashing and then had to go into hiding for a week to avoid the family's vengeance. The Italian colony did not have many conventional mechanisms for relieving the burden of immigrant life. The work day was long and the satisfactions few. The two pleasures available to the hard-working immigrant were food and drink. Food in abundance and well prepared, washed down by quantities of wine, beer, and sweet liquor, was a comfort; filling one's stomach was a sacred duty and the one acceptable solace available. Sunday dinner was looked forward to with great anticipation. Sunday was the one day of the week when friends and *paesani* could come together on common ground. To miss Sunday dinner was to miss the major social event of the week. It was a time for gorging, a time for catching up on the week's gossip, a time for the continuation of old arguments and the invention of new ones, a time for venting frustration. The emphasis on the Italian immigrant Sunday dinner has usually been about food and its preparation; little has been said about what actually went on around the table. Totonno's classic description of a Sunday dinner in Utica, New York, in the fall of 1907, fills in this gap:

I am boarding in the Oronzo household and occasionally eat with the Liuzzi family. Liuzzi has a number of brothers and assorted relatives. Yesterday (Sunday) there were about twelve of us at the table. I can barely stand their company. They are a bunch of ignorant *cafoni*. They slurp their soup, they shovel the pasta down their gullets like a bunch of pigs while smacking their lips and making the noodles whistle, they talk with their mouths full so that bits of food take flight across the table, and they belch when the occasion demands. Liuzzi's uncle is the worst offender. His shirts are always spotted with tomato sauce. One of the girls put a large towel around his neck in place of a napkin to the hilarity of everyone. There is constant bickering and jostling at the table. I must bear the insults of two of the kids who are always grabbing something that belongs to me and throwing it out the window. They do not converse; they shout. By evening everyone was drunk. Oronzo and Liuzzi's uncle got into a rough and tumble fistfight. All that exercise and excitement whetted our appetites and we went back to the table.[38]

Peace and harmony within the immigrant household was difficult to maintain for any appreciable period of time. There were too many intrusions. Loud verbal clashes would suddenly erupt to be followed by sometimes long periods of nonverbal sullenness. The precipitating factor might appear to an outsider to be a trivial matter, but a person's pride, his fear of "losing face" or his family reputation, was a subject never taken lightly. The following two incidents from Totonno's diary—the first a quarrel between spouses, and the second a clash between a brother and his sisters—illustrate the pressures of the immigrant experience and the gradual erosion of Old World ethics and standards when they contradicted American customs.

Palombo received a shipment of wine from Italy. To celebrate my 22nd birthday, I got a few bottles and walked upstairs to Turiangelo's place. On entering the front room, I heard a big commotion. Sante was being held by Turiangelo, Concetta was screaming, and Silvia was crying. Sante had struck Silvia and wanted to give her another good *battuta* when Turiangelo intervened and was rewarded with a black eye. Once we got the girls out, Turiangelo was able to persuade Sante to take a walk with him. With everyone gone, I decided to celebrate by myself. I drank some wine, played my guitar and sang a few songs. When they returned, I asked what had happened. The reply was a collective shrug of the shoulders and looks of resignation. I left the wine on the sideboard and walked over to Sisto's place. There were fourteen in the room drinking wine, eating peppers, dried figs and chestnuts, and helping themselves to a one-half wheel of cheese, which was sitting in the center of the table.

A warm and pleasant spring day. Naschetto and I took two girls out for a picnic in the woods. Walking home, I turned into Kossuth Avenue and saw Naschetto running in my direction. Donato, the brother of the two girls, had found out about our picnic and was going crazy. When we got upstairs, we saw him chasing the screaming girls around the apartment, calling them *puttane* and swinging his arms wildly in an attempt to get in a few more smacks. Once we got Donato settled down, I assured him that nothing untoward had happened in the woods, that we had brought his sisters back as we had taken them—sound and whole. It was a bad day. I went to Nanuccio's bar to eat dinner and to have a few drinks.[39]

If Totonno had pondered the brother's moral dilemma for a moment, he would have realized the extent to which America had revised his own notions of right and wrong. Donato was an immigrant valiantly fighting a rearguard battle to hold off the insidious intrusion of America on his Old World principles. A few years previously, in Italy, Totonno could not have imagined himself compromising the reputations of two unchaperoned *signorine*, nor would they have so blatantly risked soiling their own reputations. In Italy, Totonno had satisfied himself with a long and meaningful side glance at his "beloved" during the evening *passeggiata* around the village square. To go beyond that without a serious and explicit understanding between the two families was unthinkable. But in America, Totonno had "girlfriends"—plural, not singular—who were as willing as he to test the limits of their new environment and as willing to redefine the old code as they went along. The immigrants found themselves caught in the midst of the clash between the Old and New World values. Perhaps most of them, unlike the brother, were fatalistic about the outcome and did little to prevent the change, but by no means did the Italians see such change as an absolute good.

ITALIANS AND AMERICANS

"Even a simpleton can see that they do not like us."
—immigrant coal miner

An Italian was not an Italian. He was a wop, dago, duke, gin, tally, ghini, macaroni or spaghetti or spaghetti bender. He was also Hey Boy or Hey Youse, or he was given a generic name: Joe, Pete, Tony, Carlo, Dino, Gumba.[40] "Do you know why most Italians are called Tony?" "No." "Because when they land in New York they have cards on their caps that say: To NY."

Most of the terms were obviously meant to dehumanize and to degrade. Others were simply ways of addressing a worker by someone who felt no need to indicate individual identity. Sometimes they were used by the Italians themselves; visitors from Italy noted that the immigrants called each other "ghini." The most common terms were "wop" and "dago." H. L. Mencken accepted "wop" as the institutionalized term for Italians because of its widespread use. The Italian consul in New York received a letter one day with the salutation: "Dear consul of Dagoland." "Dago" was used freely in print, even in leading newspapers, although not without protest. This statement appeared in *L'Italia* (in English) in response to an article in the *Chicago Tribune:* "DAGO: The above appellation as applied to Italians is considered by them as a gross insult. In last Thursday's *Tribune* we notice that a reporter used this term in speaking of an Italian. Anyone pretending to be a gentleman would not use this term."[41]

The language applied to the Italian immigrant signified his status in the society, one of cultural, economic, and moral inferiority. The attitude of Americans toward Italians was expressed succinctly by an Italian editor:

> What has impeded the moral and material development of the immigrant Italians? The Italians are viewed by the Americans as so much meat to be consumed. Italians are maltreated, mocked, scorned, disdained, and abused in every way. The inferiority of the Italians is believed to be almost that of the Asiatics.[42]

The Yellow Peril on the west coast had its counterpart in the Italian Peril on the east coast. The worst part of the American experience, Margariti observed, was the "harsh, negative, uncompromising attitudes of the members of the Celtic race who are convinced that we were of a lower social order and treat us accordingly."[43] D'Angelo had no delusions about his status. "I was a poor laborer, a dago, a wop or some such creature—in the eyes of the world."[44] In his youthful innocence, William Murray accepted the nickname "woppo" from his schoolmates without complaint, but Ventresca knew an insult when he heard it: on the playground "a certain boy named Ralph called me a dago. I gave him one on the jaw right there, and he never indulged in derogatory names after that."[45] Maurino, a greenhorn in Boston in 1911, was stopped on the street by two men. "Are you a wop?" they asked. "No, I'm Italian." "Get off the sidewalk!" they shouted, and pushed him violently to the ground.[46]

A day did not pass that the Italian was not vilified in one manner or another. The Americans laughed at his speech, his clothes, his customs, and where and how he lived. Such treatment caused Italians to be wary of all Americans. Broughton Brandenburg, a native American, lived for a brief time with Italians in New York, but there were those who spurned his offers of friendship. He would be confronted by Italians who wanted to know what he and his wife were doing in their midst: "Who are you? What do you want of us?" One man who had been very hostile said to him later by way of explanation and apology, "You know American mans ain't good to Eyetalyuns on'y he make de graft." [47] A policeman whom Totonno had met when his store was robbed tried to befriend him. The policeman wanted Totonno to teach him Italian, and went so far as to suggest that Totonno, who was a large, well-built, and confident man, might join the department as a member of the Italian Squad. Totonno was very suspicious of the man's motives, and agreed to act as his teacher only because of the officer's persistence.

Totonno had every reason to be on his guard; he had been a victim of corruptive police practices when he was fresh off the boat. His diary for June 1906 describes his two-day encounter with the American system of justice:

The afternoon was slow and I had nothing to do. On impulse, I jumped on a bike parked in front of the store and pedaled rapidly up to 154th Street, then circled back and was returning at a brisk pace. At the corner of 152nd a streetcar came alongside, and in my attempt to keep clear of its wheels, I veered to the right. I did not see the two kids who were jostling each other in the road until I struck one of them head on. We both fell and the bike flipped over against the streetcar. The car stopped, a crowd quickly gathered, and before I knew it I was taken into custody by a policeman who escorted me into a grocery store to make sure I did not escape. The boy's leg was twisted and bleeding, he was screaming, and the crowd was getting larger and more boisterous. I understood nothing. An ambulance arrived to take the boy away. Meanwhile, the boy's father came on the scene and the policeman asked him whether he wanted me arrested. Certainly, he replied, and with that the policeman led me out of the store, pushed through the crowd, and placed me in the police wagon. My *paesani* clamored on board, as did the father and one of the boy's cousins, and down to the Police Station we went.

The interrogation continued at the station. To satisfy the father who insisted that I be jailed, they put me into a cell and slammed the door. I looked around and found myself in a steel cage about two meters long and 1.5 meters wide. On one side was an iron bunk and on the other a toilet. I paid twenty-five cents for a pillow and stretched out on the bunk. I was frightened and full of shame. How could I face my *paesani* after this disgrace? The policeman laughed and told me he would take care of things. He knew it was not my fault.

The next morning we went to the courthouse where we were placed in a steel cage with other prisoners to await our trials. One by one each prisoner was called and a short time later would return. Some of them were chained and led into other cells. When I saw that, I could hear my heart pounding and I began to tremble. My legs were jerking so much I could barely stand. When my name was announced I was escorted upstairs to the court. I was relieved to see my friends sitting there. One of them came forward to translate. It all happened very fast. I was found not guilty. The judge told me that if I felt my rights had been violated, I could take the case to civil court.

The policeman took me out the back door to the tram stop. He wanted me to pay him for his testimony. How much? I asked. Five dollars. Sisto and Turiangelo joined us on the tram. We stopped at a bar. I bought a round of beer for twenty-five cents and Sisto gave the policeman the five dollars.

The Americans formed their impressions of Italy and Italians largely on the basis of negative newspaper reportage and contact with immigrants of humble origin. When they encountered an Italian of middle-class bearing and education who did not fit their conception, they registered surprise and confusion. The middle-class Italians were alarmed by the American attitude. They were fiercely proud of their country and their noble Italian heritage, and did not care to defend themselves before every anti-Italian critic when they felt no defense should be necessary. In their desire for respect, some would carefully distinguish themselves from the "wop class," but by doing so, they were admitting to Italian inferiority. The common immigrants had to endure insults much more frequently, but the barbs were suffered more acutely by middle-class Italians, who felt compelled to argue for their honor and the honor of their nation. Those of the "wop class" often did not feel this compulsion; they had been at the bottom of the social ladder in Italy and consequently had acquired an imperviousness to harsh treatment.

Touring Italian artists quickly learned what Americans thought about Italy and the immigrants. The actor Tommaso Salvini was outraged at a depiction of Italy in the 1872 Mardi Gras carnival procession in New Orleans. The float had Pope Pius IX blessing two brigands, who were kneeling before him with knives between their teeth. Naively, Salvini demanded and fully expected an apology from the city officials. His written protest—which said, in part, "Every good person rejects the insult to a nation, which from antiquity to the present merits the respect and admiration of a civilized world"—went unanswered.[48] Giuseppe Giacosa, a celebrated Italian actor of the day, met the impresario of a Philadelphia music hall where he was to perform. The man approached Giacosa, smiled, and remarked in an affirmative tone, "You're French." "No," Giacosa replied, "Italian." The impresario was incredulous. "He looked at me again, taking in my full person, undoubtedly asking himself how this well-dressed, obvious gentleman before him could be one of those macaroni, an organ grinder, a degos, terms of insult that are used for all Italians in America."[49]

While living in Boston, Reverend Gaetano Conte and his wife were visiting some American friends when they were introduced to a proper Bostonian couple. The host presented Conte as a person who was interested in the "Italian Question." The woman immediately exclaimed, "Oh, I do not like those Italians!" After a few moments of conversation she realized that the Contes were Italian. "Well," she said, "no one would ever think that such respectable people as you would belong to that race. Italians are ignorant and illiterate." Conte assured her that there were schools in Italy. After conceding that possibility, she added that, even so, "English is not taught." The fact that the Contes were speaking English seemed to escape her attention.[50]

Rossi saw the Americans as bullheaded and hopelessly provincial. He was appalled at their distorted and superficial knowledge of anything outside of the United States. Every day in New York he had to listen to statements that summed up Italians in terms of stiletto, macaroni, brigand, and vendetta; all Italians had dark eyes and hot blood, and were musically inclined. He rarely ate macaroni, he would tell them; he could not sing or play an instrument, he would insist, and at that moment was not concealing a knife in his pocket. But his arguments fell on deaf ears.[51]

Those Italians who stepped outside their colonies with the intention of "making it" in the world of the Americans frequently had a rude awakening. Robert Ferrari went to Columbia College at the turn of the century at a time when few foreigners were admitted and those few were barely tolerated. "In my day," the handful of Italians "who made the attempt to enter the schools were met with curious glances, a stormy reception, deliberate animosity, and discouragement." When he was examined for a teaching position in English in the New York schools, he answered the questions correctly but was never called to teach. An Italian was not allowed to teach English, or any other subject, to American students. Ferrari eventually found a post teaching Italians.[52]

The Americans considered Italians much the same as gypsies. The Italians lived in groups under the guidance of a "head man," they cooked communally, and their dress and personal hygiene left much to be desired. While walking with his friends, D'Angelo noticed that Americans kept their distance on the streets and would make slurring remarks about unkempt and dirty foreigners. When Brandenburg boarded a New York streetcar with some newly arrived Italians, he heard a woman say "Oh, what dirty, dirty wretches," and a stout gentleman exclaimed, "I don't see why they let those lousy dagoes ride on the same cars other people have to use." Later in the day, Brandenburg was turned away from a hotel by the desk clerk, who remarked to his colleague, "Well, what do you think of that nerve. That dago coming in here with a push like that trying to get rooms."[53] Rossi heard immigrants called "those dirty Italians" because when they thronged from the ships, it was said, "they send out a stink that can be detected several meters away. Washing is unknown to them, and a bathtub is a strange object. They do not even change shirts once every fifteen days."[54] Even some Italians agreed with this assessment. Cianfarra had this to say about the "wop class": "For the Americans the Italian is of necessity filthy. It is part of his nature. After all, what can one

expect? We created this reputation of being worse than pigs and of il-
literacy. Some time must pass before we will be able to eliminate that
image."[55] In a country claiming to consider cleanliness next to god-
liness, sloppy personal habits such as children being sent to school unwashed and unbrushed were intolerable. One teacher sent a note home
informing the mother that her daughter had a bad odor and her hair
needed washing. The teacher received this reply: "Mary is not a rose.
Do not smell her, teach her."[56]

For the Americans, the Italians exemplified the Lombrosian concept of the born criminal: impulsive, primitive, violent. Behavior associated exclusively with the Italian, especially the private vendetta
and the "Code of Honor" (the honor of the family must be protected
by any means), evoked a sense of disgust, and the fighting tactics of
the Italians were considered cowardly and ungentlemanly. The newspapers at the turn of the century gave full exposure to accounts of
street fights in which the stiletto was always in evidence. Many Americans would have agreed with the comments of a first-class passenger as
he watched the steerage travelers aboard ship:

> These Italians are the worst of the lot. They are a dangerous ele-
> ment. Stick a knife in you in a minute. Look at the villainous-
> looking fellow standing right there on the box, smoking a cigar.
> Why, criminal instinct is written in every line of his head and
> face. See the bravado in the way he holds his shoulders and the
> nasty look in his uneasy eyes.[57]

Nevertheless, Italians were highly valued by many American employers
as toilers who took pride in their work. Mosso visited the owner of a
shoe factory who left no doubt of his respect for Italian labor. "I will
take any Italian I can hire. America has much work for unskilled laborers. There are railroads to be built as well as highways, bridges,
canals, and seaports. Italians are models of temperance. They never
get drunk and lose a day's work. You can be sure that we will never
close the door to the Italian. He is crucial to our economic progress."[58]

The factory owner might have added to his list of positive at-
tributes that the Italian would work at any job for long hours at low pay
with few complaints. He was pliable; he knew how to take orders; he
was passive. These characteristics irritated Louis Adamic, a Slovene

immigrant writer, who for a time labored with pick and shovel. His Italian coworkers were "short, squat, illiterate" men who spoke English sparingly if at all. "I felt, successively, sorry for and disgusted with them. The bosses had them cowed. Their wages were low, but they would have worked for even less. At the end of the day they trudged home, silent, uninspired, a heavy smell of hopelessness about them. They did not belong in America. They knew nothing of the country, nor had the ability or the desire to learn about it. They lived from day to day, from hand to mouth, driven by narrow selfishness." [59] Good workers, but not the stuff of American citizenship. Gherardo Ferreri maintained that the very characteristics that made the Italian a good worker also made him, in the eyes of the Americans, unwanted. To be taken seriously by Americans, Ferreri continued, Italians must not be timid and pliant, uncouth and ignorant, or their destiny would be to occupy a permanent underclass in the society. Ferreri concluded that arrogance must be met with arrogance, that respect and advancement come only from a position of strength. [60]

The Italians gave as much criticism as they received. Many immigrants considered American cultural priorities to be perverted. Italian culture emphasized simplicity, beauty, temperance, love of family, a spirit of economy—values that transcend the individual, and time and place. Americans were concerned with the here and now. They looked toward work as the Great American Savior and were motivated to action by their love of money. Cold and heartless, emotion had no place in their lives, but money did. America was infected by the accursed greed for gain. Money was the only topic of conversation, Carlo Tresca concluded after his first few days in New York: "Money, money, money. Everybody talked of money. I went home thinking of money. 'If I had money.' 'I must make money.' Money, money, money. These words began to haunt me. I asked my brother, 'Where are the Christians in America?' " [61] A person was defined in America not by his individuality but by his money. The man who could turn a profit was admired by his fellows. The businessman, the symbol of America, worshiped at the shrine of the Almighty Dollar. "The Dollar is King in America," Totonno wrote in his diary, "and truly represents the life in this country." Totonno was fascinated by the glitter of America; later he realized that behind the glitter was much ugliness. Cianfarra was forewarned by his teacher in Italy, who said to him on the eve of his departure, "You will see some nice things, but don't rush to judgment, because in no country do appearances deceive as in America." [62]

To be sure, the Italians were intrigued by the prospect of wealth; after all, that is why they had come to America. But this American obsession with the dollar was difficult to comprehend. Margariti felt that Americans were of "another world, another race." The lust for money had pinched them dry. Make money! The American child was raised to revere the father who could attract dollars to his billfold. A condition of poverty was examined as if it were the symptom of a terminal disease. Only good flowed from the constant acquisition of wealth, and only bad could come from a failure to do so. Work was the path to salvation, and the immigrants were enjoined to work and work and work. America was a nation of pragmatists; unless what one did made the cash register ring, it was not worth the effort. Talking about construction projects in America, Ventresca complained that while Italians emphasized the aesthetic side of an artifact, the Americans would say, "Never mind your art, we want efficiency," which meant the greatest return for the least outlay. [63]

The person who worked hard was held in high esteem, while anyone who refused to put in a good day's work for his day's pay was considered of no value to the community. The immigrants were expected to labor, to put their backs to the job, and to think of nothing else. Those who did not meet the expectations of the American Work Ethic, which demanded that the immigrant sweat, were called "bums" and "loafers." The Italians looked at the notion of physical labor differently. It was not viewed as a higher calling nor was it always considered dignified, as Iannace recognized:

> The most important difference between the American and non-American involves the concept of work as a worthy and ennobling activity. Coming to America, one enters a new dimension if, consciously, one accepts the concept of work as the vital source of human expression, as a hymn of life, as a way of making contact with one's being, and as the central means by which one interacts with others and the society. Work is viewed in another manner in Italy. Italians believe that work debilitates man, it reduces him to the status of a beast. Especially when one is forced to work for others, in particular for the State. [64]

The Americans were incapable of enjoying life; life for them was not a romp but a crusade pursued with design and calculation. "Americans are joyless, for joy is a fruit that the Americans eat green." They are a people "who had been pickled in the sour juices of Puritanism." To the Italians, America lacked diversity and Americans were without imagination. "*L'America, donne senza colore e frutta senza sapore.*" [65] "To my people," Pietro Di Donato wrote, "the Americans were color- less, unsalted, baloney munchers and 'gasoline' drinkers without cul- ture, who spoke with a vocabulary limited to repetitive, four-lettered words, listened to caterwauling, imbecilic music, and all looked more or less alike." [66] The Italians were most struck by the coldness of Americans, their inability or unwillingness to display public emotion. "They will go to a funeral of their best friend and keep a straight face. I believe they are ashamed if in a moment of forgetfulness they've turned to look at a flower or a beautiful sunset." [67] During his early years in America, Constantine Panunzio did not meet one American whom he could like or respect, but only rough and uncouth "persons who knew no refinement of language, of bearing or of manners; who mocked order; who defied and openly broke the law. Dignity had no place in life." [68] Panunzio could trust no one, and he was deceived re- peatedly, especially when money was involved.

The Italians were not free of their own brand of greed and ra- paciousness. "Bisinissi" was one of the first words the immigrants learned, and it was a term used to cover a multitude of sins. America was a golden opportunity for those Italians with capitalistic intent. There was money to be made in America, and those sharp business practices that were good enough for the Americans certainly suited Italian greed. Italian businessmen would cheat their fellow country- men while invoking the tenets of the American business creed. Rossi watched one day as an Italian businessman in New York cheated an immigrant rag collector by fixing the scale so that it showed ten pounds less than the actual weight. When Rossi asked the man why he had purposely cheated the poor ragpicker, who was full of innocent trust, out of a few pennies, he smiled and said triumphantly, "That is business, you know." [69] Cianfarra once worked for a man who "would cut your soul out in order to sell it." Cianfarra was selling cigars door to door, and when he returned to the tobacco firm at the end of the day, his Boss would go to great lengths to cheat him out of every possible

penny—with obvious relish. Why? Cianfarra finally asked. *"E'cosi'
che fanno gli affari gli Americani"* (That's the way the Americans
do it).[70]

ITALIAN AND IRISH CONFLICT

Despite the fact that Italians and other immigrants shared a low socio-
economic position and were often grouped in a single category by
Americans, no strong bonds of solidarity or feeling of a common fate
developed among the immigrant groups. Even in the mixed neighborhoods or on the job, there was little sustained social interaction
between Italians and others. While growing up in New York City in
the 1890s, Ferrari never met any of his non-Italian neighbors. "The
household my parents established on Mott Street was typical of those
of little Italy. We spoke only Italian, ate Italian food, celebrated Italian
holidays, and on Sundays entertained relatives and friends. We knew
nothing of the outside world." [71] The reaction of one immigrant group
to another was likely to be neutral or antagonistic rather than cooperative. They all shared a traditional distrust of outsiders, and the culture
of each group was just as alien to the others as was the American.
Those Italians who expected to be welcomed by the other immigrants
were invariably disillusioned. Margariti left the Italian colony in Philadelphia to escape Italian violence, only to discover that he had put his
life in jeopardy at a baking company employing Germans. Not an hour
went by that he was not verbally abused and threatened, and one of the
Germans finally assaulted him. When the foreman refused to intervene
decisively, Margariti quit.[72]

The Irish were the major antagonists of the Italians; they called the
Italians wops and dagoes and tormented them constantly. The Italians,
in turn, looked on Irishmen as drunkards who gave most of their salaries to the bartender, and considered Irishwomen prostitutes.[73] Moreover, the Italians resented the Irish, whom they felt were only by hap-
penstance in a position to lord it over them. They have an unfair
advantage, the Italians would say, because they have been in America
longer and arrived knowing the language.

The conflict between the two immigrant groups, both despised
by the Americans and both at the bottom of the social ladder, was perhaps inevitable. The Italians and the Irish were predominantly poor,
uneducated, slovenly in their habits, unskilled, and Catholic, with

long histories of oppression by foreign governments. Neither group wanted to be at the bottom, but it gave each group pleasure to see the other there. The Irish, however, had the satisfaction of knowing that the Italians were even more despised than they were. The average American, if asked to choose between Italian or Irish, would have chosen the latter. As one Protestant clergyman commented, "An Irish Catholic is preferable to an Italian Catholic, an Irish shillalah to an Italian knife." [74]

The Irish priests denounced the Italians from the pulpit in both the United States and Ireland. Irish parishioners were led to believe that Victor Emmanuel and Garibaldi, national heroes to the Italians, were criminals who had forced the Pope to flee from the Quirinale Palace, where he had ruled over both the city of Rome and the Church, to the Vatican, where he (and the Church) was being held captive by the new Italian government. The Italians had been criticized by the Church hierarchy around the world, and the Church in America made the most of the resulting anti-Italian propaganda. Moreover, Italian immigrants were viewed by Irish priests as only nominal Catholics: Italians were not as devoted as Irish or German Catholics; they were concerned only with the superficial and showy aspects of Catholicism, and had religious customs that the Irish considered more pagan than Christian. The Italians would shower their patron saints with money and would put aside as much as possible in order to have splendid funerals and christenings, but they were reluctant to support the Church by contributing even a small sum at Sunday service. "Why should we pay to enter a church?" the Italians would say, "The church is not a theater." Even those Italians who did comply did not find a ready welcome in the churches. They would be segregated and hear themselves referred to as intruders. This attitude extended also to the parochial schools, where Italian children were called "spaghetti" by the other students and often subjected to humiliating treatment by the nuns. [75]

Giovanni Perez was introduced to the Irish anti-Italian sentiment as soon as his ship entered New York harbor. A small craft came alongside, and the Irish on the boat called up to the Italian passengers, "Are you macaroni eaters? Are you from Italy? Sons of Garibaldi? Come on down, you rascals, you brigands!" Not more than a few days had passed before Perez realized that the New York of the 1860s was no "bed of roses" for the Italian; the Irish nourished "a special hatred toward us." [76] The belief was widespread in the Irish community, and the feelings ran very deep, that the Italians were *mangiapreti* (priest baiters), heretics, and oppressors of the Catholic Church. The "Roman Question" gave any Irish who were spoiling for a fight a convenient excuse to launch a crusade and to single out a vulnerable target—the naive greenhorn Italian immigrant.

Perez resided on Canal Street, where an Italian took his life in his hands if he chose to enter a saloon filled with Irish loafers from the neighborhood—"Irish of the worse type," Perez called them. Once inside, these thugs would "contest your exit" and wield their knives and clubs freely on those to whom they took a dislike. [77] Rosa Cristoforo recalled that in Chicago, too, the worst friction was between the Italians and the Irish, who "were all the time fighting." [78] Italians walking through Irish neighborhoods to and from work would often be confronted by groups of toughs who would line up on both sides of the sidewalk; the Italians were funneled between the two lines and slugged in turn by each of the boys. Cornering a lone Italian and subjecting him to torment was also considered "good sport" by the Irish lads. In Buffalo the Italians were forced to avoid the main thoroughfares and take to the back alleys to avoid becoming targets of Irish bottles, bricks, and fists. [79] Italian street peddlers were the victims of pillaging Irish street gangs. Among their favorite targets in the early days of Italian immigration were the Ticinesi chestnut vendors (chestnuts were introduced as human food to America by Taddeo Taddei in the 1840s); the Irish were successful in reducing their numbers significantly until the vendors devised their own form of protection. [80]

Festive gatherings of Italians were other favorite targets. Each time an Italian national holiday was celebrated or there was a picnic, Irish gangs would patrol the perimeters ready to ambush and thrash any individual who strayed, or to charge en masse into the crowd of Italian revelers. Perez was witness to a bloody battle between Irish and Italians one Sunday in June 1869 following a festival of Italians and city officials at Karl's Germania Park in New York. The Irish were seen during the day walking in the adjacent neighborhood. The crowd dispersed at ten in the evening, leaving about a dozen Sicilians listening to a Sicilian band. Suddenly a large gang of Irishmen charged into the park "screaming like demons, armed with rocks and large clubs. At first I stood there astonished. But when I saw my friend beside me struck down by a blow on the head and the flashing of knives I took to my heels and did not stop running until I had reached Canal Street." One Sicilian was killed and another gravely wounded. The next day a newspaper reported:

> Yesterday, at the termination of the Pic-Nic of the Italians at Karl's Germania Park, the few who had remained were cowardly and without provocation attacked by fifty fanatical Irish, who cried "Down with Garibaldi! Long live the Pope!" Six Sicilians fought back and put to flight the fifty Irishmen. It was a great day for the Sicilians.[81]

The "special hatred" that the Irish harbored for the Italians was also manifested in the job market. Many unskilled laboring jobs had been the almost exclusive domain of the Irish until the arrival of the Italians, who quickly replaced them in road and construction work. Even the Irish bosses hired Italians, because they were more reliable workers and, at least initially, willing to work for lower wages. The Irish workers struck back by attempting to intimidate the Italians and drive them away from the work sites.

One typical encounter occurred in Somerville, Massachusetts, on July 10, 1894. An Irish work gang was digging a sewer ditch. The men had begun drinking the night before and continued drinking on the job. Their employer, frustrated in his attempts to get any work out of the drunken and rowdy crew, fired one man as a lesson to the others and hired two Italians who happened by. The Irish workers grabbed the Italians, pushed them into the ditch and beat them senseless.[82] And there were more serious incidents. One occurred at a work site in the village of Mamaroneck, New York, where a small Italian colony had been established. Some Italian workers were receiving their monthly pay when 200 Irishmen, who were also working in the vicinity, fell on the outnumbered Italians, injuring several and forcing them and their families to abandon their homes and flee south to Morrisania in the Bronx, where they were placed under the protection of civil authorities.[83]

The Irish did not question their belief that the Italians were inferior, and they expected the Italians to agree with that assessment. They were bolstered in their conviction by the fact that the majority of

Italians were most likely to suffer attacks and ethnic slurs silently. Italian pent-up anger, however, could reveal itself in a violent display.

> Peppino resembled a gorilla, and for the hunch on his back was known as "Il Gobbo." Il Gobbo had one fear, his unnatural strength and ungovernable rage. An Irishman drinking in Tony's saloon called him a "dago ape." With one punch Il Gobbo shattered his face, and were it not for the paesanos who held him, he would have stomped him to death.[84]

Fighting prowess among the Irish gave a person prestige and standing with his peers. Fighting was proof of courage and manliness, one's ability to give and take punishment; brawling was a pastime and boxing a sport with specific rules. When the Italians refused to fight, the Irish immediately branded them as cowards. Like Peppino, most Italians had to be provoked to fight, but when they did, their purpose and therefore their means differed from those of the Irish. Once the fight began, the Italian would retaliate ferociously, with no holds or weapons barred, in order to get the advantage and to defeat his opponent. The Irish judged such behavior to be a breach of their ethics, and further distrusted the Italians for their "unpredictable" behavior.

ITALIAN NAME CHANGING

"Kelley and Ryan, Italian Bakers"

—*store sign in Cincinnati, circa 1910.*[85]

Like other European immigrants, thousands of Italians Americanized their surnames or took new ones, and transformed given names into English equivalents. Some of these changes were deliberate and permanent; some "evolved" through accident or circumstance; others were "immigrant names" assumed temporarily out of expediency.

By no means did the majority of Italians rush to drop their Italian names for American equivalents, however. Pride in an Italian name was often greater than the desire to conform to American usage.

Most immigrants retained their Italian given names officially, even though on an everyday level they were addressed by their Italian nicknames or an American form. Thus Francesco was Frank (or Ciccio, the

Italian nickname) to his friends and coworkers, but when he signed a document or answered a census enumerator's questions, he was still Francesco. In some families there were children with Italian given names and others with American ones; the latter were usually those born in the United States.

Surnames were changed with even less frequency. Other immigrant groups, the Jews and the Germans especially, modified their surnames much more often and usually more radically than did the Italians.[86] A review of the 1900 Federal census manuscripts for New York state reveals that only a fraction of the enumerated Italians, perhaps no more than 5 percent, had modified their surnames. And only a handful of these had assumed new full names that disguised completely their Italian origins. One cannot detect any uniform pattern: there were those who had Americanized their last names and retained their given names (Pasqua Rock, Sedota Anthony, Carmele Brown) as well as those who had slightly modified their surnames and had taken an American given name (Jimmie Pasarell, Thomas Perot, Maggie Leon).

The most common form of surname modification was to drop letters by one of three basic processes.

Syncope involves the removal of letters from the middle of the name, one of the vowels of a diphthong for example: Cuomo to Como; Buono to Bono; Coviello to Covello. When several letters were dropped, the simpler name might still retain an Italian character: Bardo from Bernardo. Internal transformation took place also through phonetic respellings that conformed to American patterns: Ritzo from Rizzo; Ameche from Amici; Pulise from Pugliese; Lulio from Luglio. Some alterations, even dropping a single letter, changed the entire character of the name: omitting the "i" from Contestabile (pronounced ContesTAbile) produced ConTEstable, which is American in both appearance and pronunciation.

The second process, *apocope*, involves dropping of the last part of the name: Bartolomeo to Bartolo. This practice was seen most often when the name was long and composed of two or more identifiable words: Presto for Prestogiacomo; Passo for Passalacqua; Trenta for Trentadue; as well as Loy for Loiacomo. Pietro Campolongo, at age 17, changed his name to Peter Campon "to make it more understandable and pronounceable in our common language, while deviating little from its original meaning."[87]

In *apheresis*, the first part of the name is removed: Teodoro to

Doro; Lapiscarella to Carrell. Occasionally, the preposition (da, de, di, d') or the article (li, lo, la) that constitutes the first part of many Italian surnames was dropped: Rocca for La Rocca; Verde for Lo Verde. But more likely the two parts were merged into one word, especially when an apostrophe was involved: D'Amato became Damato; Dell'Aquila became Dellaquila.

Throughout history, the alteration of names has been a dynamic process influenced by several factors; it is not always merely a product of emigration. Surnames in Italy have been written and spelled variously, in some instances freely ignoring proper Italian orthographic rules. Small clerical deviations if repeated often enough could be incorporated into the name. For instance, the cognomen La Sorte was written (correctly) as La Sorte in the eighteenth century, often as Lasorte in the nineteenth century, and in the twentieth as La Sorte, LaSorte, Lasorte, and Lasort.

Many Italian names were easily Americanized by simply changing a letter or two: Bernardy for Bernardi; Conty for Conti. In Buffalo in 1900 Nicholas Brock lived a few houses from Nicholas Bracco. The same end could be achieved by the removal of the final vowel. Cort for Corte; Ross for Rossi; Baron for Barone; Gilbert for Gilberti.

Some names were translated directly into English: Chiesa to Church; Lo Prete to Priest; Barbieri to Barber; Piccolo to Little; Papa to Pope; Giordano to Jordan. After a few weeks in America, Nicolo Quaranta had become Nick Forty. Italians living in New York State at the turn of the century included Sam Snow, Ralph Barber, Michael Rock, Nick Roberts, Joseph Balony, Nick Law, Frank Rich, and Anthony White.

Other names were transliterated: Bucci to Buckeye; Neri to Neareye. Some of the transformations by sound evolved through a number of phases. For example, Napoli was reduced to Nap, and then eventually spelled Knapp. In the same way, Paolo Vaccarelli evolved into Paul Kelley.

When a completely new name was assumed, it was often of Irish origin. Since the Irish dominated in the lives of many of the Italians, those Italian men who wanted to assimilate rapidly into American society and leave behind their Italian heritages frequently sought to do so not only by assuming Irish names but also by marrying Irish women. Such Mediterranean-Irish families lived outside the Italian colonies

and gave their children Irish first names. Among the Italians living in
New York state in 1900 were Andrew McLean (who first emigrated to
Scotland, then to the United States), Peter Mills, John Ryan, George
Kelley, Thomas Johnson, Frank Shannon, George Rogers, Charles
Drew, John Bates, Charles Patrick, John Sullivan, Rocky Foley, and
Rocky Murphy.

Other Italians took new names for the sake of success in American careers where an Italian name would have been a disadvantage.
For example, the sport of boxing was dominated by the Irish. Irish
fighters were believed to be the best; they were aggressive and colorful;
and Irish names drew large houses. Therefore, one way an Italian boxer
could contract for the lucrative bouts was to assume an Irish ring name.
Jim Flynn, the only man to knock out Jack Dempsey, was born Andrea
Chiariglione. Sandy Smash was really Alessandro Smiraglia, and Louis
Smith answered to Luigi Zampariello. In 1911, when Frances Pezzola
came up from the semipro baseball sandlots to play for the Chicago
White Sox, the manager insisted that he take the name of Ping Bodie.
At the suggestion of her editor, the novelist Francesca Vinciguerra
translated her name to Frances Winwar. Emanuel Carnevali, the poet,
sometimes passed himself off in New York as a Frenchman, "because I
had come to the conclusion that Italians were not well seen out of
Italy." [88] Frank Hopple was a real estate man in Utica, New York, and
Frank J. Ross was one of three physicians in the Utica Italian colony.
Frank C. James owned an Italian wine and liquor business in St. Paul,
Minnesota.

Not all such persons changed their names. The popular boxer Leo
Pardello retained his. And so did Francis De Billo, despite considerable pressure from his professors in college and at a Protestant seminary, who told him that his Italian name would limit his success in the
ministry. The non-Italian members of his congregation, he was assured, would not accept him. [89] (Curiously, during the same era, non-
Italian opera singers who wanted to succeed in the world of Italian
opera eagerly took Italian stage names and copied Italian behavioral
traits; some even faked an Italian accent and invented an Italian mama
and papa.)

Many proud Italians harshly criticized their name-changing compatriots. Ciarlantini was dismayed at those immigrants, many of whom
he felt were of limited intelligence, who allowed themselves to be ma-

nipulated by employers to accept new names.[90] Editors of the Italian newspapers, who considered themselves spokesmen for the Italian communities, expressed disapproval of any action that might endanger the Italian heritage. One Detroit paper criticized the immigrants who were seeking to accommodate themselves to their adopted country by forgetting that they were, first and foremost, Italian. "Shame, shame," one editorial exclaimed. "There are those Italians who feel so burdened by their Italian names that they accept American sur- names as legitimate substitutes." Instead of rejecting your heritage, they were advised, "elevate yourselves and others to a higher plane of dignity and respectability." They were cautioned not to act like fools and assume that it was possible to be accepted in America without surrendering that which makes the Italians unique.[91] (It is interesting to note, in this context, that at the turn of the century the Italian news- papers nevertheless carried advertisements for nose jobs, for those who wished to "improve" their facial features.) One of Cianfarra's acquaintances called name changing a "perverse habit" that would have a "bad outcome" for all Italians because "we all will be vic- timized by their poor examples. These people are preparing the way for future humiliations and other struggles, delaying the day of tri- umph." [92] Di Donato ridiculed those who translated their names into English, thereby robbing them of their worldly, romantic character.[93]

These criticisms might have kept some from contemplating a new name but had little effect on those who had already made the change. One exception was a young man by the name of Orfanello, a cook in an Italian restaurant. He suffered so much harassment from his *paesani* for changing his name to Johnson that he went back to court and asked to become Orfanello again.[94]

Amy Bernardy noticed that Italian laborers, particularly those who moved regularly from one job site to another, changed their names as easily as "they changed their shirts." [95] A new life called for a new name and a new personality. Name changing was part of the process of conforming. The gesture was largely symbolic, for these men were not seeking full assimilation. The fellow everyone called Kelley Smith, born Giovanni Sgobba, continued to speak Italian, to think of Italy, and to eat *pasta e fagioli*. The new name was a way in which Kelley could appear to transform himself into an American, to comfort the Americans into believing that he was anxious to do things their way, to bend to their expectations. When in Rome . . .

There is a likelihood that most of the Italian laborers to whom Bernardy referred eventually reassumed their original names. Iannace called himself Bill Rosa. He does not explain why. Nor does Adolfo Rossi, who called himself Frank. Panunzio accepted new names from his farmer employers: he was called Mr. Beefsteak and later Frank Nardi, a name he kept for several years. When he wrote to his family in Italy, he would enclose an envelope with the Nardi name on it and instruct his parents to use it for their reply. Panunzio knew many other immigrants who did the same. Some Italians, Panunzio wrote, "make a change on their own initiative, for the sake of convenience, or in order to be American at least in name. By far the greater number of changes, however, are superimposed by employers."[96] Orphaned and illegitimate children living in institutions were often given American names. Italian-born Margaret and Henry Thomas, two and three years of age respectively, were living in 1900 at the Sisters of Mercy Convent in Rochester, New York. An Italian farm laborer named Jacob Yates, who worked for a farmer in upstate New York, probably got his name from Yates County, where he lived. Another Italian laborer with a unique name, Cast Yours, lived in an adjacent county.

Name changing was a major step in the process of de-Italianization. No matter how American an Italian might appear to be in terms of speech and comportment, his name would continue to betray his origins, and some first- and second-generation Italians wanted to free themselves of the last vestiges of their Italian past. Charlotte Adams, in 1881, knew several Italians of the second generation who could easily pass for Americans and attempted to do so, "since a most unjust and unwarranted prejudice against Italians exists in many quarters, and interferes with their success in their trades and callings."[97] Decades later, Mencken stated the same argument in another context. "The Italians, in the early days of their migration to the United States, changed their names with some frequency, but with the advent of Mussolini and the rise of a new Italian national spirit this process was halted." Increased pride in one's Italianness would halt the assumption of American names, Mencken contended, but it would not halt the continuing erosion of long, complicated names.[98] Thus surnames like Pietrolungo, Gicognami, Gugielminetti, Calamandrei, Giacovelli, Biondolillo, Miglioratti, and others would have to give way to simpler versions. Mencken's prediction has not been entirely borne out; only a minority of complex names have been affected. The majority, including those in the foregoing list, have survived the process of assimilation intact.

If one examines the full range of modifications in Italian names, it is possible to conclude that most of the minor orthographic changes were a product of the wear and tear of the emigration process and the everyday abrasions of common speech. "The English languge," Sabine Baring-Gould observed, "is impatient of foreign sounds, and insists on rounding or roughing them into some semblance to a known English word."[99] Italian sounds did not issue smoothly from English-speaking lips, and Americans had difficulty with even relatively simple names. "Ventresca" is neither unusually long or difficult to pronounce. Yet one day when Ventresca went to a work site to seek employment and told the foreman his name, the man exclaimed, "What a hell of a name that is!"[100] It was much easier for the employer to hand out numbered tags or to call each worker a generic "Tony" than to remember a number of unfamiliar names. Through laziness and nonchalance, American clerks, paymasters, and other officials who had to speak and transcribe Italian names could—through repeated misspellings and mispronounciations—play a role in modifying them.

Given the pressures they faced, the Italians had to persist to maintain the integrity of their names. And most did. Even when pronunciation changed, the system of Italian spelling remained largely intact. The act of modification was either initiated by the Italian or ultimately accepted by him. The popular belief that new names were handed out by the bushelful at Ellis Island, or that the ignorant, guileless, powerless immigrant had no choice but to succumb to a permanent name change, clouds the more obvious and less acceptable explanation. Name changing was an adaptive concession that some immigrants chose to make to their new environment.

Italglish: The Immigrant Idiom

Era *smarto* il dabben uomo,
conosceva il *bisnisse*,
era amico del *polisse*
e in *colleggio* non andò.

—*an immigrant ditty*

One of the most fascinating adjustments that Italian newcomers made to American society was the way they adapted their language. The immigrants developed an idiom, simply constructed and quickly learned by any greenhorn within a few weeks, that proved to be an effective and practical medium of communication among Italians and between Italians and Americans. Italglish was a utilitarian, everyday language of great flexibility, spoken within the family, at work, and among peers. Italian businessmen developed the idiom to a fine art in order to communicate with customers of different dialectical traditions. Politicians and the *prominenti* of the Italian colonies found it very serviceable. Those Americans who associated with Italians acquired a few key phrases in order to communicate on the job and in the marketplace or because they found the "curious idiom" (which many Americans mistook for proper Italian) commodious and melodious and a delight to speak. In written form, the idiom appeared in poems, songs, and stories. And since it lent itself easily to exaggeration, irony, and humor, the limits of the idiom were fully explored by Italian dialect comedians for their appreciative Italian audiences.

Italglish existed as early as the 1860s. Adolfo Rossi first heard it spoken by worker immigrants on the streets of New York in 1879 and later in the far West. Antonio Margariti spoke it in Rochester and Philadelphia. Within a week after arriving in rural Pennsylvania in 1906, Carmine Iannace had mastered the essential vocabulary of immigrant railroad expressions. Totonno called the idiom the "New York dialect" and used it freely in corresponding with both Italians and Americans. Franco Ciarlantini was intrigued by the immigrant speech while visiting Mulberry Street: "These Italians from South Italy are an active, gay, chaotic, exuberant people, their language a conglomerate of dialect, outrageous English, and untranslatable New York slang."[1] Amy Bernardy was more alarmed than intrigued by what the Boston Italians were doing to her beloved language. "There is in the Italian colonies a special language, written and spoken, used extensively by the educated and uneducated—Italian consuls, ditchdiggers, bankers—comprising Italian words, dialectical phrases, and English terms that are remodeled and filtered through Italian lips."[2]

The speech Bernardy heard was basically Italian in structure and sound, with an admixture of English loan words that were brought into vocal harmony with the speaker's own habits of pronunciation. Giuseppe Prezzolini described the effect as a "deformation of English rather than an adaptation of Italian."[3] This was the first stage; later, the idiom gave way progressively to an approximation of American syntax and pronunciation. An uninitiated Italian, upon hearing the early idiom Bernardy heard, would be able to grasp some of what was said, while the American would understand nothing. In the later stages, as the idiom approached recognizable American English, that same Italian would comprehend nothing, or at least register considerable confusion, while the American with a trained ear and sufficient patience would comprehend some of the words. During several years of residence in an Italian colony, an immigrant often developed a speech pattern that could be understood only by another idiom speaker. Luigi Lombardi met such a man in Philadelphia in 1904, when he attempted to rent a room from an Italian who neither understood English nor spoke recognizable Italian. His speech was a "mixture of dialects" and so "broken" that Lombardi had to get an "interpreter" to understand the terms of the lease.[4]

In its fullest expression, the idiom was unique to the immigrant. The combination of spoken Italian and working-class American English produced a speech that was neither Italian nor English, and was as distinct from either language as any Italian dialect is distinct from proper Italian.[5]

A similar process occurred wherever Italian emigrants settled. Edmondo De Amicis discovered it in Argentina during the late 1880s:

> Those Italians who have lived for many years in Argentina speak a strange language. They associate with the natives and with Italians from other parts of Italy, and this has affected their language. They lose in the process of assimilation a part of their native dialects and acquire some Italian. They confound the Italian and dialect with the local speech patterns, putting Italian endings to Spanish words and vice versa. They literally translate phrases from Italian to Spanish, often changing the meaning of the phrases, and in the course of a conversation will switch repeatedly in mid-sentence from one language to another without conscious effort or apparent realization. You will hear, for example, *si precisa molta plata* for *ci vuol molto danaro* [you need a lot of money], *gustar capitali* for *spender capital* [to spend money], *son a salito con un carigo di trigo* for *son partito con un carico di grano* [I departed with a load of grain].[6]

The speech of Italians who went to Brazil or to the United States during that period underwent parallel changes.

There have been exceptions where in some places linguistic modification has not occurred, despite several generations of residence in the host country. One notable example is the community of Chipilo in Mexico, near Veracruz, now numbering 3,000 Italians, and first settled in 1881 by farmers from the province of Treviso (region of Veneto). The citizens of Chipilo, all descendants of the original settlers, continue to speak a nineteenth-century version of the Venetian dialect.

Some educated Italians were appalled at immigrant speech, regarding the idiom as a corruption of "la bella lingua," a bastardized and illiterate perversion of a proud national linguistic tradition, the gibberish of the Great Unwashed. Other opinions prevailed, however. There was a realization that even though Italglish disfigured both Italian and English, it held little threat to either and, more important, was an interesting aesthetic development and a practical necessity of the time. Linguistic purism is a luxury in certain situations; in the Italian colony there was a need for a common linguistic denominator, a lingua franca, a pidgin Italian dialect. The acquisition of the idiom was an essential first step for the greenhorn, especially in making it possible for him to communicate with Americans. Nor could one be an Italian Boss, for instance, without a full command of Italglish. The idiom revealed neither ignorance, laziness, nor whimsy on the part of the immigrant but rather the use of creative imagination to produce a necessary form of communication, which in fact evolved following the familiar laws of language development.[7]

But Italglish was much more than a practical method of conducting everyday affairs. It became an insider's language, in many respects a reflection of the immigrant experience. For example, *Americane*, or *Merichen* in the dialect, meant "American." But because the ending *cane* or *chen* means dog, the term could also connote "American dogs." Verbs would be constructed from nouns for no apparent reason other than to ridicule the idiom: *ciungarre* (to chew gum) was devised from the Italglish *ciunga* (chewing gum) because it sounded silly to the Italian ear—*io ciungo, tu ciunghi,* and so on. The Fourth of July was called *Il Forte Gelato* (The Great Freeze), a play on the similarity of sounds. A story was invented to account for this special holiday; *Il Forte Gelato* was celebrated, newcomers would be told, because on that day years ago it was so cold that all the rivers froze. Thanksgiving Day was known as *La Festa delle Galline* (Chickens Day) rather than *Il Giorno di Ringraziamento.* Why Chickens Day? one would ask. Because on the last Thursday of November the American people killed all their chickens.[8] *Re erode* was the immigrant's rendering of the word railroad. Since *Re* in Italian means king, the term implied a certain attitude toward railroad employment—the railroad as the master of the worker's fate. The possibilities for this kind of linguistic playfulness were endless. A popular singing trio as late as the 1940s took the song lyrics "Just because you think you got something" and replaced the word "because" with the immigrant word for toilet, which is a homonym—"Just *baccausa* you think you got something." Hopalong Cassidy, the cowboy movie star, was called Hopalong Chesadisci, from the dialectical equivalent of *che cosa dici* (watta ya say), which was a common immigrant salutation. Babe Ruth was known to the Italians as *Il Bambino* or *Bigga Bambino.*

Anthony Turano estimated that Italianized English words made up as much as one-fourth of the spoken language of the immigrants.[9] Such a generalization is misleading, however, because the number and kinds of terms used were contingent on several factors. A wife's vocabulary, to the extent that she remained in the home, would center on the household, while her husband's would extend to his job and other relationships in the community. Those immigrants who worked in factories or engaged in commerce had occasion to hear and adopt a variety of expressions and consequently developed a richer vocabulary than those in isolated work gangs away from the larger Italian colonies. Railroad workers learned chiefly the terms appropriate to their jobs. Iannace as a boy in Italy, listening to returned workers recount their experiences in America, concluded that America was a network of railways because only trains, tracks, and bridges were discussed. Pasquale D'Angelo and his coworkers got along by adding to their Italian speech a dozen or so practical American terms: "We learned a few words about the job. Then we added to our list such words as bread, shirt, gloves, and milk. And that is all. We formed our own little world—one of many in this country. And the people around us who spoke in strange languages might have been phantoms for all the influence that they had upon us or for all we cared for them." [10] It is not likely that any one immigrant, unless he traveled extensively and held several jobs, had occasion to hear and use the entire Italglish vocabulary. A railroad worker in Ohio would know *sciabola* and *storo* but would find the New York phrase *andare a Flabusse* incomprehensible.

As a fully developed idiom spoken by a large portion of Italians in America, Italglish did not endure more than five or six decades. With the cessation of mass migration and rapid immigrant Americanization after the First World War, the idiom began to erode long before it reached a mature stage of development. Its final vestiges are to be found within the household. In those cases where the idiom was transmitted from immigrants to their American-born offspring, it was done in piecemeal fashion—a word here, a phrase there—rather than as the major means of communication. Once the idiom had served its purpose, it was quietly aborted by the very community that had conceived it and was replaced by a working-class American English containing only trace elements of the earlier pronunciation and syntax.

Many Italians were fearful that the existence of an immigrant language was a sign that the Italians would come to occupy permanently one of the lower subclasses in American society. To the extent that the idiom becomes the chief vehicle of expression—spoken and written—in the Italian colonies, they argued, the Italians will remain separated from the mainstream of the host society, making it highly improbable that future generations will be able to achieve social, economic, and political equality.

From the perspective of the 1890s, such an outcome seemed very plausible, but there was no real chance that Italglish could have developed into a distinct sublanguage, to be transmitted from one generation to another as tenaciously as Pennsylvania Dutch or Cajun. It could not have happened because the Italians did not want it to. They always saw the idiom as a temporary expedient, an intermediate form of communication that was known to be a transitional language and not competitive with either "la bella lingua" or standard English. No one was lulled into believing that it was a "true" language, at least not for very long. For one thing, it was woefully incomplete as a general means of communication. Moreover, no one championed the idiom; even those immigrants who knew only their local dialects were acutely conscious of the noble status of the Italian language and quick to show their children the sharp distinctions between Italian, the spoken dialects, and the language of the immigrants. In the final analysis, Italglish was doomed to die because of its close association with the greenhorn status. There was too much pressure from every direction to be *appe tu dette*, modern in one's outlook and behavior. As long as an immigrant relied solely upon the idiom, he remained socially backward and could not participate fully in American life.

Characteristics of the Idiom

The immigrants altered the pronunciation (and consequently the spelling) of English terms in the same manner that loan words are adjusted by Italian linguists when they enter the Italian language. How would beefsteak or lynching be pronounced by an Italian? *Bistecca* and *linciaggio* would be the expected forms, and these are the words one finds in an Italian dictionary. One will also find *cognacche* (cognac), *alt* (halt), and *Quacquero* (Quaker).

Many Italglish terms are close enough to English to be recognizable to the American ear. English words that have vowel endings and approximate the pronunciation rhythm of Italian, such as *Bufalò* (Buffalo), *Cicago* (Chicago), and Utica, would present no problems to the outsider. Terms such as *bosso, campo, rancio, vischi, picchinicca, giobba* could be recognized if the context were made clear. But if the pronunciation or syllable stress deviates substantially from the English, the words become incomprehensible to the uninitiated listener: *scecchenze, sciumecco, monghì.* Other phrases, literal translations from the English to the Italian, could be appreciated only by the immigrant: for instance, downtown (New York) was rendered *abbasso città* (the city below). The outsider would also misunderstand certain words: *opportunità* to the immigrant meant "job." The appropriate Italian for "opportunity" is *occasione.*

The dialectical background of the speaker determined to a large extent the way in which the word was managed. Each Italian would affix his own dialectical terminations and inflect the term by reference to his prior linguistic conditioning. A Sicilian saying boat pronounced it *bottù.* A Pugliese said *botto,* or *botta,* or left off the final vowel—*bott.* A Pugliese said *la iarde* for yard, while a Neapolitan said *gliarda. Ghella* for a Toscan would be *nghella* for a Calabrian. Of an evening, the young blade from Puglia would *fa u sport* when he got dressed to go *abbasso città.* For the young man from Calabria with the same intention, it was *fa lu spurta.* The fact that each village in Italy had its own local dialect produced any amount of variation in the pronunciation of the idiom. Depending on where you came from in Sicily, you might say *abburdatu* for boarder or *bburdatu.* A Calabrese from Reggio Calabria said *spinsiru* (shirt or light jacket, from Spencer); his counterpart from Catanzaro insisted on *spinsaru.*

Not only the dialectical background of the speaker but the non-Italians with whom the immigrant came into contact shaped his pronunciation. The Italians in New York borrowed terms from the Jewish idiom and imitated Irish styles of pronunciation. A week after Totonno landed in New York, he went to a theater on Third Avenue. What he heard was *Toid* Avenue, and thereafter it became for him *Toidavenne.* The theater was near *Toiditoid* Street. Many immigrant terms, such as *vorche* (work) and *ticcià* (teacher), were directly shaped by the then prevailing New York speech patterns.

Dialect speakers from South Italy changed the English "o" to "u." Good became *gude* and good morning was approximated by *cummoni*.

The English "w" sounded like a "v." "Water" was pronounced *vuora*; the immigrant took a bath in a *vescettobbi* and traveled to *Vasciadone* to see the White House.

The aspirated "h" and "th" gave the immigrant lifelong problems. Hooray had to be *orrè*; tooth became *tutta*; teeth, *tutti*; height, *aite*. The word "though" sounded like "dough," and the closest the immigrant could get to "through" was *tru*. He ate when he was *ongri* and lived in his *ausa*. Cowboys rode on *orsi*. The "th" was handled differently depending on its position in the word: "this" was pronounced *dissi*; "nothing" was rendered *natinchi*; "month," *monte*; and "mouth," *maufu*.

There was a tendency to trill or draw out an "r." "All right" was pronounced *orraite*, and the word "farm" would sound much like this: *farrrma*.

The "a" ending corresponded to "er" in English. Daughter was rendered *dora* and lover *lova*. The rule was relaxed for terms that would have sounded awkward. For instance, *carpenta* is not a good solution for carpenter but *carpentiere* is.

The "s" sound was drawn out and often sounded more like a single or double "z." *Bisiniss* was sometimes *bisinizz*. Short phrases containing the verb "is" were combined to form one word with a double "z." Common examples are *azzonoffo* (that's enough), *azzollo* (that's all) and *vazzumara* (what's the matter). Such expressions were actually the backbone of the idiom.

The immigrants often carried over into Italglish the tendency in Italian to attach the definite article, "the," to abstract nouns, which changed the sound of the word. Thus *airisce* was usually pronounced *l'airisce*; *aisscrim* was more commonly rendered *l'aisscrim*; *ongala*, *l'ongala*.

Questions of gender and number were often handled in a haphazard manner. Those who knew the Italian rules of grammar would follow them: *trocco* (truck) became *trocchi* in the plural, and *il bosso* and *la bossa* in the plural were *i bossi* and *le bosse*. The immigrant might follow the rules of his dialect or he might ignore the matter all together: *polissiman* could be one policeman or several. Where the vowel endings were dropped, the plural might be indicated through the definite article. There could be one *ghella* or two *ghelle*, or *u ghel* (the girl) and *i ghel* (the girls). The problem seemed to lie in the inability of the immigrant to successfully grapple with the English plural "s" ending. The result was most likely a drawn out "s" or "z" sound. Shoes was approximated by *sciussi* and clams *clemisi*, with the "e" stressed. The "ice" ending was solved similarly: police, *pulissi*. *Cestenotto* meant chestnut. What about its plural form? One would expect *cestenotti*. But the immigrant's valiant attempt to add an "s" resulted in *cestenozzi*. Gender endings were far from sancrosanct. The immigrant might use either masculine or feminine as the mood struck him. A man could be a *bommo* or a *bomma*, more likely the latter, and *bomma* could also indicate a woman whose reputation in the community had a suspected taint. And a change in the vowel ending could change the meaning rather than the number or gender: *grosseria* meant "grocery store," but the plural *grosserie* signified "groceries." [11]

An Italian immigrant who died in a mining town in Nevada left behind a will. An Italian professor was asked to translate the document into English. The professor could not complete the task because a number of the words were not Italian and did not appear to be English. Turano, who had been raised in an Italian colony in the Southwest, was asked to look at the will. He quickly recognized the troublesome words, including *morgico* (mortgage) and *nota* (promissory note), as part of the immigrant vocabulary. [12]

The immigrant had to borrow words from the English language when his Italian vocabulary did not contain the appropriate word. A new environment forced the acquisition of new terms. The concepts of boyfriend and girlfriend were new to the Italians. Since their system of courtship was unlike the American, their native language did not contain such terms. Consequently, the American terms came into the immigrant idiom as *falò* (fellow) and *mia ghella* (my girl). The idiom would also respond to American changes in such expressions; when "fellow" became outmoded and was replaced by "boyfriend," the immigrants followed with their equivalent, *boifrendo*.

Not all loan words, however, were borrowed for lack of suitable Italian equivalents. Why use *bosso* when you have *padrone* in your vocabulary? Why use *sciabola* when you have the perfectly respectable *pala*? To be sure, the Italian words continued to be used in many instances, but the influence of the adapted American terms was strongly felt by Italians who heard them on the job and those who wanted to learn English.

Linguistic ingenuity among the immigrants included the construction of words from both Italian and English. What would one call a job fee paid to the Boss? *Bossatura* combined an English noun with an Italian suffix. The same procedure was used to form *canabuldogga*, a combination of *cane* (dog) and bulldog. How would one say steamshovel in Italglish? Since *stima* and *sciabola* already existed, the problem was quickly solved—*stimasciabola*.

Some Italglish words were so fully incorporated into the immigrant vocabulary that they became indistinguishable from any other Italian word. *Sciabola* (shovel) is a good example; once accepted as an Italian word, it became subject to the rules of Italian grammar and was used in different parts of speech. That person who used the *sciabola* became a *sciabolatore* or *sciabolatrice*. What does a *sciabolatore* do? Well, he shovels (*sciabola*) or he is shoveling (*sta sciabolando*) or he has shoveled (*ha sciabolato*). Invented verbs were based on English words—*spiccare* (to speak), *giumpare* (to jump), *abbordare* (to board), *strappare* (to strop a razor), *fichisare* (to fix), *loffare* (to loaf), *boxare* (to box)—and subsequently conjugated as Italian verbs. A sufficient vocabulary of this kind would make it possible for an immigrant to construct sentences consisting almost entirely of immigrant terms. The language would sound Italian, but it would not be understood by anyone except a fellow immigrant.

The Neapolitan dialect had a marked influence on Italglish. *Ncuop* corresponds to the word up. *Ncuop* was used alone or to form the words for "uptown" (*coppetane*) (the Sicilians said *oppitauni*) and "upstairs" (*coppesteso*). *Dollaro*, an obvious rendering of "dollar," never took hold among the southern Italians. Their preference was for the dialect terms *scudo* or *pezzo*. Pizza was combined with "pie" to form *pizzapaia*. Literally, the term is redundant because it means pizza pizza—or pie pie. *Pizzapaia* had sufficient ambiguity so that even the linguists of the day could only wonder at its origin and true meaning. It was used in a number of contexts: to mean pizza, a piece of pie or a specific type of pastry, or a man of questionable masculinity.

The idiom was full of easily learned phrases borrowed from non-Italians that could convey a variety of sentiments and emotions, depending on the context. Greenhorns would be initiated into the world of American working-class expressions as soon as they arrived at the job site. Without doubt, the universal Italglish phrase was *azzorrait* (that's all right), an all-purpose instrument of social intercourse. It was marvelously suited to the immigrant worker, who tended to be a man of few words and who was never quite sure whether he understood what was being said to him by an American. *Azzorrait* could mean yes; don't mention it; no harm has been done; good; very good; that's a good job; or have I done correctly? There was no limit to its usefulness. The expression accumulated other shadings of meaning, including: please do; help yourself; I don't care; suit yourself; no, I am not insulted; do a better job next time. A complete conversation could be carried on with an interchange of *azzorraits*. For example, the full text of a conversation on a road gang might go as follows. Greenhorn, pointing to the hole he had dug: "*Azzorrait?*" Foreman: "*Azzorrait.*"

The first American expression Antonio Arrighi heard was *orriope* (hurry up). Every other word from the sailors on the Brooklyn docks was *orriope*. When Arrighi entered Castle Garden, the immigration official yelled *orriope*. When a policeman chased a sleeping Arrighi from a park bench, the policeman shouted *orriope*. Arrighi got the idea that with a little effort he could make *orriope* substitute for the English he did not know. By his second day, Arrighi had added two more expressions: "get out" and "fire." So equipped, he decided to spend that night in City Hall Park. "While roaming about there I found seats long enough for a man to lie down and sleep. While sleeping I felt the blow of a heavy club on the soles of my feet. I opened my eyes and saw a policeman standing over me. So I said to him, 'Hurry up— get out—fire.' The bully struck me again." [13]

Sannemagogna (son of a gun) was another versatile phrase; it could express anger, astonishment (What do you know about that!), or bewilderment, or simply serve as a neutral filler to keep the conversation flowing. *Sciaddappa* had a more restricted function. When the mother said to her son who would not eat, "*Mangia e sciaddappa*" (Eat and be silent), her intentions were the best. But when she would say to him, "*Sciaddappa you mauta*" (Shut your mouth) and he did not, then *bigga trobolo* was close at hand.

Buona ccianza was used to indicate the hope of a favorable turn of events or an opportunity that one should pursue. A mother would say *buona ccianza* to her son in regard to a job opening and to her daughter in regard to a marriage prospect. The expression also replaced the Italian expression *buona fortuna* when someone was departing.

On the road gangs and in the factories, when the worker needed a refreshing drink of water on a hot and humid summer's day, he would yell for the waterboy—"Hey, boy!" which was pronounced *reboia*. Not only did *reboia* soon become the job title for the waterboy, it also served as the form of address to those lower in the hierarchy of command. Considering the amount of American profanity to which the immigrants were exposed, the idiom contains very few swear words that were spoken with any frequency. The most common ones were *gadem*, *godaelle*, and *sanemabicce*. *Godaelle* when combined with the Italian verb *mandare* meant to lose one's job, to be sent to Hell by the Boss; *Il Bosso mi ha mandato a godaelli*. Pronouncing the profane term directly would sometimes be sidestepped by substituting a similar-sounding Italian word while intending the profanity. Among the Sicilians, for instance, *gaddina* (chicken) was a common variation on *gadem*.[14]

Ma sciur, composed of the Italian "but" and the Italglish "sure," was an agreeable expression. It could mean certainly; of course; be happy to. Can I have this? *Ma sciur*. Are you working tonight? *Ma sciur*. Let's go eat. *Ma sciur*. The opposite of *ma sciur* was *ma no*.

The greenhorn and those who did not take on American ways were often exposed to ridicule. Old Country customs were considered in America to be *olda faesce* (old-fashioned). Pressure was applied to become *appe tu dette* (up to date). This process involved divesting oneself of the Old Country wardrobe, mannerisms, values—anything that smacked of the prior life—without delay or remorse. The pace of American life was continuous and rapid, change was expected, and one had to keep up with the latest fads and fashions. To accuse anyone of not being *appe tu dette* was to insult that person and to put him or her on the defensive. Fathers who would not allow their daughters to date American style were not *appe tu dette*. Nor were widows who wore black, or mothers who prepared pasta for their children at each and every meal.

Italglish in Context

Italianized English words were quickly incorporated into the Italian speech of the immigrant. If an immigrant did not want to purchase secondhand furniture, he might say, "*Io non voglio comprare forniture sechenenze*," using the immigrant terminology *forniture sechenenze* for secondhand furniture. *Sechenenze* could also mean a shabby situation: *Che maniera sechenenze di trattar la gente* (What a lousy way to treat people).

The idiomatic phrases became so commonplace that even in official circles they sometimes replaced the equivalent Italian. Gaetano Conte relates an episode he witnessed at Ellis Island, when an immigration officer asked a newcomer for her address. *"Avete addresso?"* he asked her repeatedly. She stood there in complete confusion. *Addresso* meant nothing to her, although *indirizzo* would have.[15] After a few weeks in America, that woman was no doubt using not only *addresso* but also many other immigrant words. The process of linguistic assimilation was rapid. Within a short period after his arrival, Totonno's diary notations were sprinkled with terms like *Broccolino, sobuè, orrait, bachcaus, ais scrim, pis vuorche,* and others. Here is an excerpt from his diary after six weeks in America: *"Dopo dormito, scendiamo per andare alla* fattoria *che si dove va prendare la paga. . . . Nella mancanza del* bosso *detti due* ponti *di carne"* (After sleeping, we went to the factory to collect our pay. . . . While the boss was out of the store I sold two pounds of meat). As his years in America progressed, Totonno's use of the idiom in his writing decreased and by the end of the First World War had all but disappeared. *Scudo* had become "dollar," *toidavenne* was transformed to "Third Avenue," and *picchinicca* was in transition from "pic a nic" to "pic nic."

Arthur Livingston collected several illustrative examples of immigrant speech. Here is a sampling from an article published in 1920.[16]

Lo trobolo *che se passa lo saccio* (I know the troubles you have seen).

La carta *serve a tante e tante cose: può ave' na* giobba *in* corte, o *fà o* polisse (You can do many things with your citizenship papers: you can get a job in court or become a policeman).

Il mio cognato Gecco, *il* faietatore, *mi fece prender questa* giobba *qua sulla* tracca (My brother-in-law Jack, the fighter, got me this job on the railroad).

Rossi constructed an imaginary conversation between an immigrant and his wife based on the immigrant *gergo* (slang) that he heard in New York in 1880. An excerpt follows.[17]

     Hai salutato o' bosso *iersera?* (Did you see the Boss yesterday?)

Sì, se vedessi che casa commifò, *che ha! L'ho trovato in* Elisabetta stretta *che si faceva* scianinare *i* botti *e m'ha condotto* incoppaustese *in camera sua. Ci ha il* carpetto *in casa, capisci e l'*aisboxa. *Sua moglie è un'irlandese, una donna che* guarda bene. *Il* bosso *era tornato l'altro giorno in* stimbotto *dall'* Albania *dove hanno* stoppato *il lavoro. E tu dove sei andato iersera?*
(Yes, and you should see what a comfortable house he has! I found him on Elizabeth Street getting his boots shined and he took me upstairs to his apartment. He has a carpet on the floor, of course, and an icebox. His wife is Irish, a good looking woman. The boss returned the other day on a steamboat from Albany because work there has stopped. Where did you go last night?)

One evening in 1909, Bernardy stood in Boston's North Square listening to a speech being given during a political campaign to a group of workers, and transcribed a portion of it. The speaker, a southern Italian, used the Neapolitan dialect mingled with terms from the immigrant idiom that the workers would understand.[18]

Tutt'a gente pote fare mistecchi; *u'* prevete mistecca *'ncoppa u'*bucco *d'a messa; u* sciabolatore *quanne* sciabole *u'*dorte *int'u* diccio *or sulle* tracche. *U* mistecco *nu ruina u galantuomo. Ma u galantuomo sape dicere sempre:* Schiusmi *aggio fatto nu grosso* mistecco *e mo' ciabbadaraggio.* (Everyone makes mistakes. A priest can make a mistake while copying a mass book. A ditch-digger can make a mistake when he shovels dirt into a ditch or on a track bed. A mistake can ruin a gentleman. But a gentleman can always say: Excuse me. I have made a big mistake, and now I have to be more careful.)

The dialect comedians made extensive use of the immigrant idiom in the Italian theater around the country. The style was derived from the *macchietta* tradition of Naples, where the colorful and robust dialect was used to develop Neapolitan character sketches, in which the literal meaning of dialect words was often accompanied by a ribald double sense. The *macchietta* in America, called the *macchietta coloniale*, was adapted to a mixed audience of Italians from different parts of Italy; it reflected the emotions, predicaments, and fantasies of the

immigrant. The following example also illustrates the frequent use of
the immigrant idiom.

*Na sera dentro na barra americana dove il patrone era
americano, lo visco era americano, la birra era americana,
ce stava na ghenga de* loffari *tutti americani; solo io non ero
americano; quanno a tutto nu mumento me mettone mmezzo e me
dicettono:* Alo' spaghetti. Iu *mericano* men? *No! No! mi* Italy
men! Iu blacco enze? *No, no! Mi* laico *mio* contri. *Mi* laico Italy!
A questo punto mi chiavaieno lo primo fait! *Dice* orrè *for America! Io tuosto:* Orrè *for Italy!* Orrè *for Italy!* Nato fait *e* nato fait,
fino a che me facetteno addurmentare; ma però, orrè *for America
nun o dicette!* (One evening inside an American bar where the
owner was an American, the whiskey was American, the beer
was American, there was a gang of loafers, each one an American. I was the only non-American. All of a sudden the gang
members crowded around me and they said, Hello Spaghetti. Are
you an American? No! No! I am an Italian. Are you a Black
Hand? No! No! I like my country. I like Italy! At this point I was
struck by a fist. Say hooray for America! I said, rather, hooray
for Italy! I was struck again. Say hooray for America! Hooray for
Italy! Hooray for Italy! I repeated. Another punch and still another, until they knocked me out. But I never said hooray for
America.)
Quanno me scietaie, me trovaie ncoppa lu marciapiedi cu nu
pulizio *vicino che diceva:* Ghiroppe bomma! *Io ancora stunato
alluccaie:* America nun gudde! Orrè for Italy! *Sapete lu* pulizio
che facette? Mi arrestò. (When I woke up I found myself on the
sidewalk with a policeman standing over me. Get up you bum,
he said. Still stunned, I yelled: America is no good! Hooray for
Italy! Do you know what he did? He arrested me.)
Quando fu la mattina, lu giorge *mi dicette:* Wazzo maro
laste naite? *Io risponetta:* No tocche *inglese! No?* Tenne *dollari.
E quello porco dello* giorge *nun scherzava, perchè le diece* pezze
se le pigliaie. (The next morning the judge asked me, What happened last night? I responded, I don't speak English! No? he said.
Ten dollars. And that pig of a judge wasn't kidding for he took the
ten bucks.)[19]

The most famous and widely acclaimed Italian comedian in America was Eduardo Migliaccio, whose stage name was Farfariello. Farfariello wrote much of his own material, capturing the essence of Italian life in America through his portrayals of immigrant stereotypes. Being a product of South Italy, he easily mastered and used the immigrant idiom (and undoubtedly contributed to it). Here is one of the *macchiette* from his repertoire, entitled *"Portame 'a casa mia"* (Take me home).[20]

Alla corte notturna	At night court
il giorge *disse: di*	the judge said: tell me,
chi t'ha venduto il dringo?	who sold you the drink?
ce voglio anda' pur'i.	I would like to go myself.
Però la legge e legge,	However the law is the law.
te truove nnanze a mme	You find yourself before me,
o il carcere or la multa	either jail or a fine.
che posso fa' per te?!	What can I do for you?!

Farfariello's talents and his astounding success forced the New York theater critics to pay attention to him, even though his performances were in Italian and his audiences made up of ordinary Italian immigrants. The following review by Edmund Wilson appeared in the *New Republic* in 1925:

> The Italian theatre in New York possesses quite a remarkable impersonator in the old music hall tradition. Farfariello is an Italian who has lived in America for now nearly thirty years, during which time he has appeared throughout the country and become known wherever Italians have a theatre to go to. He can appeal only to Italian-American audiences—and to them only on a basis of what is European in their culture. He has invented an enormous repertoire of characterizations, based on Italian types he has known or imagined, and compels his audience to recognize them.[21]

The immigrant idiom was spoken to the customers who frequented the Italian restaurants of New York. The owners of these restaurants thought that Americans knew nothing about good cooking, and these verses entitled "Spaghetti House," written in the idiom of the Italian restaurant trade, lament the lack of culinary sophistication of the typical American customer.[22]

Dica, signore, come li voule, al dente?
Tomato sauce *e parmigiano* cheese;
Tutto italiano, sa pur la padella,
il basilico, il chef e l'assistente.

Li vendon cotti now *in farmacia,*
(figli di un cane!) I mean *il* drug store,
E in tutti i presto luncheons *e* luncheonettes
Di questa terra di rabdomanzia.

Ma qui, da me, amico e servitore
D'ogni italiano e d'ogni buon custome,
C'è l'arte culinaria del Paese,
Dove ogni fiore smells *e di che odore!*

Malinconie, lo so, per questa gente,
Son le parole mie. Ma, never mind,
Ne parlevemo un'altra volta a cena . . .
Monzù: un expresso *pel signore . . . al dente!*

(Tell me. sir, how do you want your spaghetti, al dente?
Tomato sauce and parmesan cheese;
All Italian, even the pan,
the basil, the chef and his assistant.

They sell spaghetti cooked now in a farmacia,
[Son of a bitch] I mean the drugstore
And in all of the fast food places
In this country where everything is possible.

But here, with me, friend and waiter
For every Italian and every good customer,
You will find the culinary art of Italy,
Where every flower smells, and what an odor!

It is sad, I know, for these Americans,
That's my opinion. But never mind,
We will talk about it at supper . . .
Monzù: A quick dish of spaghetti for the gentleman . . . al
    dente!)

Shop signs in the Italian colonies were sometimes phrased in the immigrant idiom. Bernardy saw this notice on the window of a furniture

store in Boston: FORNITURE FOFAMILY A POCHI CENTS LA SETTIMANNA
(Family furniture, a few cents each week).[23] Even the Italian newspapers, which tended to set Italglish words in quotation marks to
indicate that they were not proper Italian, soon incorporated a few
immigrant terms. For example, *forniture* and *grosseria* completely replaced their Italian equivalents. *Yard* was used both as a measure in
advertisements—"32¢ la yard"—and to mean the back yard (of a
house) or a lawn. PULITE LE STRADE E LE YARDE (Clean the streets and
the back yards), one newspaper headline urged.[24]

Here are two examples of the use of the idiom in Italian
newspapers.

> *Da vendere o affittare*, building *in buona posizione, con
> locali adatti per* grosseria *o* barra. Bisnis *garantito* rendite cheap.
> *Rivolgersi alla* firma *P.R.&C. Carri lungo il* block. (To sell or
> rent, building in a good location, with suitable rooms for a gro-
> cery store or bar. Guaranteed business. Cheap rent. Contact the
> P.R.&C. firm. Along a streetcar route.)[25]

> *Budora Giovanni, di 34a., 4505 S. Marshfield, è stato
> arrestato e messo sotto* bondo *di $15.00 perchè accusato dai suoi*
> buordanti satirata *la loro 8nne figliuola in quel* buordo. (Giovanni
> Budora, 34 years of age, of 4505 S. Marshfield, has been arrested
> and put under a bond of $15 because he has been accused by the
> operators of his boarding house of sodomizing their 8-year-old
> daughter in that boarding house.)[26]

The first example illustrates the middle stage in the transition from the
immigrant idiom to a form of comprehensible English. The acquisition of correct English pronunciation and the habitual use of English,
when they did occur, evolved gradually. The speech of veteran immigrants was more likely to be a mixture of Italian, dialect, and English,
shifting from one to another in a sentence without conscious motive.
The domestic language that William Murray spoke with his mother is
an excellent illustration of family speech in Italian households.

> I spoke only English, interspersed with an occasional phrase
> of Italian, and conversations around our apartment sometimes
> baffled monolingual visitors. "Che fai fatto in school oggi?" my

mother might ask. "Well, I turned in my French theme, ma non era the best I could do. Non ho avuto tempo, what with all that storia of the Trojan war to read." [27]

For Gabriel Iamurri, even after several years of residence in America, English remained an insurmountable hurdle. His early encounters with Americans invariably ended badly. One day in Perry, Maine, he went into a clothing store to buy a shirt. He confronted the clerk and said, "Me, me, mister, wanda shorta, guda shorta." The clerk looked bewildered, so Iamurri tried again. "Me, me, mister, wanda shorta, guda shorta, capish?" Realizing that he was making no headway, Iamurri tried "sheet" instead of "shorta." The clerk's face brightened. "Ah, at last, I've got you this time, my boy. You want them for a single bed, don't you?" the clerk said as he put the sheets on the counter. Iamurri got agitated. "No, no, sheet! sheet! sheet!" The clerk, concluding that he was being called a four-letter word, chased the young immigrant out into the street. A month later Iamurri went to a farmhouse to buy a dozen eggs. "Me, me, mister, wada aks," he said to the farmer. The farmer took him to the shed, pointed to his axes, and invited Iamurri to help himself. [28]

Americanisms in Italy

When immigrants returned to Italy, either permanently or for a visit, they took back with them the language of the Italian colonies. Those who had not been away very long had relatively little trouble fitting back into the speech patterns of their villages. Their exposure to Italglish had been as limited as their exposure to American society. If they had associated chiefly with *paesani* in America, their Italian dialects remained pretty much intact. These returnees used their few Americanisms when they met other repatriates, or to impress the villagers, but as time wore on, the American terminology would be used less and less. The immigrant terms that appeared so often in Totonno's diary during his four-year sojourn in America completely disappeared once he returned to Italy, to be replaced by a style that was more Italianate in vocabulary and structure. If the immigrant idiom carried over in his speech, it is not evident in his writing. His conditioning to the

immigrant idiom was not thorough enough to supplant his Italian vocabulary: what was *Bosso* for him in America became once again
Padrone in Italy.

For other immigrants, however, linguistic assimilation into the
Italian colonies had gone much deeper. Just as they had replaced their
Italian values with immigrant values, they had replaced their Italian
speech with the speech of the colonies. There they spoke the immigrant idiom much more often than their native tongue, and through
repeated use the idiom had become accepted as a legitimate language.
This was particularly the case for those immigrants who had rarely
ventured outside of the Italian colonies. Progressively but uncon-
sciously, they lost command over their dialects and their ability to distinguish what was Italian from what was Italianized English. Not only
did *spiccare* replace *parlare*, but *parlare* was forgotten. Those immigrants who had been gone from Italy for many years thought they were
speaking Italian when they returned. A repatriate who said *ho* brocco
una legga rather than *mi ho rotto una gamba*, or *mi* no spiccare
inglese rather than *mi non parlo inglese*, had forgotten the Italian
words for "break," "leg," and "speak." His English was also inadequate. Not only did he not *spiccare* Italian, he did not *spiccare* English either. At first the Italians back home thought that they were hearing English, but it soon became apparent that the repatriates were
speaking a corrupted Italian, one that had been penetrated by a series
of "barbarisms." The problem was confounded when the older returnees, who would dig into their memories for the correct dialectical
expression, used phraseology that had become antiquated in Italy. The
speech that had served them so well in America was now a disadvantage. The subculture that they had developed in America had not only
made it impossible for them and their children to move into the American mainstream, it was proving to be a barrier to successful rein-
tegration into Italian society. The reaction to emigrant speech that
Leonardo Sciascia witnessed in his Sicilian village was typical. "In
Racalmuto the speech of those who were visiting from America made
us laugh. The children would chase the returnees down the street
begging them to speak so that they could scream with delight and
ridicule them." [29]

Nevertheless, studies done by Italian scholars indicate conclu-
sively that Americanisms flourished in every part of Italy where re-

patriates settled and competed with equivalent Italian terms. *Baccau'* was heard regularly in Tuscany. *Briccoliere* circulated freely in Sicily, *boxare* in Campania, and *tichetta* and *ghenga* in Marche. A. Menarini heard some Bologna workers, who had returned from America many years before, use the Italglish *assuranza* (insurance) rather than the Italian *assicurazione*. *Fattoria*, *stimbotte*, and *ferribotte* penetrated the Genovese dialect, and *bomma* became a standard term of insult in the teeming streets of lower Naples, vying with the traditional *figlio di puttana* for popularity. In 1907, Rossi heard many of the basic immigrant terms (*bosso*, *sciabola*, *bordo*, *tracche*) while interviewing returned emigrants from America in Basilicata and Calabria. A few years later Bernardy visited the same part of Italy and reported a similar experience to a Boston Italian newspaper.[30]

In 1926 Vignoli collected hundreds of Italglish terms that had become part of the dialect of Amaseno. One Amasenese meeting another on the street might ask, *"Avaia?"* (How are you?), to which the response would be, *"Mi file gudde"* (I feel good). In the province of Lucca, the response was *"puriguddi"* (pretty good). "Where are you going?" another would ask. *"Mi gone uom"* (I'm going home) would be the reply. The vernacular of Castro dei Volsci had already been significantly influenced by immigrant speech by the turn of the century. A repatriated emigrant was a *Muricano* (American) who would say *fai* (fire) rather than *fucco* when asking for a light. When the *Muricano* went into a store to negotiate a price he would ask, "Ammoccia *cheste"* (How much is this)? If someone gave the *Muricano* a difficult time, his response would be, *"Che ttemporta a tte? Chiste so* bisinissi *nostri"* (What's it to you? That's our business).[31]

La mano nera returned to Naples as the *blacco enze* (Black Hand) and *sciaine* took hold to such an extent that it threatened to replace the classic term used to refer to the street urchins of Naples—*scugnizzi*. The *scugnizzi* live by their wits. Among other activities, they are shoeshine boys. The immigrant verb *sciainare* was also used in the context of a man who had shed his work clothes, shaved, bathed and perfumed, and put on his Sunday best: *Tonio la domenica è tutte* sciainato (On Sundays Tony is all dressed up). *Bossu* and *bisinissi* became part of the Palermo argot. "To postpone *bisinissi* until later" was communicated by the expression *bai bai* (by and by). Cigarettes were lighted with a *mecciu* (match), and astonishment could be expressed by the phrase *boimerri* (by Mary), which probably is Irish in origin.

Even some American profanity survived the return trip. *Sannemabicce* was heard to echo up and down the Italian peninsula, each regional dialect giving the term its own pronunciation. A Toscan would say *sana babbicia*; a Sicilian, *salamapeci*; a Pugliese, *sanamabicci*. During the evening card games at the tables outside of the bars in Puglia, one could hear a joyful *fachingù* (fucking good) at the turn of a good hand, as well as a curt *fagoff*.

Comprehension of the immigrant idiom by the uninitiated Italian was further complicated by the phonetic similarity between several Italglish and Italian terms. The homonyms are the same in sound and spelling, but their meanings and origins differ. The first immigrant word that Turano heard when he arrived from Italy to live in an Italian colony in New México was *sciabola*. But to him, *sciabola* meant saber: "I was both puzzled and amused during my first week in America when I heard a laborer say quite casually that his daily work involved the use of a *pico* and a *sciabola*—that is to say, a pick and a saber!" [32] If Turano was confused, the Italians back home were bewildered. The immigrant word *cuccio* (church) is the Italian word for donkey. *Grosseria* and *fattoria* are Italian words for "wholesale outlet" and "farm." If a returning emigrant said that in America he had been a *genitore* (janitor), the Italians would understand "parent." If he said he shoveled *culo* (coal), the image of buttocks would appear in the listener's mind. The immigrant rendered the term "gas pipe" as *pipe del grasso*. *Pipe* in Italian is a tobacco pipe, and *grasso* means "fat." Others include,

ITALGLISH TERM	ENGLISH MEANING	ITALIAN MEANING
rendita	rent	income
boia	boy	executioner
fessa	face	fool
arte	heart	art
stinco	stink	shin bone
stima	steam	estimate
omaccio	how much	big, ugly man
guai	why	troubles
sciocchezza	showcase	joke
uliveta	elevated train	olive grove

The Italglish term for women, *uomene*, has approximately the same pronunciation as the Italian word for men, *uomini*. This similarity is humorously exploited by Francesco Perri in his novel *Emigranti*. Perri took his material from emigrants he met in Pandora, Calabria. In the following excerpt a returnee, who thinks that *uomene* is *uomini*, is patiently explaining to his relatives the status of women in America.

"In America the women rule," responded Sperli. "They are the bosses."

Rocco's eyes widened. "The women rule? What kind of country is that?"

"That is the kind of country it is. America is a republic. And in a republic the women rule. In fact in America women are called *uomini*."

The girls shouted in unison—"*Uomini!*"—and burst into loud laughter. "What are you talking about, Sperli?" Passarelli said. "How is it possible that a *donna* [woman] is called a *uomo* [man]?"

"You don't believe me? I swear to God. Ask anyone who has been there. The woman is called *uomo* and the man is called *menne*. When a man is rich he is called *riccimenne*; when he is in commerce he is a *bissini menne*."

They all stood there with their mouths wide open as they listened to the stories about the strange customs in that mysterious America. The two countries, Italy and America, were so different. Women in America are *uomini*, and they rule.[33]

Perri was not the first writer to introduce the immigrant idiom into Italian literature. Giovanni Pascoli, the Italian poet, heard the idiom in his native Tuscany at the turn of the century, and the Italian experience in America inspired some of his work. Here is a sample.[34]

Molti bisini oh yes. . . . *No, tiene un* fruttistendo.
. . . Oh yes, *vende* checche, candi, scrima. . . .
Conta moneta! Può campar coi frutti.

(Much business, oh yes. . . . No, I have a fruitstand.
. . . Oh yes, I sell cakes, candy, ice cream. . . .
Count the money! You can support yourself with fruit.)

Readers of Ignazio Silone's *Bread and Wine*[35] will remember Signor Sciaddappa, who introduced that term into the dialect of his Abruzzi mountain village. When his wife attempted to speak to him, he would put his finger to his lips to indicate *sciaddappa*. As a young man, Sciaddappa had delivered coal in New York. Each time Sciaddappa tried to speak, his Boss would tell him to *sciaddappa*. It was the only English word he knew after years in America. No matter what he was asked, his response was always the same. How did you like America? *Sciaddappa!* Say something in English. *Sciaddappa!*

Common Italglish Words and Phrases

(Unless otherwise noted, the stress is on the penultimate syllable.)

abbasso città: downtown
abbordare: to board
addresso: address
aidonchera: I don't care
aite: height
aigacciu: I've got you, I understand
airisce: Irish
airono: I don't know
ais bochs: icebox, refrigerator
aiscule: high school
ais scrim: ice cream
Albania: Albany
alò: hello
a micci, ammoccia cheste: how much is this?
andare a Flabusse: to die, a business failure
appe tu dette: up to date, Americanized
arioppa, orriope: hurry up
arte: heart
assuranza: insurance
ausa: house
auschieppe: housekeeper
avaia: how are you?
azzollo: that's all

azzonoffo: that's enough
azzorrait: that's all right
baccausa, baccaù: backhouse, toilet
bai bai: later
baisicle: bicycle
banchisto: banker
barratenda: bartender
Batteria: Battery (New York)
bisiniss: business
blacco enze: black hand
boia: boy
boifrendo: boyfriend
bomma: bum
bondo: bond
Bonveria: Bowery (New York)
bordante: Italian boarding house operator
bordo, abbordato: boarder
bossa: wife of boss, housekeeper, proprietress
bosso: boss, employer, proprietor, landlord
botta: boat
boxare: to box
briccoliere: bricklayer
broccare: to break
Broccolino: Brooklyn
bucco: book
canabuldogga: bulldog
carpetto: carpet
carpentiere: carpenter
carta: an official paper
ccianza: chance, opportunity
cecca: check
cestenotto: chestnut
checca: cake
Cialì: Charlie
Cialiston: (stress on *Cia*) Charleston
ciunga: chewing gum
colleggio: college
commifò: comfortable

Coneiland: (stress on *nei*) Coney Island
contri: country, nation
coppetane: uptown
coppesteso: upstairs
corte: court
Crismis: Christmas
cuccio: church
cuddivinni: (stress on *di*) good evening
culo: coal
cummoni: good morning
cunnaiti: good night
custome: (stress on *cus*) customer
dezzò: that's all
dicce, diecio, indiccio: ditch
Dicchì: Dicky
Dionigi: D&H (Delaware & Hudson Railroad)
dissi: this
dora: daughter
dorte: dirt, Dorothy
dringo: drink
fa ffait: to fight, to throw a punch
fai: fire
faietatore: fighter
falò: fellow, boyfriend
fare u sport: to affect a dress, posture, or mannerism
fare u stingio: to be cheap, to save every penny
farma: farm
farmaiolo: farmer
fattoria: factory
fenza, fenzata: fence
ferribotte: ferryboat
fessa: face
fichisare: to fix
file gude: feel good
Flabusse: Flatbush, Brooklyn
forniture: furniture
Franghì: Frankie
fruttistenne: fruitstand

Gecco: Jack
genitore: janitor
Gerserì: Jersey City
ghella: girl
ghenga: gang
ghiroppe: get up
giobba: job
giorge: judge, George
giumpare: to jump
globbo: club
godem: goddamn
goraelli, godaelle: go to hell
grignollo: greenhorn, newcomer
grosseria: grocery store
guai: why?
guarda bene: good looking
gubbai: goodbye
gude: good
iasse: yes
Il Forte Gelato: The Fourth of July
iu: you
La Festa delle Galline: Thanksgiving Day
la iarda, gliarda: yard, lawn
laiche: like
La Merica: America
legga: leg
licenza: license
loffaro: (stress on *lof*) loafer
lova: lover
Maighì: Mikie
mandar a goraelli: to lose one's job
ma no: no
mascina: machine, automobile
ma sciur: sure, certainly
maufu: mouth
mecciu: match
menne: men
mia ghella: girlfriend

minoiu: I know you
mistecca: mistake
monghì: monkey
monte: month
morgico, morgheggio: mortgage
muvo piccio, muffo: moving picture, movie
naise: nice
naite: night
natinga, natinchi: nothing
nato: another
Nevevano: New Haven
nota: promissory note
Nuova Iorche, Namaiorca: New York
Obrochen: Hoboken
olda faesce: old fashioned
ongala: (stress on *on*) uncle
ongri: hungry
Oribescia: Wabash Railroad
organ grainda: organ grinder
orrait: all right
orrè: hurray
orsi: horse
pezzo: dollar
picca: pickaxe
picchinicca: picnic
piccio: pinch
Pighì: Peggy
pis vuorche: piece work (factory)
Pizburgo: Pittsburgh
polisi, pulisi: police
ponce: punch, sting, pierce
Portolante: Portland
prominenti: important persons in the Italian colonies
raida: ride
rancio: ranch
rangia: range, stove
reboia: hey boy!
re erode: railroad

rendita: (stress on *ren*) rent
Ricciomondo: Richmond
ronguè: wrong way
sanguicce: sandwich
sannemabicce: son of a bitch
sannemagogna: son of a gun
scecchenze: shake hands
sciabola: shovel
sciaddappa, scialappa: shut up
sciaina: shoeshine
sciarpa: shop, factory
sciocchezza: showcase
sciumecco: shoemaker
scudo: dollar
sechenenze: secondhand
sidiollo: city hall
smarto: smart
sobuè: subway
spiccare: to speak
spinsiru: jacket
stimasciabola: steamshovel
stinco: stink
stoppare: to stop
storo: store
strappare: to strop a razor
tenne: ten
ticchetta: ticket
ticcì, ticcià: teacher
tinga: think
toccare: to talk
toidavenne: (stress on *av*) Third Avenue
tracca: track (railroad)
trobolo: (stress on *tro*) trouble
trocco: truck
trù: through
tutta: tooth
uariu: who are you?
uatsiùs: what's the use

uenni: when
uindo: window
uliveto: elevated (train)
uomene: (stress on *uo*) woman
variu vanni: what do you want?
Vasciadone: Washington
vazzumara, vostamater: what's the matter?
vescettobbi: washtub, bathtub
vischi: whiskey
vuorche: work
vuora: water

Simplified Guide to Pronunciation

a is like *a* in *ah!*
e is like *e* in *they*
i is like *i* in *machine*
o is like *o* in *oh!*
u is like *u* in *rule*
che is like *Kaye*
chi is like *key*
sci is like *she*
sce is like *Shea*

Repatriation

I came from America, the land that gathers
the rebels, the miserable, the very poor; The
Land of puerile and magnificent deeds: The
naive skyscrapers, votive candles at the head
of supine Manhattan. O Italy, O great shoe,
do not kick me away again![1]

Italians may have been unique among European immigrants in their
rate of return to their homeland. Some of these repatriates went home
permanently; either they had planned to do so, or they had become
disillusioned with America. Others, after a period of months or years
in Italy, reemigrated to the United States; conflicting loyalties and personal changes wrought by the immigrant experience made it impossible for them to fit back into Italian society.

Repatriation and Reintegration

Prior to the 1890s, relatively few Italians arrived in America with the
express intention of establishing permanent residence. Those who did
so tended to come over as family units, or the wife and children would
join the breadwinner one or two years after his arrival.

The majority of Italians in the country in those early days, however, were migrant workers, the sojourners who left Italy only to seek
better employment. Some crossed the ocean several times over a period of 10 to 20 years. For them, America was a workplace, not their
home. Their loyalties—and their families—remained in Italy.

The census data for 1870 to 1890 reveal that the sojourners were
found in large numbers on work crews of various kinds in the rural
areas and small towns. These jobs tended to be contractual and sea-

sonal; once they were terminated, most of the men would return home (although some continued to stay on as nomadic laborers for several years, and others eventually settled in one of the urban colonies). Between 1873 and 1890 more than 356,000 Italians came in, yet the 1890 census counted only 182,580 Italians residing in the United States.

Critics of the time claimed that the Italians were in America for the single purpose of exploiting work opportunities and had no interest in becoming Americans. Indeed, it was said, they seemed to reject the American way of life and hold tenaciously to their Old World heritage. Not only were they draining precious American capital from the local economy to be sent back home, therefore, but their foreignness threatened the very fabric of American society.[2]

With regard to the sojourners, such criticism had some basis in fact—these men *were* taking whatever money they could make and running—but was blind to American capitalism's exploitation of the migrant workers. A more balanced view would have recognized the sojourner as something of a victim rather than a threat.

The migrant laborers from South Italy whom Alberto Pecorini met in New York all had ambitions to work hard in America, save as much money as possible, and then return home to buy a small farm or to retire long-standing debts. They arrived in America ready to accumulate whatever they could. Everyone knew of a person like Stefano Ribera who had left Sicily shoeless and shirtless and was now sending regular remittances from Buffalo to his wife to put aside for the purchase of a house when he returned.[3]

Matteo was one of those tightwad migrant workers who came to America to accumulate a cash reserve. When he and his two compatriots arrived from Sicily in 1913, they took a room at a Brooklyn hotel and spent the next four days planning their strategy. First, they needed some money for travel. Matteo sent a telegram to his brother, who had emigrated to Philadelphia the previous year, asking for money. Receiving no response, he wired his brother-in-law in Detroit with the same request. When a few dollars arrived two days later, Matteo went to Philadelphia to look for work and found an employment office advertisement for 500 quarry workers and 500 railroad men. Matteo accepted the second job at the promised wage of $2.00 a day. When the men arrived at the isolated rural work site, they were told that the wage was $1.66. Matteo quit after three months, not having saved a penny, and joined his brother who had moved to Detroit, where a $2.00 job was waiting. When Matteo arrived, his brother took a day off from work to celebrate their reunion. At the factory the next day the Boss, in an angry outburst, not only refused to hire Matteo but fired the brother because he had taken the holiday without permission. Jobs were scarce. The two brothers remained unemployed for eight months, accumulating a debt of $115. Matteo was not bothered by the debt. He looked beyond it to the day when he would finally have his little nest egg. Once the brothers did obtain work and satisfy the debt, Matteo carefully worked out a systematic plan to save all that he could from his wages. He spent only for food and rent, and an occasional silent film.

It took Matteo seven years, but his frugality finally paid dividends. Shortly after the end of the First World War, he was able to inform his father that he had enough cash to buy a plot of farmland, and that he could not wait to return home where every blade of grass understood Sicilian. His father replied that a choice vineyard was available for sale. Without hesitation, Matteo mailed his savings to his father with instructions to buy. For the first 27 years of his life, when he lived in Italy, Matteo never had anything to show for his labor. Now he was returning as a property owner.[4]

Men who had intended to return but had no ties at home were likely candidates for permanent settlement. Rocco Corresca and his friend Francesco, both orphans, had come to America with a plan similar to Matteo's. Once they left the Brooklyn *padrone* who had recruited them at Ellis Island, their plan was to save $400 before returning to Naples, and by their second year of residence, they had accomplished this goal. But rather than return—there was no necessity for haste, they decided, since there were no relatives waiting—they invested the money in a shoeshine parlor, this time aiming for savings of $1,000. By the time they had achieved that second goal, in 1902, returning to Italy was no longer the priority. Why leave when they were doing so well? With each passing year, Italy would recede into a smaller and smaller corner of their minds.[5]

Immigrants who had strong ties with their past, however, retained a sense of Italy as their true home. They were Italians abroad, not immigrants who would be pulled inch by inch into the Great Melting Pot. "The town of Cinisi, Sicily, is forever in their minds," Gaspare

Cusumano said of the Cinisari living in New York City.[6] They counted the days, the months, the years, like convicts doing time. Their return would sometimes be long delayed—5, 10, 20 years or more—but they knew that returning was inevitable. So did their wives and relatives who had been left behind. An old newspaper story tells of an Italian who left for America before the turn of the century and reappeared decades later. He was met at the door by his wife, who said quite casually, "Hello, my husband, I knew you would come home. As you can see I have waited for you."[7] She had endured their separation with consummate patience because his reappearance was predictable, not the result of chance. They had separated out of economic necessity, and he had continued to support her with his work in America. Of course, not all husbands did return. There were some wives who waited in vain, "emigration widows" whose husbands had broken their pledges that the excursion to America would be nothing more than an interlude.

The time-delayed return phenomenon was not common; the return rate was highest among greenhorn Italians who had been living in America less than five years. The longer the period of continuous residence in America, the greater the likelihood that the immigrant would never again see his native village. Continuous residence of ten years or more was an indication that the Italian had made an adjustment of sorts to his immigrant status and intended to live out his life in America.[8] As the commitments to the new home increased—through job security, the acquisition of a wife and family, and integration into the Italian colony—the immigrant's memories of his native home would begin to blur, and a notable erosion would occur in his obligations to whatever he had left behind. A war, a father's death, or a family crisis that would have sent the newcomer scurrying home in a frantic state elicited far less response after years of residence. When Italy entered the First World War, tens of thousands of young immigrants returned to defend Italy's borders, but veteran immigrants like Totonno did not feel the same patriotic fervor. Did they owe allegiance to Italy, or was their allegiance now to America? They remained sympathetic to the Italian cause, but taking up Italian arms was an action that seemed alien. Totonno's family expected him to return to fight for his country; the Italian consuls in Utica and New York told him that it was his duty to do so, and he was advised to sail on the first available ship for

Genoa. Totonno hesitated and did nothing. Exasperated by such indecisiveness, his brother, who was at the front, told him to make up his mind once and for all whether he was an Italian or an American. The question resolved itself when America entered the war, and Totonno was drafted to serve in France with the American Expeditionary Force.[9]

Between 1902 and 1914 over 2.5 million Italians were repatriated from transatlantic countries, at least half from the United States. Ships sailing from east coast ports to Italy never lacked for Italian passengers. On November 21, 1903, the liner *Vancouver* left Boston with 1,130 Italian immigrants aboard, and another 800 who were waiting for transportation were sent by rail to New York to board another ship.[10]

Repatriation from the United States fluctuated substantially from one year to the next, however. In 1902, for instance, 58,000 returned; in 1904 the number exceeded 140,000; in 1908 the volume almost doubled to 245,000 (and only 71,000 arrived that year), yet during the following year the number of departures fell to 74,000. These fluctuations were due in part to the number of Italian job opportunities in America and to the manner in which the American economic picture was being defined in Italy.[11] Even a modest decline in factory and construction jobs would throw thousands of Italians out of work and force many of the unemployed to return to Italy.

The fiscal crisis of 1907–8, which occurred during the peak of Italian immigration, created a return rate of substantial proportions. Before the crisis Totonno, living in Utica, made several references in his diary to the brisk movement of numbers of *paesani* from Alberobello to that textile city. When the economic recession struck in 1907 and the Utica shops closed their doors, the movement was abruptly reversed; many people who had arrived only months previously packed up and went back. "Almost every day we go down to the station to see someone off. They are loaded down with packages and letters for the relatives in Italy of those who are here. I usually give them something for my family." Business was so bad that winter that several of the Italian retail establishments failed. Totonno had contingency plans to depart the following summer if nothing improved, but an economic upturn took place, and with it came an increase of newcomers to prerecession levels.

During the years 1900 to 1911 it can be estimated that one Italian left for every two or three Italians who landed. Lack of work was a reason for returning, yet many immigrants stayed on in America despite months and years of intermittent employment. Not all of the immigrants were willing to endure that kind of existence, however. While living in the South Bronx, Totonno escorted to the New York docks dozens of men who had become completely disillusioned with the immigrant life. An immigrant's lot was a demeaning one, and many an immigrant lost heart. The reality of the immigrant status was in stark contrast to the intending emigrant's mental picture of America. Totonno's friend Gianni had come to America with his wife in the hope of finding employment that would use his skills as a decorative stonecutter. He arrived to discover that America already had its quota of Italian stone artists. What remained was what most Italians did—an occasional factory job or street work. Gianni refused to consider such employment, but he did not want to live on the welfare of his friends until a job opportunity opened up. After two months, he and his wife returned to Italy. "Gianni," Totonno noted, "is too proud a man to be an immigrant."

Cosmina also had her pride. Cosmina was a young woman in her twenties when she arrived in America. She had had some education in Italy and had studied English. She worked in a clothing factory in Rochester, New York, and went to night school to improve her English. The teacher, soon perceiving that Cosmina was a cut above the other students, asked where she was from. When Cosmina told her, the teacher replied, "Funny, you don't act like an Italian immigrant." A talented and ambitious woman, Cosmina attained the position of floor supervisor in the factory, but after seven years she went home. "Why did you return to Italy?" she was asked. "You were doing fairly well in America." "Why?" she said, in a dry tone indicating that she found the query superfluous. "Because I got sick and tired of being treated like an immigrant." [12]

Immigrants like Gianni and Cosmina, those with pride, an education, or a hard-earned skill, frequently had to accept manual labor like the other Italians. As a consequence, it was not unusual to find two men laboring shoulder to shoulder in a sewage ditch, one illiterate and the other with his head full of Dante and Virgil. As many discovered, Italians with an education had a better chance of succeeding in Italy than in America, where as wops their credentials, whatever they might be, meant less; it was easier to maintain their self-respect in Italy. And parents could raise their children as Italians, a less troublesome identity than that of hyphenated Americans, who as they grew up would learn to pity and reject their parents and their heritage.

Because of their bitter experiences as immigrants, many returnees had only negative recollections of America. For them it was not the Land of Opportunity. Nino Manfredi, the Italian actor, has consistently refused to work in Hollywood because of his hatred for the country that ground up many of his immigrant relatives. Manfredi's grandfather worked in the Pennsylvania coal mines for 25 years; he returned to Italy an embittered and broken old man who felt he had wasted his life. Manfredi's mother was an immigrant child whose family lived in Albany, New York; she was treated like a "small nigger," an experience she found so humiliating that she made a point of never teaching English to her children, even though she knew the language well.[13]

Disillusionment could come in a variety of forms. Many Italians demanded more of America than America was willing or able to give. Men came to America under the impression that they would be employed in a job of their own choosing the day they landed. Farmers who sought to manage a farm were informed that Italian farm managers simply did not exist. Those with training from technical schools in Italy did not find jobs commensurate with their talents. Others had great difficulty making the necessary adjustments to American culture. Alessandro De Luca realized that he was an "Italian through and through" and could not feel or think like an American. "I cannot become mechanical like the American. The American work all the time for the dollar. The Italian love sometime to have the leisure, he love the art, he love the music."[14]

Emigration produced its share of folk proverbs, among which was one in the dialect of Basilicata: *L'America a ci acconza e a ci uasta* (America accommodates some and ruins others).[15] Many of those that America ruined returned home, having found no room for them here.

Of those who came only the strong remained—
The strong of faith and hope and stout of heart!
They worked and toiled and greater fame attained;

Others, too proud to work, just stood apart
Hoping in some manner Fortune to find!
These poor weaklings returned from whence they came,
Broken in spirit and broken in mind,
Shadows of flesh remembered by a name! [16]

In 1906, 4,961 impoverished Italians were given free passage back to Italy by the American government. The Boston Immigrants Society, partly funded by the Italian government, also assisted those who had no money but wished to return: every ship leaving Boston for Italy reserved 30 tickets at only $4.80 apiece, the cost of feeding one passenger. [17] Many of the returnees were like Giuseppe Epifanio, who had come to America hoping to support his family but through misfortune or ill health had not been able to succeed.

Dear Father, I am informing you that I have been sick and I have been able to earn only 35¢ a day. I have not worked for a month and all my money is gone. I have some small debts. I am ashamed to write, dear father, because I have been in this land three months and I have sent no money to you. I think I must return to Italy. [18]

When he was a child growing up in Sicily, the opinion Leonardo Sciascia had of America was conditioned by those villagers who wished only to forget the pain and drudgery of their immigrant years.

My father left for the United States in 1912 and returned in 1919 after having served with the American army. While living in New York he worked in a large laundry as an ironer. He never talked to us about his experiences. For him America was totally unacceptable and indescribable. Once he returned to our village, Racalmuto, he wanted to cancel from his mind those eight years, almost as if they had never happened. The others who returned were the same way. At the mention of America, they would screw up their faces. You could not get a word out of them. The people of our village have always viewed America with a mixture of fear and disgust. Never with envy. Those emigrants who returned to visit every five or six years had become so Americanized that they were viewed with contempt, as if they had become less intelligent over the years. For us America was a place where people did not know how to live correctly, where they labored like beasts, where one became progressively stupid, and where people dressed in a strange manner: loud, ostentatious neckties for the men and indescribable hats for the women. We ridiculed them and they, in turn, ridiculed us. Nothing has changed, they would say. The village is as filthy as ever, and you are old-fashioned and out of date. They were suspicious of all of their Italian relatives whom they felt were looking to get money from them. Of course, that is what the relatives had in mind.[19]

Repatriation and Reemigration

For a young, unmarried immigrant the choice between the Old World and the New, between family loyalty and personal hopes, was often emotionally difficult. He had come to America in part out of a sense of adventure, in part out of curiosity, and in part to make a living. Once in America he saw a life that was both qualitatively and quantitatively different from that of Italy—overwhelmingly so; he was both fascinated and repelled by its energy, its excesses, and its crudeness. Yes, the immigrant would say, life in America is frustrating and demanding, but there is an excitement in America that is not to be found in Italian village life. America was fresh, it was new, and it was unrestrained. One could dream in America; Totonno, for example, dreamed constantly of wealth and high status; he never had that dream in Italy.

America was not totally satisfying, however; something had been left behind in the village. The immigrant's unease could be put to rest by going back home—but being at home was not totally satisfying either, and a desire to relive America would gnaw at the returnee. Now that he was back and could realistically compare America with the native village, he felt hemmed in and dissatisfied with the old life. The village was a very small world, and fitting back into that provincial existence would exact from him many costs. It meant treating his American adventure as an insignificant interlude in his life, and he was unwilling to do that. Even if he had come back intending to stay, he remained torn between the Old World and the New World. He had to make a choice, and he often chose to go back to his immigrant status out of a conviction that he could better shape his own destiny in America than in the static, staid society of the village, where his future, he knew, had already been determined.

Much of the return migration was composed of such young men. They would cross the Atlantic several times, living in Italy and in America for varying periods, attempting to capture something tangible from both.[20] Totonno and Carmine Iannace both returned to their respective villages with intentions of settling down. They did not succeed. For men like them who remained attached, in varying degrees, to their backgrounds, America was thought to be the better of the two alternatives, but neither alternative by itself could ever be completely fulfilling.

TOTONNO

In 1910, at the age of 23, Totonno returned to Alberobello after four years in America.[21] The emotions that he felt at the prospect of a reunion with his family were typical of the repatriation experience:

> Stepping down from the train, I scanned the crowd anxiously for a familiar face. I saw no one, but as I walked through the center of town toward my house, I was greeted by many who recognized me. The tensions that had begun as the train pulled into the station continued to build inside of me when I crossed the piazza and could see my house across the way. My emotions were so great that I could not focus my eyes. There was a crowd in front of the door. When I stepped closer, a path was cleared and out stepped my family. My throat tightened and the tears began to flow freely. I threw myself into their arms. After all the thoughts and dreams of home, I was finally and really here. I could not believe it. We went into the house and sat down to eat, while we constantly looked at one another, knowing that there was so much to say and yet not finding the words. So rather than converse, my sisters and I laughed and giggled between mouthfuls of food.

The first few days were delightful. Totonno renewed old friendships, heard about the events that had occurred while he was away, and paid his respects to the families of emigrants in America. Once all this had been done, he then faced the problem of reintegrating himself into village life. What was it that he wanted to do? He could not answer that question. Indeed, he did not even know with certainty whether he had returned for a prolonged visit or permanently. Who knows? Totonno kept telling himself; something is bound to happen that will give me the direction I need. Maybe, he thought, I can rekindle the old flame with my former girlfriend. We will get married, settle down in Alberobello or a nearby village, I can get some capital together, buy my own meat shop. . . .

Totonno spent most of 1910 working in his brother's shop. In the early months of 1911, more out of boredom than a sense of vocation, he took the tax collector's exam, passed it, and was assigned to the small Calabrian mountain town of Satriano, near Catanzaro. Totonno had not been in that part of Italy before, and the poverty of the region shocked him:

> I arrived in Satriano at 3:30 and walked up to the village—if that is what it can be called. The houses are dug into the hillsides. Pigs run wild through the streets. Pigshit is everywhere. The walkway between the houses is only about a meter wide, and I had all I could do to avoid the pigs, who appeared to resent my intrusion on their domain, and to tiptoe through the pigshit.

The contrast with Alberobello, a quaint village where the inhabitants swept the streets each day and whitewashed their impressive stone dwellings each year, was stark and disconcerting. He could not believe that this backward region was in fact Italy; it was worlds away from what he knew. "Given the economic conditions of Satriano," Totonno wondered, "what does a tax collector do here? What taxes could these people pay? They are totally destitute." Indeed, Totonno was to discover that the job required very little effort. He spent most of his day chatting with the townfolk and flirting with the women whose husbands were in America. Within six months he resigned the post and returned to Alberobello to attempt to develop a wine and oil business. When this venture failed because of his inexperience and his partner's dishonesty, he went back to butchering.

Totonno's family had always considered his sojourn in America as a foolish waste of time, but they had indulged his fantasies of becoming rich. Now that he had gotten that notion out of his head, it was time for him to settle down and establish himself in some kind of profession or business, no matter how minor. His brother Michele, the guiding light of the family, left no doubt as to his opinions of the phenomenon of mass emigration. He despised America and what it stood for, and had nothing good to say about the Italians who went there. His point of view was one common to middle-class Italian society: the emigrants are the dregs of Italy who, incapable of achievement in their own country, give up their birthright to scratch out a living in a hostile environment. Michele openly expressed his anti-American sentiments when one of his sisters became engaged to an intending emigrant. "Trisolina confided to me," wrote Totonno, "that Michele is very displeased over her plans to marry the young man from Locorotondo. In my brother's view, he is unsuitable as a marriage partner because his family background is ordinary. But most of all, Michele does not want Trisolina to struggle in America as the wife of one more common immigrant among a multitude of common immigrants."

Totonno experienced frustration each time he tried to conform to his family's values and expectations. He was demoralized by his inability to accommodate to the old life and felt trapped by the restrictive customs of southern Italy. "I have become tired of this little town: the same old routine, the endless squabbles between the municipality and the butcher's cooperative, the predictable lack of response from my father to anything I propose, my brother's pompous and interminable digressions." He soon longed to return to his immigrant status even though, he admitted to himself, he had accomplished nothing in America. He had been home for two years and was thoroughly depressed when he confided to his diary, "I do not like Italy anymore. This country has too many problems. Life is tedious here." Two months later he was once again back in the Bronx behind a meat counter.

Totonno's dilemma was not uncommon. When an emigrant returned from abroad to be greeted by relatives he had not seen for years, the air would be thick with unbridled joy: tears, screams of ecstasy, suffocating embraces, full-mouth kisses—a moment of pure happiness and contentment. All was forgiven. Old resentments were thrust aside. But all too soon, the emotional release he experienced at his return was replaced by the same anxieties and irritations that had caused him to leave initially.

IANNACE

One year of backbreaking labor in America, and Carmine Iannace was returning home with empty pockets.[22] Recurring periods of unemployment had made it impossible for him to save any money. In the fall of 1907, Iannace arrived back in Belvedere just as his family was preparing to move to its winter home. Iannace decided to go along as he had done as a young boy to help tend the sheep, cow, goat, and pig.

Like Totonno's family, Iannace's assumed that the boy had gotten the emigration fever out of his system and was ready now to assume the life of a small-plot subsistence farmer. And Iannace was sincere in his attempts to satisfy his father, but the more he tried to reacquaint himself with activities he had once performed without much thought, the clearer was the contrast between what he had been and what he had become. He was amazed at the transformation that had taken place in his personal values. His new American perspective kept intruding upon all his attempts to adjust to the old life and its customs. He had an American self and an Italian self; his every thought and every action had two reference points. "It was like living a double life, not two lives diverse and independent, but one with two sides to it." Try as he did to adjust, he soon concluded that as long as he remained in Italy he would not be able to resolve his dilemma. He wanted to develop this emerging American self. Its dominating element was a new drive to succeed, but he knew his ambitions would never flower if he remained under his father's thumb.

His plans to return to America included taking Agnesella, his betrothed, with him as his bride. He thought that by doing so, he could work in America and at the same time, through his wife, maintain his identification with the many village traditions to which he remained attached. By all means, marry Agnesella his father responded, but you must live in Belvedere and follow in my footsteps. A bitter argument ensued when Iannace told his father that he had no intention of subjecting his wife to the harsh and unrewarding life that his mother had had to endure. Nor did he intend to throw his own life away tilling land that refused to yield despite heroic efforts. "The thought that this life would be all I would ever have were I to remain made me tremble with fright."

Iannace made his proposal to Agnesella. She was not surprised that he wanted to return to America; she had noticed the change in him from the very first day: "Your eyes light up every time you talk about

America. You are here but you wish to be there." He admitted that he yearned to go back. "I can breathe freely in America," he told her. "I do not want to spend my days in the fields working for nothing." Come with me, he urged. Agnesella shook her head. "I do not want to go because I am in line to inherit the family property." America did not interest her. Her place, she decided, was by her widowed mother's side. "I can't abandon my family. Since my papa's death, mother has been helpless. She cries all the time; she can do nothing without me." Go, she told Iannace; I belong here, and you belong there.

There was nothing else to say to anyone. Iannace went to see Varricchio, the travel agent, and said to him, "Make the papers. I want to return to America." No member of his family had walked with him to the station when he departed the first time, nor did anyone when he left for the second and final time. "I did not experience the painful disappointment I felt then. Instead, I was relieved. By making a clear break with my family, by not glancing back, it was as if *La Merica* began at the edge of town."

Many immigrants had brought on board balls of yarn, leaving one end of the line with someone on land. As the ship slowly cleared the dock, the balls unwound amid the farewell shouts of the women, the fluttering of the handkerchiefs, and the infants held high. After the yarn ran out, the long strips remained airborne, sustained by the wind, long after those on land and those at sea had lost sight of each other.[23]

NOTES

PREFACE

1. Richard N. Juliani, "American Voices, Italian Accents," *Italian Americana* 1 (1974): 1–25.
2. Rudolph J. Vecoli, "Cult and Occult in Italian American Culture: The Persistence of a Religious Heritage," in Randall M. Miller and Thomas D. Marzik, eds., *Immigrants and Religion in Urban America* (Philadelphia: Temple University Press, 1980), 26.
3. Rudolph M. Bell, *Fate and Honor, Family and Village: Demographic and Cultural Change in Rural Italy since 1800* (Chicago: University of Chicago Press, 1979).
4. Virginia Yans-McLaughlin, *Family and Community: Italian Immigrants in Buffalo, 1880–1930* (Ithaca, N.Y.: Cornell University Press, 1977).
5. Josef J. Barton, *Peasants and Strangers: Italians, Rumanians and Slovaks in an American City, 1890–1950* (Cambridge, Mass.: Harvard University Press, 1975).
6. Juliani, "American Voices, Italian Accents."
7. Ann Cornelisen, *Strangers and Pilgrims: The Last Italian Migration* (New York: Holt, Rinehart and Winston, 1980).
8. John Bodnar, *Workers' World: Kinship, Community and Protest in an Industrial Society, 1900–1940* (Baltimore: Johns Hopkins University Press, 1982).
9. Nuto Revelli, *Il mondo dei vinti: Testimonianze di Vita Contadina* (Torino: Einaudi, 1977).
10. Hubert Blumer, *Critiques of Research in the Social Sciences: I. An Appraisal of Thomas and Znaniecki's "The Polish Peasant in Europe and America"* (New York: Social Science Research Council, 1939), 41.
11. Information on the lives and works of D'Angelo, Panunzio, and Ventresca can be found in Olga Peragallo, *Italian-American Authors and Their Contributions to American Literature* (New York: Vanni, 1949).

ONE

1. Guglielmo Josa, "L'emigrazione nel Molise," *Bollettino dell'emigrazione* 10 (1907): 50.
2. A. Savona and M. Straniero, *Canti dell'emigrazione* (Milano: Garzanti, 1976), 36.

3. Adolfo Rossi, "Vantaggi e danni dell'emigrazione," *Bollettino dell'emigrazione* 13 (1908): 11.

4. Ibid., 29.

5. Francesco Cordasco, ed., *La società Italiana di fronte alle prime migrazione di massa* (New York: Arno, 1975), 39–41.

6. *La Gazzetta del Massachusetts*, April 30, 1910. Data on remittances were published regularly in the *Bollettino dell'Emigrazione*. See Francesco Cordasco, *Italian Mass Migration* (Totowa, N.J.: Rowman and Littlefield, 1980).

7. Rossi, "Vantaggi e danni," 42.

8. Diego Delfino Papers, 1912–29 (University of Minnesota, Immigration Research Center).

9. George R. Gilkey, "Italian Emigrant Letters: The Teramesi Write Home from America" (University of Minnesota, Immigration History Research Center), 36, 16, 30.

10. Fortune T. Gallo, *Lucky Rooster: The Autobiography of an Impresario* (New York: Exposition, 1967), 39–41.

11. F. Paul Miceli, *Pride of Sicily* (New York: Gaus' Sons, 1850), 51.

12. Robert Ferrari, "Autobiography" (University of Minnesota, Immigration History Research Center), 8.

13. Personal interview.

14. Pietro Greco, *I ricordi d'un immigrato* (Brooklyn: Gaus' Sons, 1964), 49.

15. Carmine B. Iannace, *La scoperta dell'America* (Padova: Rebellato, 1971), 45.

16. Matteo's life story appears in Danilo Dolci, *Banditi a Partinico* (Bari: Laterza, 1956), 173–89.

17. The Totonno material in this chapter is from either his 1906 diary (when he left for America) or his 1910 diary (when he returned to Italy).

18. C. Ianni, *Il sangue degli emigrati* (Milano: Edizioni di Communità, 1965), 6.

19. Angelo Mosso, *Vita moderna degli Italiani* (Milano: Treves, 1906), 12.

20. Fernando Manzotti, *La polemica sull'emigrazione dell'Italia unita* (Milano: Società Editrice Dante Alighieri, 1969), p. 78.

21. "Protezione ed assistenza degli emigranti in patria e durante il viaggio," *Bollettino dell'emigrazione* 11 (1907): 114.

22. E. La Riccia, "Vite allo sbaraglio," *Il messaggero di Sant'Antonio*, Dec. 1980, pp. 38–39.

23. Broughton Brandenburg, *Imported Americans* (New York: Stokes, 1903), 157–64.

24. For examples of emigrant exploitation, see ibid.

25. Ibid., 15.

26. "Noli massimi per il trasporto degli emigranti dal 1 Maggio al 31 Agosto 1906," *Bollettino dell'emigrazione* 6 (1906): 57; "Movimenti dell' emigrazione Italiana nell'anno 1905," *Bollettino dell'emigrazione* 1 (1906).

27. Amy A. Bernardy, *Italia randagia attraverso gli Stati Uniti* (Torino: Fratelli Bocca, 1913), 13.

28. Federico Garlanda, *The New Italy* (New York: Putnam, 1911), 219. For a general documentation of steerage conditions in the eighteenth and nineteenth centuries, see Edith Abbott, *Immigration: Select Documents and Case Records*, pt. 1 (Chicago: University of Chicago Press, 1924).

29. Edmondo De Amicis, *Sull'oceano* (Milano: Treves, 1889), 12.

30. Adolfo Rossi, *Un Italiano in America* (Treviso: Buffetti, 1907).

31. Francesco Ventresca, *Personal Reminiscences of a Naturalized American* (New York: Rueson, 1937), 18.

32. Ibid.

33. Ibid., 20.

34. Aldobrando Piacenza, "Memorie di Aldobrando Piacenza," 1956 (University of Minesota, Immigration History Research Center), 9.

35. Brandenburg, *Imported Americans*, 135, 175.

36. Ibid., 177–78, 31.

37. Ibid., 184.

38. Ventresca, *Personal Reminiscences*, 23.

39. Brandenburg, *Imported Americans*, 187.

40. Iannace, *La scoperta*, 24.

41. Brandenburg, *Imported Americans*, 137.

42. Bernardy, *Italia randagia*, 12.

43. Iannace, *La scoperta*.

44. "Protezione ed assistenza," 117.

45. *Bollettino dell'emigrazione* 9 (1908): 159.

46. Pietro Pisani, *L'emigrazione: Avvertimenti e consigli agli emigranti* (Firenze, 1907), 40.

47. Brandenburg, *Imported Americans*, 161.

48. Pisani, *L'emigrazione*, 40–42.

49. Brandenburg, *Imported Americans*, 200–202.

50. Ibid.

51. Ibid., 195.

52. "Protezione ed assistenza," 118.

53. The Totonno Diaries (March 1919) mention a few of these techniques.

54. R. Corresca, "The Biography of a Bootblack," *Independent* 5 (Dec. 4, 1902): 2863–67.

55. Personal interview.

56. Brandenburg, *Imported Americans*, 323.
57. Bernardy, *Italia randagia*, 323.
58. Dolci, *Banditi*, 76.
59. Antonio Margariti, *America! America!* (Salerno: Galzerano, 1980), 19.
60. Ibid., 75.
61. Constantine Panunzio, *The Soul of an Immigrant* (New York: Macmillan, 1921).

Two

1. Carlo Tresca, "Autobiography" (University of Minnesota, Immigration History Research Center), 90.
2. For information on the history of the immigration laws, see Helen Silving, *Immigration Laws of the United States* (New York: Oceana, 1948); E. E. Proper, *Colonial Immigration Laws* (New York: Columbia University Press, 1900).
3. For a history of Castle Garden and Ellis Island, see Thomas M. Pitkin, *Keepers of the Gate: A History of Ellis Island* (New York: New York University Press, 1975).
4. Antonio Arrighi, *Antonio, the Galley Slave* (New York: Revell, 1913).
5. Adolfo Rossi, *Un Italiano in America* (Treviso: Buffetti, 1907), 42.
6. Richmond Mayo-Smith, *Emigration and Immigration* (New York: Scribner, 1904), 219–21.
7. Edward A. Steiner, *On the Trail of the Immigrant* (New York: Revell, 1906), 76.
8. Marie Hall Ets, *Rosa: The Life of an Italian Immigrant* (Minneapolis: University of Minnesota Press, 1970), 166.
9. Francesco Ventresca, *Personal Reminiscences of a Naturalized American* (New York: Rueson, 1937), 24.
10. Gaetano Conte, *Dieci anni in America: Impressioni e ricordi* (Palermo: Spinnato, 1903), 116–23.
11. For one view of the Ellis Island administration by an Italian immigrant who later became the superintendent, see Edward Corsi, *In the Shadow of Liberty: The Chronicle of Ellis Island* (New York: Macmillan, 1935).
12. Broughton Brandenburg, *Imported Americans* (New York: Stokes, 1903), 207.
13. Ibid., 213.
14. Ibid., 216–17.

15. Amy A. Bernardy, *Italia randagia attraverso gli Stati Uniti* (Torino: Fratelli Bocca, 1913), 25.

16. Ibid., 27.

17. Brandenburg, *Imported Americans*, 272.

18. "Circolari del commissariato dell'emigrazione," *Bollettino dell'emigrazione* 8 (1907): 92.

19. Steiner, *On the Trail of the Immmigrant*, 80–81.

20. *Bollettino dell'emigrazione* 8 (1905): 36.

21. *La Gazzetta del Massachusetts*, Nov. 7–8, 1903.

22. *La Fiaccola*, Buffalo, New York (Aug. 1909).

23. Fortune T. Gallo, *Lucky Rooster: The Autobiography of an Impresario* (New York: Exposition, 1967), 45.

24. This interchange was overheard by an Italian journalist. *L'Avennire* (Utica, N.Y.), June 29, 1901.

25. Pietro Greco, *I ricordi d'un immigrato* (Brooklyn, Gaus' Sons, 1964), 52.

26. Gerardo Ferreri, *Gli Italiani in America: Impressioni di un viaggio agli Stati Uniti* (Roma: Farro, 1907), 24.

27. Bartolomeo Vanzetti, *The Story of a Proletarian Life* (Boston: New Trial League, 1923), 12.

28. Pasquale D'Angelo, *Son of Italy* (New York: Macmillan, 1924), 59.

29. *L'Avennire*, June 29, 1901.

30. Amy A. Bernardy, *Paese che vai: Il mondo come l'ho visto io* (Firenze: Le Monnier, 1923), 288.

31. Brandenburg, *Imported Americans*, 207.

32. Ibid., 207–8.

33. Ibid., 209–10.

34. Angelo Mosso, *Vita moderna degli Italiani* (Milano: Treves, 1906), 20.

35. Rossi, *Italiano in America*, 76.

36. Max Nomad, "Carlo Tresca, Rebel without Uniform," pt. 1: "The Seed and the Seedling" (University of Minnesota, Immigration History Research Center), 28.

37. Conte, *Dieci anni in America*, 123.

38. Ets, *Rosa*, 168.

39. Personal interview.

40. Brandenburg, *Imported Americans*, 223.

41. Gabriel Iamurri, *The True Story of an Immigrant* (Boston: Christopher, 1951), 38.

42. Mosso, *Vita moderna*, 32.

43. Quoted in ibid., 217.

44. *Bollettino dell'emigrazione* 13 (1907): 91–92.

THREE

1. Emanuel Carnevali, *The Autobiography of Emanuel Carnevali* (New York: Horizon, 1967), 76.

2. Napoleone Colajanni, *Gli Italiani negli Stati Uniti* (Napoli: Rivista Popolare, 1909), 44.

3. Gaetano Conte, *Dieci anni in America: Impressioni e ricordi* (Palermo: Spinnato, 1903), 41.

4. Camillo Cianfarra, *Diario di un emigrante* (New York: L'Araldo Italiano, 1900), 76.

5. Adolfo Rossi, "Vantaggi e danni dell'emigrazione," *Bollettino dell'emigrazione* 13 (1908): 16; Stewart E. Perry, *San Francisco Scavengers* (Berkeley: University of California Press, 1978); Alberto Pecorini, "The Italian in the United States," *Forum*, Jan. 1911, pp. 15–29.

6. Translated from the first four lines of the "Canto di Tessitore" by A. Agresti, published in *La Questione Sociale* (Paterson, N.J.), Dec. 30, 1895, p. 3.

7. Calculated from Department of Commerce and Labor, Bureau of the Census, *Special Reports, Occupations at the Twelfth Census* (Washington, D.C., 1904); *Annual Reports of the Commissioner General of Immigration, 1911–1920* (Washington, D.C.); G. E. Di Palma, "L'immigrazione Italiana negli Stati Uniti dell'America del Nord dal 1820 al 30 Giugno 1910," *Bollettino dell'emigrazione* 12 (1914): 108.

8. Alberto Pecorini, *Gli Americani nella vita moderna* (Milano: Treves, 1909). For a listing of Italian businessmen and professionals by city, see *Italian Business Directory*, 1907–8 (New York: Italian Directory Company, 1907).

9. F. Paul Miceli, *Pride of Sicily* (New York: Gaus' Sons, 1950), 60.

10. Angelo Mosso, *Vita moderna degli Italiani* (Milano: Treves, 1906), 116.

11. H. Frederic, *The Damnation of Theron Ware* (N.Y.: Doubleday, 1896), 31–32.

12. Carnevali, *Autobiography*, 167.

13. Pecorini, *Gli Americani*, 390; Colajanni, *Gli Italiani*, 11–16.

14. Totonno Diaries (Sept. 1913).

15. Carnevali, *Autobiography*, 77.

16. Bartolomeo Vanzetti, *The Story of a Proletarian Life* (Boston: New Trial League, 1923), 13.

17. Ibid., 15.

18. Richmond Mayo-Smith, *Emigration and Immigration* (New York: Scribner, 1904), 128–31.

19. Broughton Brandenburg, *Imported Americans* (New York: Stokes, 1903), 30.

20. *La Gazzetta del Massachusetts*, Feb. 20–21, 1904.

21. "Le agenzie di collocamente nello Stato di Nuova York," *Bollettino dell'emigrazione* 1 (1906): 30–38.

22. The general features of the Boss System are discussed in Ziffero Ciuffoletti, *L'Emigrazione nella storia d'Italia, 1868–1975*, vol. 1 (Firenze: Vallecchi, 1978), 241–47; John Koren, "The Padrone System and Padrone Banks," *U.S. Department of Labor Bulletin* 9 (March 1897): 113–29; Humbert Nelli, "The Italian Padrone System in the United States," *Labor History* 3 (1964): 153–67; Francesco Cordasco, ed., *La Società Italiana di fronte alle prime migrazioni di massa* (New York: Arno, 1975), 305–23, 483–506.

23. Adolfo Rossi, *Un Italiano in America* (Treviso: Buffetti, 1907), 70; George E. Pozzetta, "The Mulberry District of New York City: The Years before World War One," in Robert F. Harney and J. Vincenza Scarpaci, eds., *Little Italies in North America* (Toronto: Multicultural History Society of Ontario, 1981), 7–40.

24. Cianfarra, *Diario*, 121.

25. Carmine B. Iannace, *Uomini e Galantuomini* (Firenze: Grafica Toscana, 1970), 22.

26. Emanuelle Masi was given a three-month jail sentence for collecting a one dollar *bossatura* from 100 workers for nonexistent jobs (*La Gazzetta del Massachusetts*, May 21–22, 1904).

27. Cianfarra, *Diario*, 72.

28. Pietro Greco describes such an event and its violent aftermath in *I ricordi d'un immigrato* (Brooklyn: Gaus' Sons, 1964), 67–72.

29. Amy A. Bernardy, *Italia randagia attraverso gli Stati Uniti* (Torino: Fratelli Bocca, 1913), 84.

30. Antonio Mangano, "The Effect of Emigration upon Italy: Threatened Depopulation of the South," *Charities and the Commons* 19 (1908): 113.

31. Conte, *Dieci anni in America*.

32. Colajanni, *Gli Italiani*, 27.

33. Fortune Gallo, *Lucky Rooster: The Autobiography of an Impresario* (New York: Exposition, 1967), 50.

34. Brandenburg, *Imported Americans*, 1–2.

35. Greco, *I ricordi d'un immigrato*, 85.

36. Colajanni, *Gli Italiani*.

37. Francesco Ventresca, *Personal Reminiscences of a Naturalized American* (New York: Rueson, 1937).

38. Pasquale D'Angelo, *Son of Italy* (New York: Macmillan, 1924), 99.

39. Ibid., 132.

40. See ibid. and Antonio Margariti, *America! America!* (Salerno: Galzerano, 1980).

41. Ventresca, *Personal Reminiscences*, 28.

42. Carlo Tresca, "Autobiography" (University of Minnesota, Immigration History Research Center), 27.

43. Cianfarra, *Diario*, 54.

44. Gerolamo Moroni, "Il peonage nel sud degli Stati Uniti," *Bollettino dell'emigrazione* 5 (1910): 4–10; Luigi Villari, "Gli Italiani nel sud degli Stati Uniti," *Bollettino dell'emigrazione* 10 (1907): 42; Gino C. Speranza, "Forced Labor in West Virginia," *Outlook* 74 (June 13, 1903): 407–10.

45. Bernardy, *Italia randagia*, 104.

46. Ibid., 104–5.

47. Gabriel Iamurri, *The True Story of an Immigrant* (Boston: Christopher, 1951), 40.

48. Ibid., 41–46.

49. Ibid., 47.

50. Constantine Panunzio, *The Soul of an Immigrant* (New York: Macmillan, 1921), 79.

51. Miceli, *Pride of Sicily*, 65.

52. Michael Novak, *The Rise of the Unmeltable Ethnics* (New York: Macmillan, 1972).

53. A. Dosch, "Just Wops," *Everybody's Magazine* 25 (1911): 578.

54. Iamurri, *True Story*, 48–49.

55. Angelo M. Pellegrini, *Americans by Choice* (New York: Macmillan, 1956), 82–83.

56. Bernardy, *Italia randagia*, 162–86.

57. Enrico Sartorio, *Social and Religious Life of Italians in America* (Clifton, N.J.: Kelley, 1918, 1974), 27.

58. Antonio Stella, *Some Aspects of Italian Immigration* (New York: Putnam, 1924), 94.

59. Conte, *Dieci anni*, 59.

60. Iannace, *La scoperta*.

61. *La Gazzetta del Massachusetts* (Boston), July 16, 1910, April 30, 1910.

62. Bernardy, *Italia randagia*, 184. For a general discussion of the immigrant and the legal system, see K. H. Claghorn, *The Immigrant's Day in Court* (New York: Harper, 1923).

63. Quoted in Bernardy, *Italia randagia*, 186.

64. *L'Avvenire* (Utica, N.Y.), Jan. 26, 1901.

65. *Zarathustra* (New York), May 15, 1926, p. 24.

66. Rocco Corresca, "The Biography of a Bootblack," *Independent* 5 (Dec. 4, 1902): 2866. See also Antonio Pasche's story in Blake McKelvey, "The Italians in Rochester: An Historical Review," *Rochester History* 22 (1960): 3.

67. George R. Gilkey, "Italian Emigrant Letters: The Teramesi Write

Home from America" (University of Minnesota, Immigration History Research Center), 38.

   68. D'Angelo, *Son of Italy*, 63.

   69. Cianfarra, *Diario*, 13.

   70. Most of the following discussion has been taken from these sources: Margariti, *America! America!*; Ventresca, *Personal Reminiscences*; Carmine B. Iannace, *La scoperta dell'America* (Padova: Rebellato, 1971); Totonno Diaries (1906–10).

   71. *L'Italia* (Chicago), Dec. 20, 1886.

   72. Pecorini, *Gli Americani*, 397.

   73. Iannace, *La scoperta*, 72.

   74. Ibid., 123–24.

   75. Personal interview.

   76. Ernest Tummolillo Papers, 1876–1916 (University of Minnesota, Immigration History Research Center).

   77. Rossi, *Italiano in America*, 131.

FOUR

   1. Adolfo Rossi, *Un Italiano in America* (Treviso: Buffetti, 1907), 65–71.

   2. Angelo Mosso, *Vita moderna degli Italiani* (Milano: Treves, 1906), 33.

   3. Emanuel Carnevali, *The Autobiography of Emanuel Carnevali* (New York: Horizon, 1967), 73; Franco Ciarlantini, *Al paese delle stelle* (Milano: "Alpes," 1931), 22.

   4. Gaetano Conte, *Dieci anni in America: Impressioni e Ricordi* (Palermo: Spinnato, 1903), 34.

   5. Emily F. Robbins, "If One Speak Bad of Your Mother, How You Feel?" *Red Cross Magazine*, Sept. 1919, p. 45.

   6. F. Paul Miceli, *Pride of Sicily* (New York: Gaus' Sons, 1950), 5. For a review of urban immigrant housing, see G. P. Morton, "Chicago Housing Conditions, VII: Two Italian Districts," *American Journal of Sociology* 18 (1912–13): 509–42; Robert F. Harney and J. V. Scarpaci, eds., *Little Italies in North America* (Toronto: Multicultural History Society of Ontario, 1981); Donna R. Gabaccia, *From Sicily to Elizabeth Street: Housing and Social Change among Italian Immigrants, 1880–1930* (Albany, N.Y.: SUNY Press, 1984); Jacob A. Riis, "The Italian in New York," in *How the Other Half Lives: Studies among the Tenements of New York* (New York: Scribner, 1890).

   7. For the analysis in this section the data on Italian colonies in New York state were gathered from the 1900 United States Federal manuscript census, National Archives, Washington D.C.

8. Rocco Corresca, "The Biography of a Bootblack," *Independent* 5 (Dec. 4, 1902): 2865.

9. Francesco Ventresca, *Personal Reminiscences of a Naturalized American* (New York: Rueson, 1937), 37.

10. Angelo Pellegrini, *Americans by Choice* (New York: Macmillan, 1956), 144.

11. Carmine B. Iannace, *La scoperta dell'America* (Padova: Rebellato, 1971), 101. For an excellent overview of the boarding phenomenon, see two articles by Robert F. Harney: "Boarding and Belonging: Thoughts on Sojourner Institutions," *Urban History Review* 2 (1978): 8–37; "Men without Women: Italian Migrants in Canada, 1885–1930," in Betty Boyd Caroli, Robert F. Harney, Lydio F. Tomasi, eds., *The Italian Immigrant Woman in North America* (Toronto: Multicultural History Society of Ontario, 1978).

12. Camillo Cianfarra, *Diario di un emigrante* (New York: L'Araldo Italiano, 1900), 107.

13. Domenick Ciolli, "The Wop in the Track Gang," *Immigrants in America Review* 2 (July 1916): 62.

14. Ventresca, *Personal Reminiscences*, 26.

15. Pasquale D'Angelo, *Son of Italy* (New York: Macmillan, 1924), 110; Iannace, *La scoperta*.

16. Gabriel Iamurri, *The True Story of an Immigrant* (Boston: Christopher, 1951), 45.

17. Ciolli, "Wop in the Track Gang."

18. Carlo Tresca, "Autobiography" (University of Minnesota, Immigration History Research Center), 100.

19. Broughton Brandenburg, *Imported Americans* (New York: Stokes, 1903), 21; see also *Italian Business Directory*, 1907–8 (New York: Italian Directory Company, 1907), 14–19.

20. For an example, see Cianfarra, *Diario*, 122–27.

21. Ibid., 155–56.

22. See Brandenburg, *Imported Americans*, 21–22; Conte, *Dieci anni in America*, 129–32; Federico Garlanda, *The New Italy* (New York, 1911), 223.

23. Giuseppe Giacosa, *Impressioni d'America* (Milano: Cogliati, 1908), 225.

24. *Boston Herald*, Aug. 11, 1904.

25. Cianfarra, *Diario*, 167–70.

26. Antonio Margariti, *America! America!* (Salerno: Galzerano, 1980).

27. D'Angelo, *Son of Italy*, 58.

28. Ziffiro Ciuffoletti, *L'emigrazione nella storia d'Italia, 1868–1975*, vol. 1 (Firenze: Vallecchi, 1978), 67.

29. Ferdinando D. Maurino, *Dal cavo delle mani: Pagine di vita attuale in Italia e in America* (Cosenza: Pellegrini, 1968).

NOTES 213

30. Robert Park and H. A. Miller, *Old World Traits Transplanted* (New York, 1921), 104.

31. Leonardo Sciascia, *La Sicilia come metafora* (Milano: Mondadori, 1979), 30. For a thorough discussion of southern Italian stereotypes by region, province, and city, see Giuseppe Galasso, *L'altra Europa* (Milano: Mondadori, 1982), 143–90.

32. Totonno Diaries (June 1906).

33. D'Angelo, *Son of Italy*.

34. Iannace, *La scoperta*, 81.

35. Margariti, *America! America!*, 55.

36. Ibid., 47.

37. Ibid., 51; quarrels and violence are common themes in Margariti, *America! America!*; D'Angelo, *Son of Italy*; Totonno Diaries (1906–20).

38. Totonno Diaries, Oct. 1907.

39. Ibid., Dec. 1908, April 1914.

40. L. Berrey and M. Vandenbark, *The American Thesaurus of Slang* (New York: Macmillan, 1945), 361. *Gumba* is a dialect version of *compare*.

41. *L'Italia* (Chicago), Nov. 8, 1886. See also Amy A. Bernardy, *Italia randagia attraverso gli Stati Uniti* (Torino: Fratelli Bocca, 1913), 245; H. L. Mencken, *The American Language*, 4th ed. (New York: Knopf, 1936); Salvatore La Gumina, *WOP! A Documentary History of Anti-Italian Discrimination in the United States* (San Francisco: Straight Arrow Books, 1973).

42. *La Tribuna* (Detroit), June 5, 1909.

43. Margariti, *America! America!*, 75.

44. D'Angelo, *Son of Italy*, 138.

45. William Murray, *Italy: The Fatal Gift* (New York: Dodd, Mead, 1982); Ventresca, *Personal Reminiscences*, 41.

46. Maurino, *Cavo delle mani*.

47. Brandenburg, *Imported Americans*, 237.

48. Tommaso Salvini, *Ricordi, aneddotti ed impressioni* (Milano: Dumolard, 1895), 285.

49. Giacosa, *Impressioni*.

50. Conte, *Dieci Anni*.

51. Rossi, *Italiano in America*, 171–75.

52. Robert Ferrari, "Autobiography" (University of Minnesota, Immigration History Research Center), 96.

53. Brandenburg, *Imported Americans*; D'Angelo, *Son of Italy*, 225.

54. Rossi, *Italiano in America*, 90.

55. Cianfarra, *Diario*, 51.

56. Domenico Siciliani, *Fra gli Italiani degli Stati Uniti d'America* (Roma: Stabilimento per l'Ammistrazione della Guerra, 1922), 31.

57. Brandenburg, *Imported Americans*, 105.

58. Mosso, *Vita moderna*, 113.
59. Louis Adamic, *Laughing in the Jungle* (New York: Harper, 1932), 113.
60. Gherardo Ferreri, *Gli Italiani in America* (Roma: Farro, 1907), 14.
61. Tresca, "Autobiography," 92.
62. Cianfarra, *Diario*, 10.
63. Margariti, *America! America!*, 20; Ventresca, *Personal Reminiscences*, 28.
64. Iannace, *La scoperta*, 106.
65. "America: women without substance and fruit without character" (Carnevali, *Autobiography*, 160–70).
66. Pietro Di Donato, *Three Circles of Light* (New York: Messner, 1960), 32.
67. D'Angelo, *Son of Italy*, 80.
68. Constantine Panunzio, *The Soul of an Immigrant* (New York: Macmillan, 1921), 129.
69. Rossi, *Italiano in America*, 84.
70. Cianfarra, *Diario*, 115.
71. Ferrari, *Autobiography*, 20.
72. Margariti, *America! America!*, 55.
73. Park and Miller, *Old World Traits Transplanted*, 149.
74. D. B. Davis, "Baptist Response to Immigration," *Journal and Messenger* 63 (March 1894): 125.
75. See Rudolph J. Vecoli, "Prelates and Peasants: Italian Immigrants and the Catholic Church," *Journal of Social History* 2 (1969): 217–68; S. W. Halperin, *Italy and the Vatican at War* (New York: Greenwood, 1939); Christopher Perrotta, "Catholic Care of the Italian Immigrant in the United States," Ph.D. diss., Catholic University of America, Washington, D.C., 1925.
76. Giovanni Perez, *Ricordi d'America* (Genova: Tomati, 1873), 35–41.
77. Ibid., 75.
78. Marie Hall Ets, *Rosa: The Life of an Italian Immigrant* (Minneapolis: University of Minnesota Press, 1970), 232.
79. Virginia Yans-McLaughlin, *Family and Community: Italian Immigrants in Buffalo, 1880–1930* (Ithaca, N.Y.: Cornell University Press, 1971), 113; see also George Schiro, *Americans by Choice: History of the Italians in Utica* (New York: Arno, 1940, 1975), 93–94.
80. Perez, *Ricordi d'America*, 35.
81. Ibid., 42–45.
82. Conte, *Dieci anni*, 57.
83. Perez, *Ricordi d'America*, 42.
84. Di Donato, *Three Circles of Light*, 63.
85. Bernardy, *Italia randagia*, 95.
86. See Mencken, *American Language*.

87. Peter F. Campon, *The Evolution of an Immigrant* (Brooklyn: Gaus' Sons, n.d.), 2.

88. Carnevali, *Autobiography*, 88.

89. Frances De Billo, "Protestant Mission Work among the Italians in Boston," Ph.D. diss., Boston University School of Theology, Boston, 1945, 175.

90. Ciarlantini, *Al paese*, 203.

91. *La Tribuna Italiana d'America*, June 5, 1909.

92. Cianfarra, *Diario*, 101.

93. Di Donato, *Three Circles of Light*, 32.

94. Maurice Marchello, *Black Coal for White Bread: Up from the Prairie Mines* (New York: Vantage, 1972), 109.

95. Bernardy, *Italia randagia*, 173.

96. Panunzio, *Soul of an Immigrant*, 107.

97. Charlotte Adams, "Italian Life in New York," *Harpers* 62 (1881): 678.

98. Mencken, *American Language*, 493.

99. Louis Adamic, *What's Your Name?* (New York: Harper, 1942), 27. See also Joseph Fucilla, *Our Italian Surnames* (Evanston, Ill.: Chandler, 1949).

100. Ventresca, *Personal Reminiscences*.

FIVE

1. Franco Ciarlantini, *Al paese delle stelle* (Milano: "Alpes," 1931), 23.

2. Quoted in Mario Girardon, "La Lingua dell'Yesse in U.S.A.," *Nuova antologia* 446 (1949): 69.

3. Giuseppe Prezzolini, *I trapiantati* (Milano: Longanesi, 1963), 275.

4. Luigi Lombardi, *Pages of My Life, by Lu-Lo* (Fond du Lac, Wis., 1943), 53.

5. For a discussion of the evolution of immigrant speech to English, see Robert Di Pietro, "Language as a Marker of Italian Ethnicity," *Studi emigrazione* 42 (1976): 202–17.

6. Edmondo De Amicis, *Sull'oceano* (Milan: Treves, 1889), 56. Post–World War II Italian emigrants to various countries have also developed immigrant idioms. Ann Cornelisen discusses the Italo-German idiom: "Many nouns, especially those having to do with the local management of life, are German words tricked out with Italian endings and arbitrary endings. The pronunciations are a bizarre compromise. Other nouns are more or less Italian or specific dialect words that have caught the immigrants' fancy—all welded together with a common solder of Italian conjunctions, adverbs, and prepositions" (*Strangers and Pilgrims: The Last Italian Migration* [New York: Holt,

Rinehart and Winston 1980], 121). See also A. Menarini, *Ai margini della Lingua* (Firenze: Sansoni, 1947), 200–208; Temistocle Franceschi, *Lingua e cultura di una comunita' Italiana in Costa Rica* (Firenze: Valmartina, 1970), 278.

7. A low rate of literacy is not an essential precondition for the development of an immigrant idiom. The Finns had one of the highest rates of literacy (over 90 percent) of all the American immigrant groups and yet developed a highly refined immigrant idiom called Finglish. For examples of the idioms of other American immigrant groups, see H. L. Mencken, *The American Language*, 4th ed. (New York: Knopf, 1936).

8. Angelo di Domenica, *Protestant Witness of a New American: Mission of a Lifetime* (Chicago: Judson, 1956), 17.

9. Anthony Turano, "The Speech of Little Italy," *American Mercury* 26 (1932): 358.

10. Carmine D. Iannace, *La scoperta dell'America* (Padova: Rebellato, 1971); Pasquale D'Angelo, *Son of Italy* (New York: Macmillan, 1924), 70.

11. For a different treatment of the Italian pronunciation of English, see Lewis Herman and Marguerite Herman, *Foreign Dialects: A Manual for Actors, Directors and Writers* (New York: Theatre Art Books, 1943), 169–93.

12. Turano, "Speech of Little Italy," 357.

13. Antonio Arrighi, *Antonio, the Galley Slave* (New York: Revell, 1913), 187.

14. H. Vaughan, "Italian and Its Dialects Spoken in the United States," *American Speech* 8 (1926): 433.

15. Gaetano Conte, *Dieci anni in America: Impressioni e ricordi* (Palermo: Spinnato, 1903), 122.

16. Arthur Livingston, "La Merica Sanemagogna," *Romantic Review* 9 (1920): 220. See also Alberto Menarini, "L'Italo Americano degli Stati Uniti," *Lingua nostra* 1 (1939): 152–60.

17. Adolfo Rossi, *Un Italiano in America* (Treviso: Buffetti, 1907), 86.

18. Amy A. Bernardy, *Italia randagia attraverso gli Stati Uniti* (Torino: Fratelli Boccà, 1913), 80.

19. Ciarlantini, *Al paese*, 259. For a discussion of dialects see G. Devoto and G. Giacomelli, *I dialetti delle regioni d'Italia* (Firenze: Sansoni, 1972).

20. Eduardo Migliaccio Papers (University of Minnesota, Immigration History Research Center).

21. *New Republic*, Oct. 21, 1925, p. 230.

22. Giuseppe Prezzolini, *Maccheroni & Co.* (Milano: Longanesi, 1957), 80.

23. Bernardy, *Italia randagia*, 88.

24. *La Luce* (Utica, N.Y.), April 18, 1914. The New York newspaper *Il Progresso Italo-Americano* used the idiom in its advertisements after the Sec-

ond World War. One example: "*Affittasi casa di* bricchi, *senza* stima, *senza genitore, con lunga* lista, *prossima* olivetta" (Brick house for rent, without heat, without a janitor, with a long lease, nearby elevated railroad). For an appraisal and criticism, see Di Pietro, "Language as a Marker," and Prezzolini, *I trapiantati*, 350–54.

25. Cited in Bernardy, *Italia randagia*, 39.

26. *La Tribuna Italiana Trans Atlantica* (Chicago), Jan. 20, 1923.

27. William Murray, *Italy: The Fatal Gift* (New York: Dodd, Mead, 1982), 18.

28. Gabriel Iamurri, *The True Story of an Immigrant* (Boston: Christopher, 1951), 55–57.

29. Leonardo Sciascia, *La Sicilia come metafora* (Milano: Mondadori, 1979), 25.

30. Adolfo Rossi, "Vantaggi e danni dell'emigrazione," *Bollettino dell'emigrazione* 13 (1908): 77. The Bernardy article appeared in *La Gazzetta del Massachusetts*, March 5, 1910. For listings of Americanisms in Italy, see Giovanni Alessio, "Americanismi in Calabria," *Lingua nostra* 4 (1942): 41; Oronzo Parlangeli, "Anglo-Americani Salentini," *Lingua nostra* 9 (1948): 83–86; Giuliano Pellegrini, "Americanismi in Lucchesia," *Lingua nostra* 6 (1944–45): 78–80; G. Tropea, "Americanismi in Sicilia," *Lingua nostra* 18 (1957): 82–85. Italians continue to be exposed in print to Italglish terms. The title of a recent book about Italians in Montreal is one example: Pietro Corsi, *La Giobba* (Campobasso: Enne, 1982).

31. From Menarini, *Ai margini della lingua*, 187–93.

32. Turano, "Speech of Little Italy."

33. Francesco Perri, *Emigranti* (Milano: Mondadori, 1928), 36.

34. Giovanni Pascoli, *Poesie*, vol. 2 (Bologna: Zanichelli, 1904), 195.

35. Ignazio Silone, *Bread and Wine* (New York: Harper, 1937).

SIX

1. Emanuel Carnevali, *The Autobiography of Emanuel Carnevali* (New York: Horizon, 1967), 198.

2. See, for example, John Foster Carr, "The Coming of the Italian," *Outlook* 82 (Feb. 29, 1906): 419–31; Edward A. Ross, "Italians in America," *Century* 66 (July 1914): 439–45.

3. Alberto Pecorini, *Gli Americani nella vita moderna* (Milano: Treves, 1909).

4. Matteo's life is described in Danilo Dolci, *Banditi a Partinico* (Bari: Laterza, 1956), 173–89.

5. Rocco Corresca, "The Biography of a Bootblack," *Independent* 5 (Dec. 4, 1902): 2863–67.

6. Robert E. Park and H. A. Miller, *Old World Traits Transplanted* (New York: Harper, 1921), p. 150.

7. Martha Weinman, "Thirty-nine Years, $23,000 . . . Then Home to His Wife in Italy," *Colliers* 130 (July 12, 1952): 62–63.

8. Ercole Sori, *L'emigrazione Italiana dall'Unita' alla Seconda Guerra Mondiale* (Bologna: Il Mulino, 1979), 342.

9. Totonno Diaries (1916–18).

10. *La Gazzetta del Massachusetts*, Nov. 28–29, 1903.

11. For repatriation statistics, see Massimo Livi Bacci, *L'immigrazione e l'assimilazione degli Italiani agli Stati Uniti secondo le statistiche demografiche Americane* (Milano: Gioffrè, 1961); *Bollettino dell'Emigrazione* 2 (1902): 4, and 9 (1908): 33–34; J. Ferenezi, "A Historical Study of Migration Statistics," *International Labor Review* 20 (1929): 356–84. One will find in various sources different time periods and different rates. Statistics from the Instituto Centrale di Statistica show that between 1902 and 1914 a total of 3,217,283 Italians went to the United States and 1,161,713 returned during the same period. Caroline Golab in her book *Immigrant Destinations* (Philadelphia: Temple University Press, 1977), 58, quotes a 62 percent return rate of those who came between 1902 and 1924.

12. Personal interview.

13. From an interview in *Oggi*, June 23, 1982.

14. Emily Robbins, "If One Speak Bad of Your Mother, How You Feel?" *Red Cross Magazine*, Sept. 1919, p. 47.

15. Nino Calice, *Basilicata tra passato e presente* (Milano: Teti, 1977), 207.

16. F. Paul Miceli, *Pride of Sicily* (New York: Gaus' Sons, 1950), 65.

17. *La Gazzetta del Massachusetts*, Jan. 22, 1910, p. 4; "Protezione ed assistenza degli emigrati in patria e durante il viaggio," *Bollettino dell'emigrazione* 11 (1907): 119.

18. George Gilkey, "Italian Emigrant Letters: The Teramesi Write Home from America" (University of Minnesota, Immigration History Research Center), 9.

19. Leonardo Sciascia, *La Sicilia come metafora* (Milano: Mondadori, 1929), 25. One of Sciascia's relatives fled back home to Sicily after only three months in the United States. He summed up his immigrant venture in these words: "*Si lavora, si lavora e poi si muore*" (You work, you work and then you die).

20. For many of these Italian men, navigating freely between their villages and America became a way of life. Once work migration from the villages got underway, it turned into routine, ritualized behavior, which needed

no further push of any kind to keep it in motion. Those who had left and returned would leave again for no apparent reason, or for a reason that appeared trivial. After her visit to America, Bernardy traveled throughout Calabria and talked to the returnees. Her impressions were that many went abroad "because it was the thing to do" or "out of habit." When springtime approached, groups of prospective emigrants would form. Why were they going? What did they intend to do? "Perhaps nothing," they would respond. But they went just the same. Was an explicit reason needed? Was not wanting to go enough? (Amy A. Bernardy, *Italia randagia attraverso gli Stati Uniti* [Torino: Fratelli Bocca, 1913], 315).

21. Most of the following material has been taken from the Totonno Diaries (1910–12).

22. The material on Iannace has been derived from Carmine Iannace, *La scoperta dell'America* (Padova: Rebellato, 1971).

23. Luciano De Crescenzo, "Il Gomitolo di Lana," in Paola Cresci and Luciano Guidobaldi, *Partono i bastimenti* (Milano: Mondadori, 1980), 21.

SOURCES AND FURTHER READING

This is a very selective bibliography that lists the sources most central to the development of this book and some additional works for those seeking a broader perspective on the Italian in America.

Since the 1860s a very large and diverse literature has accumulated on transatlantic Italian emigration. Much of this literature in English has been brought together by Francesco Cordasco in a number of bibliographic guides. These are (with Salvatore La Gumina) *Italians in the United States: A Bibliography of Reports, Texts, Critical Studies and Related Materials* (New York: Oriole, 1972); *The Italian American Experience: An Annotated and Classified Bibliographical Guide, with Selected Publications of the Casa Italiana Educational Bureau* (New York: Franklin, 1974); and *Italian Americans: A Guide to Information Sources* (Detroit: Gale, 1978). In addition, Professor Cordasco has compiled a guide to the *Bollettino dell'emigrazione* (a publication of the Italian Emigration Commission), *Italian Mass Migration, the Exodus of a Latin People: A Bibliographical Guide to the "Bollettino dell'emigrazione," 1902–1927* (Totowa, N.J.: Rowman & Littlefield, 1980).

A more recent publication by Pietro Russo offers an index to the Italian immigrant press, *Italian American Periodical Press, 1836–1980: A Comprehensive Bibliography* (Staten Island, N.Y.: Center for Migration Studies, 1984). Many of the earlier books and articles in English on Italian immigrants are cited in Ralph W. Janeway, *Bibliography of Immigration in the United States, 1900–1930* (Columbus, Ohio: Hedrick, 1934). Several articles about Italians first published in *Charities* have been reprinted in *The Italian in America: The Progressive View, 1891–1914* (Staten Island, N.Y.: Center for Migration Studies, 1972) edited by Lydio F. Tomasi.

An extensive listing of largely Italian works is presented in the overview of Italian emigration by Grazia Dore, *La democrazia e l'emigrazione in America* (Brescia: Morcelliana, 1964). These titles have been in part duplicated and the bibliography updated (with content summaries of the major works) by Vittorrio Briani in *Emigrazione e lavoro Italiano all'estero: Elementi per un repertario bibliografico* (Roma: Ministero degli Affari Esteri, 1967).

One of the largest collections of unpublished and unedited writings, papers, letters, photos, reports, and general memorabilia by and about Italian immigrants and their institutions is located at the Immigration History Research Center (IHRC), 826 Berry Street, St. Paul, Minn. 55114. IHRC publications routinely list holdings and recent acquisitions. The Summer 1983 issue (vol. 4, no. 2) of *Spectrum*, the center's newsletter, contains an article on immigrant autobiographies. The newsletter of the American Italian Historical Association (AIHA, 209 Flagg Place, Staten Island, N.Y. 10304) lists new publications and ongoing research.

MEMOIRS AND ITALIAN IMPRESSIONS OF THE IMMIGRANTS

Arrighi, Antonio. *Antonio, the Galley Slave*. New York: Revell, 1913.

Bernardy, Amy A. *Italia randagia attraverso gli Stati Uniti*. Torino: Fratelli Bocca, 1913.

———. *America Vissuta*. Torino: Fratelli Bocca, 1911.

Brandenburg, Broughton. *Imported Americans*. New York: Stokes, 1903.

Campon, Peter F. *The Evolution of an Immigrant*. Brooklyn: Gaus' Sons, n.d.

Carnevali, Emanuel. *The Autobiography of Emanuel Carnevali*. Compiled and prefaced by Kay Boyle. New York: Horizon, 1967.

Cianfarra, Camillo. *Diario di un emigrante*. New York: L'Araldo Italiano, 1900.

Ciarlantini, Franco. *Al paese delle stelle*. Milano: "Alpes," 1931.

Conte, Gaetano. *Dieci anni in America: Impressioni e ricordi*. Conferenze riguardanti l'emigrazione Italiana nell'America del Nord. Palermo: Spinnato, 1903.

Corresca, Rocco. "The Biography of a Bootblack." *Independent* 5 (Dec. 4, 1902): 2863–67.

D'Angelo, Pasquale. *Son of Italy*. New York: Macmillan, 1924.

Di Donato, Pietro. *Three Circles of Light*. New York: Messner, 1960.

Dolci, Danilo. *Banditi a partinico*, 173–89. Bari: Laterza, 1956.

Domenica, Angelo di. *Protestant Witness of a New American: Mission of a Lifetime*. Chicago: Judson, 1956.

Ets, Marie Hall. *Rosa: The Life of an Italian Immigrant*. Minneapolis: University of Minnesota Press, 1970.

Gallenga, Antonio. *Episodes of My Second Life*. Philadelphia: Lippincott, 1885.

Gallo, Fortune T. *Lucky Rooster: The Autobiography of an Impresario*. New York: Exposition, 1967.

Giacosa, Giuseppe. *Impressioni d'America*. Milano: Cogliati, 1908.

Greco, Pietro. *I ricordi d'un immigrato*. Brooklyn: Gaus' Sons, 1964.

Iamurri, Gabriel A. *The True Story of an Immigrant*. Rev. ed. Boston: Christopher, 1951.

Iannace, Carmine B. *La scoperta dell'America*. Padova: Rebellato, 1971.

————. *Uomini e galantuomini*. Firenze: Grafica Toscana, 1970.

Juliani, Richard N. "American Voices, Italian Accents." *Italian Americana* I (1974): 1–25.

La Gumina, Salvatore J. *The Immigrants Speak: Italian Americans Tell Their Story*. Staten Island, N.Y.: Center for Migration Studies, 1979.

La Sorte, Michael A. "Diary of an Immigrant." *Attenzione* 3 (Jan. 1981): 31–36.

Lombardi, Luigi. *Pages of My Life, by Lu-Lo*. Fond du Lac, Wis.: n. pub., 1943.

Manganiello, Giuseppe F. L. *Reminiscenze: Pagine di vita vissuta*. Revere, Mass.: n. pub., 1963.

Marchello, Maurice R. *Black Coal for White Bread: Up from the Prairie Mines*. New York: Vantage, 1972.

Margariti, Antonio. *America! America!* Salerno: Galzerano, 1980.

Massari, Angelo. *The Wonderful World of Angelo Massari: An Autobiography*. New York: Exposition, 1965.

Maurino, Ferdinando D. *Dal cavo delle mani: Pagine di vita attuale in Italia e in America*. Cosenza: Pellegrini, 1968.

Mosso, Angelo. *Vita moderna degli Italiani*. Milano: Fratelli Treves, 1906.

Orlando, Guido. *Confessions of a Scoundrel*. Philadelphia: Winston, 1954.

Panunzio, Constantine. *The Soul of an Immigrant*. New York: Macmillan, 1921.

Pellegrini, Angelo M. *Americans by Choice*. New York: Macmillan, 1956.

————. *Immigrant's Return*. New York: Macmillan, 1951.

Perez, Giovanni. *Ricordi d'America*. Genova: Tomati, 1873.

Piacenza, Aldobrando. "Memorie di Aldobrando Piacenza," 1956. University of Minnesota, Immigrant History Research Center.

Quattrociocchi, Niccolo. *Love and Dishes*. Indianapolis: Bobbs-Merrill, 1967.

Robbins, Emily F. "If One Speak Bad of Your Mother, How You Feel?" *Red Cross Magazine*, Sept. 1919, pp. 44–47.

Rondina, F. S. "L'emigrante Italiano, racconto." *Civilita' Cattolica* (Roma), ser. 15, pts. 1, 2 (1892). (A serialized semifictionalized account of an immigrant group.)

Rossi, Adolfo. *Un Italiano in America*. Treviso: Buffetti, 1907.

Sermolino, Maria. *Papa's Table D'Hote*. Philadelphia: Lippincott, 1952.

Tresca, Carlo. "Autobiography." University of Minnesota, Immigrant History Research Center. (Copy at New York Public Library.)

Turco, Luigi. "The Spiritual Autobiography of Luigi Turco," 1969. University of Minnesota, Immigrant History Research Center.

Vanzetti, Bartolomeo. *The Story of a Proletarian Life*. Boston: New Trial League, 1923.

Ventresca, Francesco. *Personal Reminiscences of a Naturalized American*. New York: Rueson, 1937.

THE IMMIGRANT IDIOM

Alessio, Giovanni. "Americanismi in Calabria." *Lingua nostra* 4 (1942): 41.

Di Pietro, Robert. "Language as a Marker of Italian Ethnicity," *Studi emigrazione* 42 (1976): 202–17.

Girardon, Mario. "La lingua dell'Yesse in U.S.A." *Nuova antologia* 446 (1949): 68–80.

Gisolfi, Anthony. "Italo-American: What It Borrowed from American English and What It Is Contributing to the American Language." *Commonwealth* 30 (1939): 311–13.

Livingston, Arthur. "La Merica Sanemagogna." *Romantic Review* 9 (1920): 206–25.

Menarini, Alberto. *Ai margini della lingua*. Firenze: Sansoni, 1947.

———. "L'Italo Americano degli Stati Uniti." *Lingua nostra* 1 (1939): 152–60.

Mencken, H. L. *The American Language*. 4th ed. New York: Knopf, 1936.

Parlangeli, Oronzo. "Anglo-Americani Salentini." *Lingua nostra* 9 (1948): 83–86.

Pellegrini, Giuliano. "Americanismi in Lucchesia." *Lingua nostra* 6 (1944–45): 78–80.

Prezzolini, Giuseppe. "La Lingua della Giobba." *Lingua nostra* 1 (1939): 122.

Simoncini, Forrest. "The San Francisco Italian Dialect: A Study." *Orbis* (Louvain) 8 (1959): 342–54.

Turano, Anthony. "The Speech of Little Italy." *American Mercury* 26 (1932): 356–59.

Tropea, Giovanni. "Americanismi in Sicilia." *Lingua nostra* 18 (1957): 82–85.

Vaughan, Herbert. "Italian and Its Dialects Spoken in the United States." *American Speech* 8 (1926): 431–35.

CASTLE GARDEN AND ELLIS ISLAND

Brownstone, David M., Irene M. Franck, and Douglass L. Brownstone. *Island of Hope, Island of Tears*. New York: Rawson, Wade, 1979.

Corsi, Edward. *In the Shadow of Liberty: The Chronicle of Ellis Island*. New York: Macmillan, 1935.

Heaps, Willard. *Story of Ellis Island*. New York: Seabury, 1967.

Novotny, Ann. *Strangers at the Door*. Riverside, Conn.: Chatham, 1971.

Pitkin, Thomas M. *Keepers of the Gate: A History of Ellis Island*. New York: New York University Press, 1975.

Tifft, Wilson, and Thomas Dunne. *Ellis Island: A Picture Text History*. New York: Norton, 1971.

IMMIGRANTS AND COLONIAL LIFE

Barton, Josef J. *Peasants and Strangers: Italians, Rumanians and Slovaks in an American City, 1890–1950*. Cambridge, Mass.: Harvard University Press, 1975.

Bodnar, John. *Lives of Their Own: Blacks, Italians and Poles in Pittsburgh, 1900–1960*. Urbana: University of Illinois Press, 1982.

Bohme, Frederick G. *A History of Italians in New Mexico*. New York: Arno, 1958, 1975.

Briggs, John W. *An Italian Passage: Immigrants to Three American Cities, 1890–1930*. New Haven: Yale University Press, 1978.

Churchill, Charles W. *The Italians of Newark: A Community Study*. New York: Arno, 1942, 1975.

Cinel, Dino. *From Italy to San Francisco*. Palo Alto, Calif.: Stanford University Press, 1982.

Colajanni, Napoleone. *Gli Italiani negli Stati Uniti*. Napoli: Rivista Popolare, 1909.

Cordasco, Francesco, ed. *La società Italiana di fronte alle prime migrazioni di massa. Il contributo di Mons. Scalabrini e dei suoi primi collaboratori alla tutela degli emigranti*. New York: Arno, 1975.

Federal Writers' Project. *The Italian of New York*. New York: W.P.A., 1938.

Gabaccia, Donna R. *From Sicily to Elizabeth Street: Housing and Social Change among Italian Immigrants, 1880–1930*. Albany, N.Y.: SUNY Press, 1984.

Harney, Robert F., and J. V. Scarpaci, eds. *Little Italies in North America*. Toronto: Multicultural History Society of Ontario, 1981.

La Piana, George. *The Italians in Milwaukee, Wisconsin*. San Francisco: R & E Research Associates, 1915, 1970.

Mangione, Jerry. *Mount Allegro*. Boston: Houghton Mifflin, 1943. Reissued and expanded; New York: Columbia University Press, 1981.

Nelli, Humbert. *Italians in Chicago, 1880–1930: A Study in Ethnic Mobility*. New York: Oxford University Press, 1970.

Perilli, Giovanni. *Colorado and the Italians in Colorado*. Denver, Colo.: Smith Brooks, 1923.

Perry, Stewart E. *San Francisco Scavengers*. Berkeley: University of California Press, 1978.

Radin, Paul. *The Italians of San Francisco: Their Adjustment and Acculturation*. New York: Arno, 1935, 1975.

Rolle, Andrew. *The Immigrant Upraised: Italian Adventurers and Colonists in an Expanding America*. Norman: University of Oklahoma Press, 1968.

Sartorio, Enrico. *Social and Religious Life of Italians in America*. Clifton, N.J.: Kelley, 1918, 1974.

Schiro, George. *Americans by Choice: History of the Italians in Utica*. New York: Arno, 1940, 1975.

Schiavo, Giovanni. *The Italians in Missouri*. New York: Arno, 1929, 1975.

———. *The Italians in Chicago: A Study in Americanization*. New York: Arno, 1928, 1975.

Workers of the Writers' Program. *The Italians of Omaha*. New York: Arno, 1941, 1975.

Yans-McLaughlin, Virginia. *Family and Community: Italian Immigrants in Buffalo, 1880–1930*. Ithaca, N.Y.: Cornell University Press, 1977.

GENERAL HISTORIES

Amfitheatrof, Eric. *The Children of Columbus: An Informal History of the Italians in the New World*. New York: Little, Brown, 1973.

Foerster, Robert F. *The Italian Emigration of Our Times*. Cambridge, Mass.: Harvard University Press, 1919.

Gallo, Patrick J. *Old Bread, New Wine: A Portrait of the Italian Americans*. Chicago: Nelson-Hall, 1981.

Iorizzo, Luciano, and Salvatore Mondello. *The Italian Americans*. Rev. ed. Boston: Twayne, 1980.

Lopreato, Joseph. *Italian Americans*. New York: Random House, 1970.

Lord, Eliot. *The Italian in America*. New York: Buck, 1905.

Nelli, Humbert. *From Immigrants to Ethnics: The Italian Americans*. New York: Oxford University Press, 1983.

Pisani, Lawrence. *The Italian in America: A Social Study and History.* New York: Exposition, 1957.

Rolle, Andrew. *The Italian Americans, Troubled Roots.* New York: Free Press, 1980.

————. *The American Italians: Their History and Culture.* Belmont, Calif.: Wadsworth, 1972.

Villari, Luigi. *Gli Stati Uniti d'America e l'emigrazione Italiana.* New York: Arno, 1912, 1975.

PHOTO ESSAYS

Barolini, Helen. *Images: A Pictorial History of Italian Americans.* Staten Island, N.Y.: Center for Migration Studies, 1981.

Cresci, Paolo, and Luciano Guidobaldi. *Partono i bastimenti.* Milano: Mondadori, 1980.

Scarpaci, Vincenza. *A Portrait of the Italians in America.* New York: Scribner, 1982.

MISCELLANEOUS

Adamic, Louis. *What's Your Name?* New York: Harper, 1942.

Adams, Charlotte. "Italian Life in New York." *Harpers* 62 (1881): 676–84.

Bodio, Luigi. "Della protezione degli emigranti italiani in America." *Nuova Antologia* 60 (1895): 628–44.

Caroli, Betty. *Italian Repatriation from the United States.* Staten Island: Center for Migration Studies, 1973.

Ciarlantini, Franco. *Incontro col Nord America.* Milano: "Alpes," 1929.

Ciolli, Domenick. "The Wop in the Track Gang." *Immigrants in America Review* 2 (July 1916): 61–64.

Ciuffoletti, Zeffiro, and Maurizio Degl'Innocenti. *L'Emigrazione nella storia d'Italia, 1868–1975.* Firenze: Vallecchi, 1978.

Claghorn, Kate H. *The Immigrants' Day in Court.* New York: Harper, 1923.

Cordasco, Francesco, ed. *La società Italiana di fronte alle prime migrazione di massa.* New York: Arno, 1975.

Curinga, Nicola. *An Italian Tragedy: The Story of a Humble People.* New York: Liveright, 1945.

Dosch, A. "Just Wops." *Everybody's Magazine* 25 (Nov. 1911): 579–89.

Felici, Icilio. *Father to the Immigrants: The Servant of God, John Baptist Scalabrini.* New York: Kenedy, 1955.

Fenton, Edwin. *Immigrants and Unions: Italians and American Labor, 1870–1920.* New York: Arno, 1957, 1975.

Flamona, Ario. *Italiani di America: Enciclopedia Biografia.* New York: Cocce, 1936.

Fucilla, Joseph G. *Our Italian Surnames.* Evanston, Ill.: Chandler, 1949.

Gilkey, George. "The United States and Italy: Migration and Repatriation." *Journal of Developing Areas* 2 (1967): 23–36.

Josa, Guglielmo. "L'Emigrazione nel Molise." *Bollettino dell'emigrazione* 10 (1907): 50–69.

Koren, John. "The Padrone System and Padrone Banks." *U.S. Department of Labor Bulletin* 9 (1897): 113–29.

La Gumina, Salvatore. *WOP! A Documentary History of Anti-Italian Discrimination in the United States.* San Francisco: Straight Arrow Books, 1973.

Livi Bacci, Massimo. *L'immigrazione e l'assimilation degli italiani agli Stati Uniti secondo le statistiche demografiche Americane.* Milano: Gioffrè, 1961.

Massara, Giuseppe. *Viaggiatori italiani in America, 1860–1970.* Roma: Edizioni di Storia e Letteratura, 1976.

Mayo-Smith, Richmond. *Emigration and Immigration.* New York: Scribner, 1904.

Miceli, F. Paul. *Pride of Sicily.* New York: Gaus' Sons, 1950.

Moreno, Celso. *History of a Great Wrong: Italian Slavery in America.* Washington, D.C.: Department of Labor, 1895.

Moroni, Gerolamo. "Il peonage nel sud degli Stati Uniti." *Bollettino dell'emigrazione* 5 (1910): 3–20.

Morrison, Joan, and Charlotte Fox Zabusky. *American Mosaic: The Immigrant Experience in the Words of Those Who Lived It.* New York: Dutton, 1980.

Murray, William. *Italy: The Fatal Gift.* New York: Dodd, Mead, 1982.

Nelli, Humbert. "The Italian Padrone System in the United States." *Labor History* 3 (1964): 153–67.

Park, Robert E., and Herbert A. Miller. *Old World Traits Transplanted.* New York: Harper, 1921.

Pecorini, Alberto. *Gli Americani nella vita moderna.* Milano: Treves, 1909.

Prezzolini, Giuseppe. *I trapiantati.* Milano: Longanesi, 1963.

———. *Maccheroni & Co.* Milano: Longanesi, 1957.

Ross, Edward A. "Italians in America." *Century* 66 (1914): 439–45.

Rossi, Adolfi. "Vantaggi e danni dell'emigrazione." *Bollettino dell'emigrazione* 13 (1908): 3–99.

Savona, A., and M. Straniero. *Canti dell'emigrazione.* Milano: Garzanti, 1976.

Speranza, Gino C. "Forced Labor in West Virginia." *Forum* 74 (June 13, 1903): 407–10.

Steiner, Edward A. *On the Trail of the Immigrant.* New York: Revell, 1906.
Stella, Antonio. *Some Aspects of Italian Immigration.* New York: Putnam, 1924.
Vecoli, Rudolph J. "Prelates and Peasants: Italian Immigrants and the Catholic Church." *Journal of Social History* 2 (1969): 217–68.
Villari, Luigi. "Gli Italiani nel sud degli Stati Uniti." *Bollettino dell'emigrazione* 10 (1907): 39–49.

INDEX